NEW PERSPECTIVES ON MIDDLE ENGLISH TEXTS
A Festschrift for R. A. Waldron

The essays in this volume celebrate the career of the distinguished medievalist, R. A. Waldron. Fittingly, they focus on the Middle English alliterative tradition, but do not exclude material in other areas. Acting as a linking theme is a concern with the relationship of texts to their contexts, whether historical, philosophical, linguistic, or codicological. Topics discussed include feasting in Middle English alliterative poetry; setting and context in the works of the *Gawain*-poet; Henryson's *Testament of Cresseid*; Layamon; and Middle English verse in chronicles.

Ron Waldron (centre) with the editors at the Early Book Society Conference at the
University of Glasgow, July 1999.

NEW PERSPECTIVES ON MIDDLE ENGLISH TEXTS

A Festschrift for R. A. Waldron

Edited by Susan Powell and Jeremy J. Smith
with a personal memoir by Derek Pearsall

D. S. BREWER

First published 2000
D. S. Brewer, Cambridge

ISBN 0 85991 590 5

D. S. Brewer is an imprint of Boydell & Brewer Ltd
PO Box 9, Woodbridge, Suffolk IP12 3DF, UK
and of Boydell & Brewer Inc.
PO Box 41026, Rochester, NY 14604-4126, USA
website: http://www.boydell.co.uk

A catalogue record of this publication is available
from the British Library

Library of Congress Cataloging-in-Publication data
New perspectives on Middle English texts: a festschrift for R.A. Waldron /
edited by Susan Powell and Jeremy J. Smith.
p. cm
Includes bibliographical references and index.
ISBN 0–85991–590–5 (alk. paper)
1. English Literature – Middle English, 1100–1500 – Criticism, Textual.
2. English language – Middle English, 1100–1500 – Grammar, Historical.
3. Mansucripts, English (Middle) – Editing.
I. Waldron, Ronald. II. Powell, Susan, 1948– III. Smith, J.J. (Jeremy J.)
PR275.T45 N48 2000
820.9'001–dc21   00–036035

This publication is printed on acid-free paper

Set in Times New Roman by Bookcraft Ltd, Stroud, Gloucestershire

Printed in Great Britain by St Edmundsbury Press Ltd,
Bury St Edmunds, Suffolk

CONTENTS

PREFACE

LIKE THE HERO of his favourite poem, Ron has always seemed to his students and colleagues a type of courtesy and kindness, and it is for this reason that these essays by former students and close friends and collaborators are offered to him. We hope that he will take pleasure in them.

Texts, we all now know, are not beamed down from outer space but are a reflection of the circumstances which give them birth, and it is for this reason that we asked Derek Pearsall to provide a short memoir at the beginning of this volume. The relevance of this memoir to the themes of the remaining essays is covert rather than overt, but will become very clear to the attentive reader, for Ron is someone in whom human sympathy and scholarship are completely and happily integrated. We are most grateful to Professor Pearsall for undertaking this (albeit pleasant) task, and also for his enthusiastic advice, encouragement and support.

The body of the collection falls into two sections. The first part is to do with the interpretation of alliterative poetry from the Middle English period, a genre which has engaged Ron's interest from the very outset of his academic career and with which he has enthused many generations of his students. Malcolm Andrew, who co-edited with Ron the works of the *Gawain*-poet, analyses how setting and context are exploited in these poems. In particular, Andrew investigates the way the poet's settings complement distinct stages in his protagonists' psychological, moral and spiritual development. Ros Allen's interest in contemporary performance theory leads her to use considerations of performance in arguing for a symmetrical seven-part structure for a key work from the period: *The Alliterative Morte Arthure*. Ralph Hanna examines the role of the feasting-*topos* in a wide range of alliterative verse, especially *Sir Gawain and the Green Knight*. George Kane brings his unparalleled experience with the editing of *Piers Plowman* to bear on the interpretation of a series of complex problems in the various texts of the poem. Jane Roberts's essay on Layamon's *Brut* is similarly concerned with cruces; she uses recent lexicological research for the detailed interpretation of a poem whose considerable significance for the literary history of the Middle English period is currently being re-evaluated. Finally in this section, the editors' essays also address issues to do with lexis. Sue Powell focuses on the *Gawain*-poet's use of the term *knot* and the related term *knytte*, and argues for an heraldic context for both the *endeles knot* of the pentangle and for Gawain's other blazon, the *bende of blame*. And Jeremy Smith attempts to link Ron's interests in alliterative verse and semantics, using current research in the historical study of meaning and phonaesthetic analysis to present new readings of key lines in *Sir Gawain and the Green Knight*.

The second part of the volume may seem at first sight to be a somewhat eclectic collection of studies of Middle English texts, but it soon becomes clear that all follow, from a range of different angles, the approach to our subject which Ron has always favoured: close textual analysis, combined with intense sympathy for the processes whereby poets and readers (including scribes) interact. Norman Blake's account of a neglected MS of the *Canterbury Tales* emphasises the value of scribal outputs hitherto ignored because they have been outside the established stemmatic tradition. Having started the Ellesmere-Hengwrt controversy some years ago, Blake now, through his contention that Chaucer was responsible for several versions of the links, sets off a new hare for the Chaucer hounds to course. Janet Cowen's work on the neglected Middle English version of Boccaccio's *De Mulieribus Claris* – a paper forming part of a larger research programme – demonstrates the way in which a translator has read, reordered and reworked a highly influential Latin original to provide a selection which is of interest not least because of its emphasis in the women's lives selected on the exemplary role of 'masculine' qualities. Julia Boffey and Tony Edwards, in a survey of Middle English verse set within prose chronicles, suggest some of the complex processes of interaction whereby such texts emerged and sketch a programme for future research in this area. Verse situated in such contexts appears for contemporary chroniclers to perform a function which is supplementary and incidental, and marginalised in the context of the dominant prose mode. Roger Dahood presents a detailed case study of pen strokes in a manuscript containing Mirk's *Festial* and eight saints' lives. He demonstrates how scribal practices which can seem trivial and thus capable of being ignored by modern editors are in fact systematic and of considerable textual interest. Elton Higgs draws attention to the frequency of occurrence of the lexeme 'debt' in the *Canterbury Tales*; in relating the meaning of the term for a medieval audience, Higgs offers a new interpretation of the *Tales* in terms of conjugal debt and other examples of temporal, rather than spiritual indebtedness. Derek Pearsall's essay sees the *Testament of Cresseid* as emerging through the dynamic interaction of Henryson, a great reader of Chaucer, with his Chaucerian model. Pearsall engages with current issues in literary theory and argues, amongst other things, for the poem *qua* poem rather than as meta-history.

The editors would like to thank the contributors to this volume for their cooperation and patience, and to Boydell and Brewer (especially Caroline Palmer) for their encouragement. Finally, they and Professor Pearsall would like to express their particular thanks to Mary Waldron.

Susan Powell (Salford) and Jeremy Smith (Glasgow)
September 1999

RON WALDRON: A PERSONAL MEMOIR

DEREK PEARSALL

IRST, the facts of life. Ronald Alan Waldron was born on 9 January 1927 at Teignmouth, Devon, the fourth of five children. He was educated at local primary schools and then at Teignmouth Grammar School. He left school in December 1942 and worked as a stores clerk for the Teignmouth Electricity Company until February 1945, when he was called up to do his National Service in the Royal Navy. After preliminary training at Malvern and Portsmouth, he went out to South Africa as a 'Jack Dusty' or stores assistant, stationed at the naval base at Simonstown, near Cape Town, happily out of the way of British rationing and perishing winters for almost two years. He returned to Britain in 1947 aboard *HMS Belfast*, now moored as a tourist attraction in St Catherine's Dock on the Thames (a plaque indicating where Ron swung his hammock has not yet been installed).

Offered the option of a university place with financial support under the government's Further Education and Training Scheme for ex-service personnel, Ron applied successfully for a place at the University College of the South West (now the University of Exeter), which then offered University of London external degrees, and graduated in 1951 with an Upper Second in English. He went on to a postgraduate studentship at Royal Holloway College, and received the MA degree of the University of London with mark of distinction in 1953. The title of his thesis was 'The Diction of English Alliterative Romances'. From 1952 to 1957 he was Engelsk Lektor at the University of Aarhus in Denmark. During his time there he married Mary, in 1955, and their first child, John, was born in Aarhus. Sarah, the second child, was born in London in 1959, and Tom, the third, delayed his arrival until 1969.

Ron was appointed Assistant Lecturer in English at King's College London in 1957, and was subsequently Senior Lecturer and Reader. He retired early (1982) as Reader Emeritus. Since then he has taught from time to time at King's and Birkbeck and for the American Institute for Foreign Study in London. He is a Member of the Council of the Early English Text Society.

*   *   *

I first met Ron Waldron when I arrived at King's College London as a very junior assistant lecturer in 1959. To me, coming from four years of schoolteaching, he seemed a very wise and experienced scholar and 'don' (as we were later to learn was the correct term for what we did). He was enormously kind to me, and we became fast friends, but there was never any question about who was the junior colleague. We shared a suite of rooms in 33 Surrey Street, a crumbling Dickensian tenement next door to where Joseph Conrad used to stay when he was in London, reached by underground corridors from the main college building (which was also, oddly enough, accessible through Aldwych Tube station). I call it a 'suite of rooms', but it was actually a normal-sized room with a large cupboard. Ron had the normal-sized room; I had the cupboard. It was a large cupboard but a small room and if I had a tutorial with three students we had to put all the chairs on the table while the students squeezed in and could only put the chairs back on the floor when the door was shut. And of course if Ron and I were teaching at the same time – as was often the case – I had to wait until Ron had finished before I could get out.

Ron looked then exactly as he looks now. We have talked about this, and concluded that going bald early has its advantages. A man looks older when he is younger, but he stays looking the same age, and so looks younger when he is older. Ron has always seemed to me, though, a young person in lots of ways – in his vigour, his enthusiasm, his inexhaustible cheerfulness, and his adventurousness. He was always the first one, in my experience, to be trying out some new invention or gadget, and I was not surprised when he became one of the first people I know to get into computers. Ron was always something of a technological wizard, and he was always experimenting with new bits of machinery: he is perhaps the only person I know in our profession who does not go pale when he opens the bonnet of his car. The love of new ideas and new-fangled gadgets was evident in Ilford, then in Blackmore, and most recently in Chatham Green. I think they had the first magnetic soap-holder I had ever seen, the first electric toothbrush, the first electronic games. He was much encouraged in all this by his son John, who had a precocious child's passion for science and curiosity about everything. The house was always bulging with telescopes, geological specimens, dodecahedrons, board games newly invented by John with rules of such fiendish subtlety that only John understood them. John, by the way, is now a geology professor at Halifax, Nova Scotia. He and his sister Sarah both have families. Sarah works as practice manager of a law firm partly run by her solicitor husband, and lives in Colchester: Ron and Mary are devoted grandparents and frequent full-day full-time carers. Tom, the youngest son, has gone into finance and is prospering.

When I first met him, Ron was the author of a very important article on oral-formulaic theory in Middle English alliterative verse. This was a hot topic at the time. Larry Benson had recently demonstrated some of the extravagances of the theory in relation to Anglo-Saxon verse, and Ron's account of the

Middle English evidence was so thorough and judicious that it has been neither added to nor improved upon in the years since. Much of our work at King's was on the history of the language, or 'The Development of the English Language as a Medium of Literary Expression', as it had come recently to be more tactfully called, perhaps in an attempt to restrain our senior colleague, John Sheard, who regularly stoned the students practically senseless with hypothetical Indo-European forms. But he encouraged Ron in his first book, *Sense and Sense Development* (1967), on a subject which was then something of a battlefield of conflicting opinion, and which is still central to linguistic debate. Ron's book on meaning and meaning change was, and has remained, the standard non-specialist account of the topic.

He also taught, year after year, a year-long class on *Sir Gawain and the Green Knight*. It was classic *explication de texte*, and it was famous. Kenneth Sisam once said of the great German scholar Julius Zupitza that to him, as an editor, 'every blur was a challenge'. I would say this of Ron's work on *Gawain*, too, with the addition that he sometimes recognised as blurs what no-one previously had realised were blurs at all. His edition of *Gawain*, which later came out revised in the magnificent edition of the *Poems of the Pearl Manuscript* that he did with Malcolm Andrew, is to my mind the best annotated edition of a Middle English text that we have.

Ron is held in universal affection: even those who make it a point of pride to fall out with everyone have not been able to fall out with him. His smile and sunny demeanour have brightened up many a conference and other academic occasion for colleagues and friends and have warmed the hearts of generations of students. He is inexhaustibly patient, generous and knowledgeable, and also very shrewd. His project for his retirement – an edition of Trevisa's translation of Higden's *Polychronicon* – was wonderfully well chosen. There is much to find out, little done, many visits to be made, infinite opportunities for ingenious computerisation, and problems to solve that need all of Ron's erudition, experience and wise judgement. Mary too has found a late-blossoming career as a scholar of late-eighteenth-century women's writing, and already has a Ph.D. and a book to show for it. All who know them will wish them many years of happiness.

PART I

SETTING AND CONTEXT IN THE WORKS OF THE *GAWAIN*-POET

MALCOLM ANDREW

I

EDITORS AND CRITICS working on the four poems regularly attributed to the *Gawain*-poet – *Pearl, Cleanness, Patience,* and *Sir Gawain and the Green Knight* – have often identified in them some distinctive and characteristic quality.[1] A few examples should suffice to provide an impression of the nature and the range of these suggestions. A. C. Spearing observes that the poems deal with confrontations between human protagonists and 'some more than human power', and argues that they convey a 'tragi-comic view of man'.[2] D. S. Brewer maintains that courtesy, as 'an ideal of personal integrity', is 'variously explored ... throughout all these remarkable poems'.[3] This idea is later developed by Jonathan Nicholls into a book-length study of the poems in relation to medieval courtesy books.[4] Charles Muscatine contends that 'the richness of the poems combined with their artistic purity ... the sublime control and assurance with which they are composed ... suggest a man for whom the

---

1   In this essay I shall assume that the poems are, indeed, the work of a single poet, while trusting that at least some of my comments may have a degree of validity independent of this supposition.

2   'Patience and the *Gawain*-Poet', *Anglia* 84 (1966), 305–29 (quotations from pp. 306–7). These views are repeated, in revised form, in Spearing's book, *The Gawain-Poet: A Critical Study*, Cambridge, 1970, pp. 29–31.

3   'Courtesy and the Gawain-Poet', in J. Lawlor (ed.) *Patterns of Love and Courtesy: Essays in Memory of C. S. Lewis*, London, 1966, pp. 54–85 (quotations from pp. 85, 78).

4   *The Matter of Courtesy: Medieval Courtesy Books and the Gawain-Poet*, Cambridge, 1985.

perfection of his art has become a kind of defense against crisis'.[5] In marked contrast, W. A. Davenport takes one of the defining characteristics of the poet to be his 'interest in difficult cases'.[6] Robert J. Blanch and Julian N. Wasserman perceive him as a poet especially interested in the theme of 'the first shall be last', and emphasize the importance of beginnings and endings in his work.[7]

During the period – now (sobering thought) some quarter of a century ago – in which I had the privilege of working with Ron Waldron on our joint edition of these poems,[8] I gradually came to recognize another distinctive quality in them. This I have attempted to encapsulate in the title of the present essay, 'setting and context'. The idea, in essence, is that the poet handles the main settings of the poems with exceptional skill and ingenuity, and that, as a consequence, they become remarkably subtle and resonant contexts for the actions, events, and episodes which take place within them. In formulating and developing this idea, I use 'setting' in a fairly narrow sense, to signify the physical locus of a fictional event.

II

The poet's subtle and sophisticated use of settings is, perhaps, most readily apparent in *Pearl*. The crucial stages in the development of the poem's central narrative are marked by the progression from one of the three settings to the next: from the initial setting of the garden to the dream setting of the earthly paradise; from there to the visionary setting of the New Jerusalem; and finally back again to the garden. This progression offers a means of both representing and exploring the emotional, psychological, and spiritual development of the protagonist (a pattern which recurs in *Patience* and *Sir Gawain and the Green Knight*).[9] In *Pearl*, the garden setting provides the first and essential context in which the protagonist laments the loss of his *perle* – a loss which is evocatively described but not fully explained. Though the protagonist can define the means by which his sorrow might be resolved, he is, as yet, unable to achieve such resolution:

> Bifore þat spot my honde I spennd
> For care ful colde þat to me caȝt;
> A deuely dele in my hert denned,
> Þaȝ resoun sette myseluen saȝt.
> I playned my perle þat þer watz penned,

5 'The *Pearl* Poet: Style as Defense', in his *Poetry and Crisis in the Age of Chaucer*, Notre Dame, 1972, pp. 37–69 (quotation from p. 69).

6 *The Art of the Gawain-Poet*, London, 1978, p. 198.

7 *From Pearl to Gawain: Forme to Fynisment*, Gainesville, 1995, pp. 1–2.

8 This was originally published as *The Poems of the Pearl Manuscript*, London, 1978, and has been through various reprints and revisions. All subsequent quotations are from the latest revised edition (Exeter, 1996).

9 See below, pp. 7–9, 11–12.

> Wyth fyrce skyllez þat faste faȝt.
> Þaȝ kynde of Kryst me comfort kenned,
> My wreched wylle in wo ay wraȝte.   (49–56)

This overwhelming sense of loss leads directly to the dream. The dream setting of the earthly paradise might be regarded as a setting-within-a-setting, since the body of the protagonist – who can now be termed the Dreamer – remains in the garden while his spirit goes forth in *auenture þer meruaylez meuen* (64). The bulk of the poem takes place in this second setting, where the cause of the Dreamer's sorrow is revealed and explored, and the essential issues of loss and consolation, innocence and culpability, faith and salvation, are debated between the Dreamer and the Pearl Maiden. The final setting, the visionary New Jerusalem, is experienced from within the earthly paradise. Thus it is, in a sense, a setting-within-a-setting-within-a-setting. The New Jerusalem serves to confirm and to provide biblical authority for the truths already propounded by the Maiden. It also indicates the limits of the extent to which the Dreamer's *resoun* has yet succeeded in mastering his *wreched wylle*. His undeniably wilful (yet entirely understandable) attempt to wade across the paradisal river and join the Maiden in the New Jerusalem results in his abrupt return to the initial setting of the garden.

While it is clear that the three settings of *Pearl* function as contexts for successive stages of the narrative, the poet also utilizes metaphors of setting and offers some consideration of setting as a concept. The opening image of the poem is that of a pearl radiantly set in gold for the pleasure of a prince. Though the main purpose of this opening is to establish the pearl as the rich and complex symbol at the heart of the poem, it also serves to introduce the idea of setting – in this case, the literal setting of a pearl in gold for purposes of worldly pleasure and adornment. The idea is taken up in the recognition scene (157ff) where the Dreamer meets his lost daughter in the form of a transfigured maiden *in perlez pyȝte* (i.e., set).[10] The significance of these words may be indicated by their use as the concatenation phrase for the fourth section of the poem. It is here that the initial exchanges between the Dreamer and the Maiden take place; with them come several further images of setting. The Maiden describes herself as *in cofer so comly clent* (259) and represents this *cofer* to the Dreamer as, potentially, *a forser for þe* (262). The notion of the paradisal garden as a coffer or a casket is developed in the following stanza, where the Maiden gives her essential reason for asserting that the Dreamer's sense of loss is worldly and misconceived:

> For þat þou lestez watz bot a rose
> Þat flowred and fayled as kynde hit gef;

---

10   These comments will indicate that I subscribe to the literal reading of the poem – not that this greatly affects my argument on the settings.

> Now þur3 kynde of þe kyste þat hit con close
> To a perle of prys hit is put in pref.   (269–72)

The image of the *kyst* (chest) and of enclosing or setting becomes a central
metaphor of transformation from the earthly to the heavenly state. Such
potential is implicit in the garden setting from the beginning, and develops the
antithetical ideas established there: of death, burial, and enclosing contrasted
with growth, hope, and resurrection. In establishing this setting, the poet draws
on both courtly and Christian traditions, so that the garden represents both the
worldly, cultured, aristocratic values of medieval romance and the potential
for spiritual growth suggested by scriptural and liturgical echoes and
associations. With hindsight, it is, perhaps, possible to identify these
respectively with will and reason. Be that as it may, worldly and spiritual
values are seen as both related to and in conflict with each other throughout the
poet's treatment of the two subsequent settings. While the earthly paradise is
presented mainly as a transformed and perfected garden which the Dreamer
enters through an *auenture þer merualylez meuen* (64), there is a recurring
sense that he has no right to be there – that he is a visitor of uncertain status,
whose position is akin to that of a trespasser in the grounds of an aristocratic
estate.[11] When the Maiden gains him special dispensation for the vision of the
New Jerusalem, she makes plain the terms which will apply:

> Vtwyth to se þat clene cloyster
> þou may, bot inwyth not a fote.   (969–70)

The effect is to stress not only the Dreamer's relatively unprivileged status but
also the stark fact of his exclusion – and thus his separation from the Maiden.

These ideas are directly developed from the subtly and elusively resonant
initial setting of the garden. There, as I have observed, the Dreamer's desperate
grief is perceived in terms of a conflict between will and reason – a conflict
which can be resolved through the *kynde of Kryst* (55). The implications of this
paradigm are explored in the two subsequent settings. It is through his debate
with the Maiden in the earthly paradise that the Dreamer is obliged to acknowledge the fundamental differences between his values and those of the Maiden,
to learn that there is more than one basis on which to judge pearls or to organize
social hierarchies, and to confront the paradoxes (such as the first shall be last,
and by losing life we gain it) which lie at the heart of Christian belief. The
vision of the New Jerusalem serves mainly to confirm these ideas in graphic
form and to represent the life of the Maiden as a Bride of Christ.

The Dreamer's sudden return to the initial setting of the garden provides a
final perspective on this process. Though he still feels an acute sense of loss, he

---

11   See especially lines 133–56. Ron Waldron and I comment on this in our edition: see
     note to lines 149–54.

can now see this in relation to the pattern of Christian consolation. At the beginning of this process, the Dreamer (not yet a dreamer) faces a fundamental problem: while he knows in theory that the *kynde of Kryst* offers a means of coming to terms with his devastating loss, he is, as yet, unable to master his *wreched wylle* sufficiently to gain access to this consolatory structure. The process by which he learns to do so is explored through the related context of the three interlinked settings.

III

There are interesting parallels in *Patience*. Though the poem is mainly based on the Old Testament Book of Jonah, the poet shows remarkable freedom and independence in his treatment of his source, elaborating some episodes and leaving others relatively undeveloped.[12] He retains all the settings of the biblical story, but develops three in particular: the ship in which Jonah attempts to escape, the belly of the whale, and the *wodbynde* (446) under which he shelters after the pardoning of the Ninevites. In each of these settings, Jonah seeks refuge. The ship, sailing from Joppa to Tarshish, represents an attempt at evading the unwelcome duty which God has imposed on him. Fearful of the storm, Jonah finds a secluded spot in *þe boþem of þe bot* (184) and is sleeping uneasily when one of the sailors, seeking out the cause of their misfortune, finds him. The fact that he ends up inside the belly of the whale provides a stark indication of the failure of Jonah's attempt to escape from God. Once he has expressed contrition in the celebrated prayer from the belly, Jonah seeks and finds a *hyrne* (289) – a place of refuge from the *fylþe* that surrounds him – in which he can sleep. The poet explicitly links this refuge with the previous one in *þe bulk of þe bote þer he byfore sleped* (292). The third of these settings is the *bour* (437)[13] which Jonah builds for himself after leaving Nineveh in rebellious frustration at the mercy shown by God to the contrite citizens. Here, once more, Jonah seeks refuge and sleeps, while God sends a splendid *wodbynde* (446) to grow over the *bour* and turn it into a kind of *hous* (450).

The shaping of the narrative strongly suggests that these places are related to each other.[14] Since each is sought out by Jonah at a moment of crisis, it is clear that these settings represent stages in his psychological and spiritual development. Unlike that of the Dreamer in *Pearl*, this does not constitute a steady (if difficult) progression from wilful rebellion against God's will to wise and chastened acquiescence, but, rather, describes a pattern of rebellion,

12 I offer a detailed analysis of the poet's treatment of the Book of Jonah in a forthcoming essay, 'Biblical Paraphrase in the Middle English *Patience*'.

13 It may be worth noting that the poet also refers to the whale's belly as a *bour* (line 276).

14 This point is made by Laurence Eldredge, 'Sheltering Space and Cosmic Space in the Middle English *Patience*', *Annuale Medievale* 21 (1982), 121–33.

followed by contrition, followed by repeated rebellion, which accords with the penitential implications of *Patience*.

In *Patience*, as in *Pearl*, the effectiveness of the settings as contexts depends partly on the poet's skilful handling of associations from various traditions. This is apparent especially in his treatment of the whale. The poet's extraordinarily bold realization of the whale's belly as a setting is derived partly from the exercise of a remarkably fertile imagination, partly from the subtle evocation of traditional ideas.[15] He creates a vivid impression of actually entering the belly, imagining Jonah's disorientation and loss of balance, and describing his surroundings as not only dark, but also full of foul smells and of muck and slime. These qualities are represented as both literal and figurative, through the skilful manipulation of such ideas as the association of light with enlightenment, of hell with foul smells, and of sin with mire. While the poet concentrates mainly on imagining what it would have been like inside the whale's belly, he also offers several brief glimpses of the whale from the outside. Twice the whale is described moving in response to God's orders (247, 239–40), in implicit contrast to the reluctant prophet; on another occasion the demanding aspect of his task is emphasized, as he is observed making his way through dangerous underwater terrain (297–98).

Though the ship and the *wodbynde* are relatively simple settings, they too reflect the poet's attention to detail in the development of his settings. It is, for instance, conspicuous that the storm, sent by God, destroys the ship's sails and steering gear – equipment with which Jonah's desire to escape had earlier been implicitly identified.[16] Similarly, by describing the corner where Jonah secretes himself and the process by which he is found sleeping there, the poet intensifies the sense of his guilt and his responsibility for the plight of the sailors. In the *wodbynde* episode, the poet turns the mere *hedera* of the Vulgate into something far more elaborate and engaging:

> Such a lefsel of lof neuer lede hade,
> For hit watz brod at þe boþem, boȝted on lofte,
> Happed vpon ayþer half, a hous as hit were,
> A nos on þe norþ syde and nowhere non ellez,
> Bot al schet in a schaȝe þat schaded ful cole.
> Þe gome glyȝt on þe grene graciouse leues,
> Þat euer wayued a wynde so wyþe and so cole;
> Þe schyre sunne hit vmbeschon, þaȝ no schafte myȝt
> Þe mountaunce of a lyttel mote vpon þat man schyne.   (448–56)

---

15 I discuss this aspect of the poet's treatment of the whale's belly in my essay 'The Realizing Imagination in Late Medieval English Literature', *English Studies* 76 (1995), 113–28 (esp. pp. 121–22).

16 See lines 97–110. The effect is discussed in my forthcoming essay, cited in footnote 12 above.

One might suspect that this exuberant description is a virtuoso display made largely for its own sake. Nonetheless, the elaboration renders this a far more effective setting for the exposure of Jonah's childish delight and possessiveness than it could otherwise have been.

The settings in *Patience*, like those in *Pearl*, contribute significantly to the representation and exploration of the spiritual and psychological concerns, crises, and development of the protagonist. The first major setting, the ship, provides the context in relation to and within which Jonah is represented as he progresses from absorption in his desire to escape from God to acknowledgement of his duty and of his guilt. His hasty flight is echoed in the activity of the sailors as they prepare the ship for departure (97–108), and his joyful relief at the apparent success of his escape in the welcome movement as the wind *swenges me þys swete schip swefte fro þe hauen* (108). Before long, of course, the wind is instructed by God to cause the storm, from which Jonah seeks refuge below while the ship is battered by the elements. The poet's elaboration and realization of the effects of the storm on the stricken ship enriches its potential as a setting for Jonah's acknowledgement of his guilt – both in trying to avoid his duty to God and in bringing misfortune on the sailors. It is the coincidence of Jonah's change of heart with the constancy of divine will that brings about his rapid transfer from the ship to the whale. As in the Old Testament account, this is the setting for the prayer in which Jonah acknowledges not just his guilt but also his total dependence on God, and pledges complete obedience to the divine will in the future. The remarkable elaboration of the setting serves to intensify the reader's understanding of and identification with this process. The third of these settings, the *wodbynde*-covered *bour* in the desert outside Nineveh, provides the context for Jonah's final rebellion. This begins with a combination of angry frustration at the mercy God has shown to the Ninevites with self-important outrage at thus being proved a false prophet. The poet's extravagant elaboration of the *hous*, considered above, renders it a richly evocative context for the presentation of Jonah's state of mind in the process of changing, with the arrival of the lovely *wodbynde*, from angry resentment to irresponsible euphoria. Similarly, Jonah's sense of loss at the destruction of this singularly desirable shelter seems particularly vivid and acute – though also comic. It is conspicuous that the reader[17] visualizes Jonah listening to God's final consolatory argument in the ruins of the *hous* which has been, albeit briefly, so precious to him.

---

17   The point would apply equally to someone hearing the poem read aloud. Here and elsewhere in this essay I use the word 'reader' to refer both to readers and to listeners.

IV

Memorable and subtly handled settings are also found in *Cleanness*, though –
as a consequence of its relatively episodic and loosely woven character –
without the symmetrical patterning which is so conspicuous in *Pearl* and
Patience. Nonetheless, it is clear that in *Cleanness* the poet develops and
elaborates some of the settings derived from scriptural sources much as he
does in *Patience*, and to broadly similar effect.

The most striking of these settings are, perhaps, the ark and Belshazzar's
palace. In his treatment of the former, the poet realizes much of what is left
implicit in the Old Testament account, and creates a palpable sense of a ship
and its fittings, while not losing sight of the ark's symbolic significance. It is
striking that, in the process, he uses metaphors of enclosing similar to those in
Pearl, describing the ark as both a *cofer* (310 etc.) and a *kyst* (346 etc.). For
Belshazzar's feast, the poet creates a complex setting which has parallels with
the castle of the lord in *Sir Gawain and the Green Knight* (discussed below). In
a passage conspicuous for its flamboyance and sense of wonder (1377 ff), the
poet describes the fine and exotic city of Babylon, the magnificent palace of
Belshazzar, and the hall itself, *so brod bilde in a bay þat blonkkes myȝt renne*
(1392). This, clearly, is a setting designed for the exotic and exuberant account
of Belshazzar's Feast which follows.

Elsewhere in the poem there are settings which, while not so obviously
striking, provide similar evidence of the poet's subtlety and of his creative
imagination. One of these is the house of Lot, setting for the poet's version of
the story, based on Genesis (19:1–11), in which the Sodomites threaten to
inflict homosexual rape on the visiting angels. This episode forms the central
part of a narrative sequence leading up to the destruction of the five cities. It is
preceded by the story of the angels' visit to Abraham and Sarah (based on Genesis 18), with which it has several parallels. Each episode deals with an
encounter between God (mainly in the form of the angels) and a powerful and
well-meaning man; in each, the respective wife finds it hard to accept a particular aspect of the divine as it impinges on her life.

There is, however, a sense of increasing danger and difficulty as the focus
moves from Abraham to Lot. While Abraham's dismay at the impending
destruction of the cities leads him to a process of anxious bargaining with God,
and Sarah's awareness of her advanced age leads her to laugh furtively in dis-
belief at the promise of a son, the encounter between the human and the divine
in this episode remains essentially harmonious. In the following episode of Lot
and his wife, it is far more fraught. The poet describes the disobedience of
Lot's wife – not mentioned in Genesis – in adding salt to the angels' food, contrary to explicit instructions.[18] He sharpens the effect of this by providing a

---

18   It was pointed out long ago that the episode in which Lot's wife puts salt in the angels'

brief but graphic account of her muttering rebelliously as she cooks, and indulging in a singularly disrespectful pun about *vnsaueré hyne* (822).

The main focus of this episode is, of course, the difficulty faced by Lot in trying to protect his guests from the unwelcome attention of the Sodomites. While this central situation is taken directly from the Old Testament source, the poet elaborates the story, making it more realistic and explicit. In the process, Lot's dwelling is imagined as the house of a wealthy burgher in a medieval town, complete (for instance) with a *loge dor* (784), a *wyket* (857), and ჳ*ates* (884) which are finally barred. The Sodomites are represented as a riotous and threatening mob, armed with clubs, with which they *clatter* on the walls of Lot's house (839). It might be argued that this increased specificity serves to intensify awareness of the crisis faced by Lot, and thus provide a context which helps to justify his extreme ploy of offering his daughters as sexual bait to distract the Sodomites. On the other hand, the poet does nothing to reduce the awkwardness of the moment, which – as described in Genesis (19:8) – caused biblical commentators some consternation.[19] Rather, he tends to exacerbate matters, by giving Lot a speech extolling the sexual attractions of his daughters with what might reasonably be regarded as excessive relish (861–72). It seems inevitable that this speech would put the reader in mind of the story of Lot's subsequent drunken incest with these same daughters (Genesis 20:30–36), which was much cited in exemplary writings. If the effect of all this is to force the reader to acknowledge the potential complexity of moral issues, it has much in common with the poet's handling of the episode as a whole. While the changes which he makes to the biblical narrative would have rendered the setting more recognizable to a medieval audience, they would also, paradoxically, have intensified awareness of the essential strangeness of the story.

V

The sense of strangeness is a quality which typifies *Sir Gawain and the Green Knight* – as a consequence both of the essential nature of the story itself and of various techniques used by the poet. In this poem, as in *Pearl* and (to a lesser extent) *Patience*, there are three main settings: Camelot, the lord's castle, and the Green Chapel. These are presented in ways which encourage the reader to relate them to each other, and to perceive a complex range of parallels and contrasts between and among them.

Again, as in *Pearl* and *Patience*, the three settings mark distinct stages in the psychological, moral, and spiritual development of the protagonist. Gawain may be seen to progress from implied identification with a code which mingles

---

food is well known in Hebraic tradition: see O. F. Emerson, 'A Note on the Middle English *Cleanness*', *Modern Language Review* 10 (1915), 373–5.

19 Ron Waldron and I cite an example in our edition: see the note to lines 861–72.

the values of courtliness and Christianity at Camelot, to enforced examination of the difficulties inherent in maintaining such a balance at the castle, to painful acknowledgement of his failure to do so at the Green Chapel. While each setting is presented and developed with great subtlety, the treatment is by no means uniform; and consideration of the differences between the ways in which each setting is handled can be illuminating.

Thus, for instance, variations in the use of viewpoint are striking. The poet does not describe Camelot from the outside, either at the beginning or at the end of the poem. It is, rather, seen entirely from within: from the shared viewpoint of Arthur's court and the specific viewpoint of Gawain. The lord's castle, on the other hand, is first seen, most emphatically, from the outside, by Gawain in his role of questing knight. Subsequently, Gawain encounters it as a complex and multifarious setting, in which he undergoes a wide range of experiences – alone, in intimate conversation with the lady, in small social groups, and in larger, more formal, groups. The third setting, the Green Chapel, is experienced as an enigmatic idea long before Gawain eventually reaches it. The actual process of discovery and arrival has the fundamental character of the lone quest: it is essentially one of determined search and bemused speculation on Gawain's part.[20] The recurring sense of uncertainty and unease, so characteristic of the poem once the Green Knight has made his challenge, derives substantially from the poet's treatment of his three main settings.

Among these, the most significant and the most complex is the lord's castle. This functions as a setting for the central part of the poem, and for roughly half of its total length. The castle is a complex or multiple setting, in that it contains or provides the focus for several others, notably a range of land used for hunting, a hall, various other rooms, a chapel, and Gawain's bedroom. The poet describes how Gawain's lone quest, in which he seeks a return blow from the Green Knight, has lasted until Christmas Eve, and how he prays to God and the Virgin that he will find a place in which he can hear mass on Christmas Day (753–58). Somewhat as in *Patience*, where Jonah finds the *hyrne* in the whale's belly just after his initial prayer (282–92),[21] Gawain's prayer seems to be answered immediately:

> Nade he sayned hymself, segge, bot þrye
> Er he watz war in the wod of a won in a mote,

---

20   I consider this aspect of the poem in my essay 'The Diabolical Chapel: A Motif in *Patience* and *Sir Gawain and the Green Knight*', *Neophilologus* 66 (1982), 313–19 (esp. pp. 313–15).

21   This prayer has no scriptural source, and precedes the 'prayer from the belly' (lines 305–36) which is closely based on Jonah 2:3–10 (2:2–9 in the Authorized Version). It may be worth noting that there is a partial parallel in *Sir Gawain and the Green Knight*, where the reader is told of Gawain's prayer to the Virgin well before the prayer itself is narrated (lines 736–39 and 753–58).

Abof a launde, on a lawe, loken vnder boȝez
Of mony borelych bole aboute bi þe diches,
A castel þe comlokest þat euer knyȝt aȝte,
Pyched on a prayere, a park al aboute,
With a pyked palays pyned ful þik,
Þat vmbeteȝe mony tre mo þen two myle.
Þat holde on þat on syde þe haþel auysed,
As hit schemered and schon þurȝ þe schyre okez.   (763–72)

It may be worth noting precisely what is stated here: not that the castle has appeared in answer to Gawain's prayer, but that, the moment he has finished praying and crossing himself, Gawain becomes aware of the castle. His aware-ness is expressed in an appreciative description of a magnificent building, seen from a distance. The identification of the castle as the finest Gawain has ever seen may, perhaps, imply an unflattering comparison with Camelot. Be that as it may, the poet's willingness to engage creatively with his protagonist's imag-ined response to the castle is indicated more fully in the next passage, which describes Gawain thanking God and St Julian (patron saint of hospitality), uttering a cheerful cry of relief, riding swiftly up to the *chef gate* – and finding himself excluded by a raised drawbridge, barred gates, and sturdy walls.[22] At this juncture, the poet offers a more detailed account of the impressive build-ings, facilities, and architectural features which can be seen within the walls, but ends by stressing Gawain's desire to be inside (803–06). Though the impli-cation that this description is based on what Gawain actually sees may involve poetic licence – since a man on horseback positioned close to the castle would not command an extensive view within the walls[23] – the fundamental point is clear. Gawain's experiences on his quest have deprived him of many things, including comfort, human company, and divine services. He desires admission to the castle as a refuge from such deprivation.

It has regularly been pointed out that the place of refuge becomes a place of testing. While Gawain is no longer exposed to the danger and deprivation he faced in the outside world – both from assorted opponents (including *wormez*, *wodwos*, and *etaynez*) and from cold and discomfort (713–35)[24] – he is, para-doxically and with hindsight, exposed within the castle to a more invidious threat, from dangers which are attractive, difficult to resist, and elusive of defi-nition. The main source of danger proves to be the sexual temptation offered by the lord's wife. It seems particularly apt that Gawain should see her first not

---

22 One might compare the exclusion of the Dreamer in *Pearl* from the New Jerusalem, discussed above, p. 6.
23 For this point I am indebted to my colleague Tom McNeil in his *English Heritage Book of Castles*, London, 1992, pp. 110–11.
24 The relative brevity of this passage may suggest the relative insignificance of the danger described in it.

in the hall (or some more or less neutral room), but in the chapel.[25] While in his prayer before he catches sight of the castle, Gawain expresses the fervent wish to find a place to hear mass on Christmas Day, when he actually attends his first service in the castle (evensong on Christmas Eve) he is immediately attracted by the lady, and distracted by his feelings from due concentration on spiritual things. His reported judgment, that the lady is more beautiful than Guinevere (945), may be related to the earlier comment, that the castle is the finest Gawain has ever seen (767), and contribute to a pattern of implied comparison between Camelot and the lord's castle – to the disadvantage of the former. More important by far, the encounter with the lady sets up the subsequent process of temptation, and contributes to the sense that this confronts Gawain with a tension between worldly and spiritual values.

Much has been written about the accounts of the lady's three attempts to seduce Gawain, and about the pattern of parallel and contrast between them and the juxtaposed accounts of the lord's three hunts. I should, therefore, not wish to revisit familiar arguments, but, rather, to consider one particular aspect of this substantial and crucial part of the poem. Each account of temptation is set within an account of hunting, and followed by an account of an exchange of 'winnings' between Gawain and the lord. The exchanges of 'winnings' serve to fulfill the terms of a second 'game'[26] into which Gawain enters, unguardedly, shortly after Christmas (1088–1113). With hindsight, this 'game' can be seen to serve two main purposes: to keep Gawain within the castle and thus vulnerable to temptation, and to face him with the need to render a public account of his private conduct.[27] The way in which the poet handles these passages reflects consummate skill. Each begins with an account of the lord rising early and going out to hunt. The focus then switches sharply to the lady's attempt to seduce Gawain, thus generating a strong sense of contrast – between a noisy, crowded, outdoor setting and a quiet, intimate, indoor one – while retaining an equally strong sense of thematic linkage. At the end of each attempted seduction, attention switches back to the end of the hunt, and the lord's return home. This leads naturally to the exchanges of 'winnings', which takes place indoors, in the presence of the assembled members of the lord's household – thus reinforcing the sense of public accountability. The pattern, once established, is twice repeated. It reveals the resources of the castle as a complex setting – one to which the specific settings (the hunting grounds, the bedroom, the hall) all belong. These individual settings come to function as

---

25 Though there are parallels in romance, including the *Earl of Toulous*, this motif (if such it can be called) is handled here with a unique delicacy and subtlety.

26 The first *game* is, of course, the exchange of blows.

27 Commentators have noted the various parallels between the two games: in particular, that both involve public accountability, the testing of reputation, and rules expressed in markedly legalistic terms.

settings-within-a-setting,[28] and to derive much of their resonance from their relationships with each other and with the overall setting of the castle.

VI

While the castle in *Sir Gawain and the Green Knight* is the most complex setting found in the poems attributed to the *Gawain*-poet, its essential characteristics are shared by several others. I have argued in this essay that analysis of the main settings used in the four poems suggests the poet's acute awareness of the potential of settings as contexts. While the settings themselves reflect various sources and influences – including narratives from the Old and the New Testaments, traditions of biblical commentary, and the conventions of romance and dream vision – it is conspicuous that all are handled with consummate skill and imagination. In this way, the episodes, actions, and events which they encompass are provided with contexts of unusual subtlety, richness, and resonance.

---

28   There are similarities and differences between these and the settings within the garden setting in *Pearl*: see above, p. 5.

PERFORMANCE AND STRUCTURE IN THE
ALLITERATIVE MORTE ARTHURE

ROSAMUND ALLEN

IN 1957 Ronald Waldron published an article analyzing formulaic structure in the *Alliterative Morte Arthure* (henceforth the *Morte*) compared with the rhythmic-syntactic patterns of fifteen other poems of the 'Alliterative Revival'.[1] In the course of his survey he remarks that while its formulas are not those of the truly orally composed text, yet the *Morte* is 'decidedly unliterary in appearance',[2] a view which, though modified by subsequent scholarship,[3] has been given a recent new twist: Britton Harwood affirms that the poem 'seems to be oral because ... that is the way [the poet] wishes it to sound'.[4] The *Morte* is surely a written text which probably imitates truly orally composed and formulaic works known to the aged, at least, among the audience, not nobles, but from the administrative class of the gentry.[5] The underlying

---

1 'The Oral-Formulaic Technique and Middle English Alliterative Poetry', *Speculum* 32 (1957), 792–801.
2 Waldron, 'Oral-Formulaic Technique', p. 800.
3 For a summary of recent work on the interrelationship of literacy and the vocalization of written texts, with full bibliography, see Mark C. Amodio, 'Oral Poetics in Post-Conquest England', introductory chapter in Mark C. Amodio (ed.) *Oral Poetics in Middle English Poetry*, New York, 1994, pp. 1–21. There is now agreement about the poet's artificial evocation of oral-formulaic style: Valerie Krishna has demonstrated that the heavily formulaic character of the language makes the *Morte* more formulaic and more paratactic in syntax than *Beowulf* ('Parataxis, Formulaic Density, and Thrift in the *Alliterative Morte Arthure*', *Speculum* 57 (1982), 63–83: 75, n. 48).
4 Britton J. Harwood, 'The *Alliterative Morte Arthure* as a Witness to Epic', in Amodio (ed.) *Oral Poetics*, pp. 241–86: 247; Harwood believes the *Morte* imitates a lost oral epic (248).
5 Jutta Würster, 'The Audience', in Karl Heinz Göller (ed.) *The Alliterative Morte Arthure: A Reassessment of the Poem*, Cambridge, 1981, pp. 44–56: 50, 54. In its turn, the *Morte* is read intertextually in later poetry. For echoes of the *Morte* in *The Awntyrs off Arthure* see Ralph Hanna (ed.) *The Awntyrs off Arthure at the Terne Wathelyn*, Manchester, 1974, pp. 38–43.

assumption is that the text was designed for public recitation.[6]

But little has been said about the logistics of such a performance. Would the poem have been recited in its entirety? This is unlikely: its nearly four and a half thousand lines would take over three-and-a-quarter hours to read aloud. If, on the other hand, it was performed as a series of recitations, how might the work have been divided into sections for serialization, and what bearing does this possibility have on its structure? This paper offers a reading of the poem in terms of a possible 'performance structure', which also suggests a close relationship between form and content. I argue that the *Morte* has a symmetrical structure of seven parts, with the conquest of the Roman Emperor (1950–2384) forming its apex and fourth section. As previous scholarship on the *Morte* has shown, episodes in the latter part of the poem explicitly echo earlier action and dialogue.[7]

In the seven-section performative structure I propose, the second half of the poem forms a mirror contrast with the first. The poem is structured on a rising-falling curve in a similar fashion to the five-part structure of Chaucer's *Troilus and Criseyde* and, as in that poem, Fortune's Wheel directs the action and the poem itself imitates its rise and fall. However, this is no 'tragedy', classical or accidental; Arthur is a great king and conqueror, but like all men, merely mortal.

The *Morte* has been much commended for its realistic – if for some brutal – treatment of warfare and death; realism becomes parody of Arthurian legend when Arthur dies in bed at his manor of Avalon in Glastonbury.[8] However, there are also romance motifs, and idealized knightly single combat is contrasted with the mass mêlée,[9] provoking continuing debate on two counts. One is the presentation of Arthur himself: is he accorded a just reprisal for his abuse of power, or does he suffer the vagaries of Fortune?[10] The other area of

---

6 This is well demonstrated by J. Finlayson (ed.) *The Morte Arthure*, London, 1967, p. 24; see also D. L. Rondolone, '*Wyrchipe*: the Clash of Oral-Heroic and Literate-Ricardian Ideals in the *Alliterative Morte Arthure*', in Amodio (ed.) *Oral Poetics*, pp. 208–35: 216.

7 The most detailed account of the echoic structure is J. Ritzke-Rutherford, 'Formulaic Macrostructure: the Theme of Battle', in Göller (ed.) *Reassessment*, pp. 83–95.

8 For a summary of critical opinion to 1979, see Karl Heinz Göller, 'A Summary of Research', in Göller (ed.) *Reassessment*, pp. 7–14. Lesley Johnson gives an excellent survey of the *Morte* criticism in W. R. J. Barron (ed.) *The Arthur of the English: The Arthurian Legend in Medieval English Life and Literature*, Cardiff, 1999, pp. 90–100. Larry D. Benson's dating of the poem (1399–1400) seems to have been generally accepted ('The Date of the *Alliterative Morte Arthure*', in Theodore M. Andersson and Stephen A. Barney (eds) *Contradictions: From Beowulf to Chaucer: Selected Studies of Larry D. Benson*, London, 1995, pp. 155–74).

9 Ritzke-Rutherford, 'Macrostructure', pp. 89–90.

10 For Mary Hamel the *Morte* is structured as a distorted romance where Arthur changes from questing hero to tyrant ('Adventure as Structure in the *Alliterative Morte Arthure*', *Arthurian Interpretations* 3 (1988), 37–48). W. Matthews (*The Tragedy of*

dissension is the genre of the work: is it a very atypical romance, or a *chanson de geste* out of due time (and place), or a chronicle, or even a tragedy?[11]

There is even less agreement about the structure of the work. Those who do not find it lacking any coherent structure at all have found it variously a four-, five- or a six-part narrative.

For example, Finlayson compares the poem to a *chanson de geste* in four sections, corresponding to the four parts of *Chanson de Roland*: Prelude (1–553), Roman War (554–2393), Further conquests (2394–3217), Mordrede (3218–4346).[12] For James Boren, on the other hand, the Prologue (1–77), precedes a six-part structure, each stage being determined by the arrival of messengers whose news impels the action onwards.[13] Ritzke-Rutherford, however, points out that messengers form the opening sequence of a battle macrostructure, and the five sections she identifies are focused on battle scenes.[14]

Eadie's quite different five-part structure uses dreams as structural divisions.[15] For Obst, meanwhile, the poem is themed on the ascent of Arthur in

Arthur: A Study of the Alliterative Morte Arthure, Berkeley, 1960) sees Arthur's career as a descent into excessive pride and illegal conquest, a view which is largely (not exclusively) held by the contributors to *Reassessment* (e.g. M. Fries, 'The Poem in the Tradition of Arthurian Literature', pp. 30–43); see also W. Obst, 'The Gawain-Priamus Episode in the *Alliterative Morte Arthure*', *Studia Neophilologica* 57 (1985), 9–18, but is countered by J. Eadie, 'The *Alliterative Morte Arthure*: Structure and Meaning', *English Studies* 63 (1982), 1–12, and by H. A. Kelly, 'The Non-Tragedy of Arthur', in G. Kratzmann and J. Simpson (eds.) *Medieval English Religious and Ethical Literature: Essays in Honour of G. H. Russell*, Cambridge, 1986, pp. 92–114, both of whom see Arthur as a great hero; Larry Benson also denies that Arthur is flawed but sees him at fault in forgetting his worldly limitations ('The *Alliterative Morte Arthure* and Medieval Tragedy', *Tennessee Studies in Literature* 11 (1966), 75–87). Elizabeth Porter believes 'the portrait of Arthur ... is indeed celebratory' ('Chaucer's Knight, the *Alliterative Morte Arthure*, and Medieval Laws of War: A Reconsideration', *Nottingham Medieval Studies* 27 (1983), 56–78: 57). Lee Patterson redefines the issue as 'Arthur's tragic submission to the iron law of historical recurrence', and sees this echoed in the circularity of the wheel emblem ('The Romance of History and the *Alliterative Morte Arthure*', in *Negotiating the Past*, Wisconsin, 1987, pp. 197–239: 217).

11   For a bibliography of debate on the genre, see M. Ball, 'The Knots of Narrative: Space, Time, and Focalization in the *Morte Arthure*', *Exemplaria* 8 (1996), 355–74: 374; the 'epic conundrum' contributes to the poem's plurality of meaning. Ritzke-Rutherford ('Macrostructure') identifies the *Morte* as a tragedy in five acts.

12   The *Morte Arthure*, edition, p. 13.

13   78–839, preparations for war; 840–1221, Giant; 1222–2385, Lucius; 2386–3175, conquests in Metz and Italy; 3176–455, dream of fortune; 3456–4341, Cradoke, English campaign; concluding with the Epilogue (4342–46), 'Narrative Design in the *Alliterative Morte Arthure*', *Philological Quarterly* 56 (1977), 310–19.

14   1–1221, battle with giant; 1222–2385, campaign against Lucius; 2386–3083, Metz-Priamus; 3084 (Hamel: 3068)–3590, Italy, Dream of Fortune, Cradoke; 3591–4346 English campaign, so combining the conquest of Italy and the dream of Fortune, 'Macrostructure', pp. 85 and 92.

15   1–755, outline of plans; 756–831, first dream; 832–3217, working out of plans;

four stages of opposition to tyrants, the second subdivided among Gawain, Cador and Arthur, and the third and fourth focused on Gawain: the descent is in two stages, Gawain's fall (3724–996) and Arthur's defeat (3997–4261), the opening, central and closing frames being state occasions: court, journey, funeral.[16]

The only discrete episode these analyses agree on is Arthur's fight with the giant. Their proposed structures are dictated by the writers' subjective views of what the poem is saying. As Lesley Johnson notes, however, the poem continues to provoke debate;[17] if it was written to be read to an audience, it was surely constructed for that very purpose.

Where all do agree is that the *Morte* is a performative text par excellence. The Prologue of the *Morte* defines the audience and primary topic. This, it claims, is a text for listeners:

> 3e that liste has to lyth   or luffes for to here
> Off elders of alde tym   and of theire awke dedys ...
> Herkynes me heyndly   and holdys 3ow styll
> And I sall tell 3ow a tale   þat trewe is and nobyll ...
> Herkenys now hedyr-warde   and herys this storye.   (12–25)[18]

The chief episode is highlighted in the oral equivalent of a bookjacket 'blurb' before the narrative begins: this will be a tale of the *ryeall renkes of the Rownnde Table* (17) and their chivalry, skill at arms, fear of disgrace, and courtesy (19–21). They gained many *wyrchippis* (22) through warfare and

> Sloughe Lucyus þe lythyre,   that lorde was of Rome,
> And conqueryd that kyngryke   thorowe craftys of armes.   (23–24)

The Prologue locates the work in a context of courts and chivalry and signals the killing of Emperor Lucius and conquest of Rome. This is the climax of the *storye*: the audience is to hear an instructive history (*storye*), *trewe and nobyll* if strange (*awke*).[19]

Joyce Coleman has recently demonstrated that even chronicles and devotional material were frequently read aloud, or 'prelected', and their significance debated among the audience.[20] Although public readings of chronicles

---

3218–455, second dream; 3456–4346, consequences of second dream, conclusion, 'Structure and Meaning', p. 2.

16 1–1221; 1222–616 (Gawain)/1617–945 (Cador)/1946–2415 (Arthur); Priamus (Gawain); Lorraine's subjection (Gawain) ('The Gawain-Priamus Episode', pp. 11–12).

17 'The *Alliterative Morte Arthure*', in *The Arthur of the English*, pp. 93 and 99.

18 All quotations are taken from Mary Hamel (ed.) *The Morte Arthure: A Critical Edition*, New York and London, 1984.

19 MED s.v. *auk(e)* (c) 'strange, marvellous'.

20 *Public Reading and the Reading Public in Late Medieval England and France*, Cambridge, 1996.

before a royal or noble patron are less well attested for the British Isles than in the noble courts of France and Burgundy,[21] Coleman presents much evidence that public reading was commonplace until the sixteenth century. The *Morte* suggests that the gentry imitated the practice of using historical narrative for exemplary purposes. The realism of the *Morte* marks it as a vernacular equivalent to a chronicle of past times, and in just the same way as Continental courts discussed the moral and instructive import of history, so, the opening prayer implies, the audience of the *Morte* can discuss its *plesande and profitabill* matter in which nothing should be useless or worthless (*voyde ... ne vayne*, 10) but all to the glory of God.

Missing from the Prologue's plot summary is the decline of Arthur's fortunes after Lucius's death, on which so much modern controversy depends. The events which occur between Lucius's death and the dream of Fortune are outlined in Arthur's own agenda for action before leaving Britain: he will be in Lorraine or Lombardy by Lammas, will conquer Milan and remain six weeks at Viterbo unless sued for peace (349–56, cf. 3134–65). His vow to revel in Rome (379) is about to be fulfilled: *Now may we reuell and riste, for Rome es oure awen!* (3207), when Fortune fails him, denying him his last ambition, *To reuenge the Renke   that on the Rode dyede* (3216–17) by regaining Jerusalem. It is possible that a lacuna in Thornton's text or its exemplar cut out the remaining summary of the full action, or perhaps the poet set up for his audience exactly the kind of surprise that awaits Arthur himself: this is not the traditional ending the audience would expect.[22]

The kind of performance flagged in the Prologue is not specified: did the poet envisage his work recited in 'hall', like the original *chansons de geste*, or for an audience in chamber?[23] What is more, what kind of reader did Thornton copy the poem for? His decorative scheme highlights earthly power, Arthur's claims and conquests and his lament for Gawain.[24] Even a solitary reader would

21   '... the public reading of histories [in France and Burgundy] served the ... goal of imparting information and influencing individuals towards a single approved understanding of history and the key social values it is presented as illustrating', *Public Reading*, p. 127; 'no British king subsidized the formulation of monarchist political theory and historiography in the manner of Charles V, and no British (sic) nobles sought to legitimize their own dynastic claims by commissioning official histories' (*Public Reading*, p. 128).

22   Just possibly the Prologue reflects an earlier stage of the text before the events immediately preceding the fall were included; Patterson accepts the view that this was a growing narrative, and Hamel believes that it was over thirty years in composition. If prelected by its author, the poem might have grown through contributive composition resulting from audience discussion.

23   Coleman, *Public Reading*, pp. 131–6.

24   Signalled by means of large initials, irregularly placed: see P. Hardman, 'Reading the Spaces: Pictorial Intentions in the Thornton MSS, Lincoln Cathedral MS 91, and BL MS Add. 31042', *Medium Aevum* 63 (1994), 250–74: 256. The facsimile, *The*

be likely to read the manuscript text aloud, a more time-consuming process than sweeping the eye over the printed page, and would need 'relief breaks' in this physically tiring process. How long would a performed instalment of a medieval text last, and how much text can be covered in each performance? Alliterative long-lines take longer to read aloud than a text in octosyllabic couplets. W. R. J. Barron reckons that four hundred lines of Laȝamon's *Brut* – long lines, it will be remembered, of approximately twelve syllables – could be performed in a sitting; indeed, Audley Hall finds only eight narratives in Laȝamon's *Brut* longer than 400 lines, suggesting that the *Brut* could have been read in instalments of discrete episodes, with longer episodes subdivided.[25] Four hundred lines of Laȝamon take about thirty to thirty-five minutes to 'prelect', without slowing down for special effects. This is around the average TV or radio programme of half to three-quarters of an hour.[26]

As Coleman shows, a prelection of a vernacular text formed part of a mixed after-dinner programme of readings, discussion of what was read, with music, dance, games of chess and backgammon and other entertainment, and must have lasted well under an hour.[27] Six hundred lines of the *Morte* take about thirty-five minutes to read aloud, and more would overtire the reader and probably the audience.[28] A medieval reader might have recited faster, though even a contemporary reader and his/her audience would have found the diction of the

---

Thornton Manuscript (Lincoln Cathedral MS 91), introd. D. S. Brewer and A. E. B. Owen (London, 1975) shows comic-tragic faces in many of the initials, such as a grieving face at 4060 where Mordrede attacks, and there are marginal line drawings, e.g. a man spears a seated warrior at 2123 where Arthur attacks Golapas, where, oddly, a woman's face fills the bowl of the 'H'.

25 A. S. Hall, 'The Fiction of History: A Structural Analysis of Layamon's *Brut*', Ph.D. Dissertation, University of Arkansas, 1987, p. 27: Arthur's is one of the eight longer narratives, all of which develop the theme of the ideal king. My own analysis of *The Brut* sees it as comprising 35 sections of between 315 and 626 lines ('Counting Time and Time for Recounting: Narrative Sections in Laȝamon's *Brut*', in Herbert Pilch (ed.) *Orality and Literacy in Early Middle English. Scriptoralia 83*, Tübingen, 1996, pp. 71–91).

26 Although the 'viewer relaxing at home' consumes text very differently from the audience community of medieval texts, the *awke* deeds of Arthur are interpenetrated by contemporary issues in a similar way to the pattern in nightly sequences of TV screening of everyday stable normality into which problematic fictional or actual dilemmas intrude (J. Ellis, *Visible Fictions: Cinema: Television: Video*, London, 1992, pp. 145–59: I owe this reference to Professor Morag Shiach).

27 Coleman, *Public Reading*, pp. 83 and 96 cites *Havelok* 2327–30 and Edward IV's household book, *Liber Niger*; a wholly private prelection could last as long as two hours, however (pp. 111 and 120).

28 This was assuming that final *-e* was certainly not pronounced except when followed by *-d* or *-s*, so accounting for the difference in reading time from the *Brut*. The timing of the seven sections to be discussed below was: 1: thirty-five minutes, 2: thirty-five minutes, 3: forty minutes, 4: twenty-five minutes, 5: thirty-five minutes, 6: thirty minutes, 7: forty minutes.

Morte far from everyday, and the prelector would hampered by using a manuscript text in artificial light. But a 'good' reader would probably read quite slowly anyway, 'pointing' the natural emphases in the plot, dwelling on poetic or graphic passages (fighting, notably, in the *Morte*!).[29]

Surprisingly, the *Morte* does seem to fall naturally into sections of between five and seven hundred lines, with one section of four hundred lines. Such sections, directed by reader-fatigue, do seem to correspond to natural divisions in the material. In fact all but two occur at a phrase of the kind 'When/then Arthur ...': *Qwen sir Arthure the kynge had kylled þe gyaunt* (1222), and one of the remaining two has 'now the bold king'.[30] Such markers would provide 'pick-up points' for resuming narrative by briefly summarizing the previous action and appropriately beginning a new section with the conqueror himself.

Using performance as a guide, then, it is possible to identify seven episodes in the work, forming a prelude to the climax at lines 2119–256, with a progressive descent from there to Arthur's death at the close of the poem:

Prologue	1–25		
Part 1	26–624	Conquests, embassy, challenge	613 lines
Part 2	625–1221	Departure, dream of dragon, Giant of Mont St Michel	597 lines
Part 3	1222–1949	Embassy to Lucius; ambush, Cador rebuked	728 lines
Part 4	1950–2385	Battle of Sessye CLIMAX Death of Emperor and Kay	436 lines
Part 5	2386–3067	Germany; Metz: Priamus: Duchess	682 lines
Part 6	3068–3590	Lorraine, Italy: Como, Milan; Dream of Fortune; Cradoke	523 lines
Part 7	3591–4346	Last battle. Deaths of Gawain, Mordrede, Arthur	756 lines

29 Coleman provides evidence that the best readers did indeed 'point' their readings for dramatic and instructive effects, pp. 121–2.

30 12 *Qwen that the Kynge Arthur*; 625 *At the vtas of Hillary syr Arthure*; 1222 *Qwen sir Arthure the kynge*; 1950 *whene the senatours*; 2386 *thane sir Arthure onone*; 3068 *When þe Kyng Arthure*; 3591 *Nowe bownes the bolde kynge*. Only 1950 and 2386 do not have a large capital in the Lincoln Thornton manuscript; for 1950 see below, p. 24. Thornton (or his exemplar) seems to have regarded adverbs of time as junctions; of the eighty large capital letters in the *Morte*, only 26 do not correspond to 'when', 'then' or 'now' beginning or within the line; of these, eight mark a speech, and six begin with 'but/and', while three of the remaining twelve mark a temporal division. Most of Thornton's paraphs also occur at 'then' or 'after' in the text. Whether or not Thornton recognized any larger section divisions, he organized smaller sections of his material in a way which would have made his copy easier to use when reading aloud from it.

Each of these episodes is between five and seven hundred lines long, with the exception of Part 4. Exactly equal division of the whole would have sections of just over six hundred lines apiece, but Parts 3 and 7 are over a hundred lines longer, while 4 is nearly two hundred lines and 6 one hundred lines shorter, and it is impossible to identify junctures which would construct an exactly symmetrical text.

Possibly some episodes, notably in Part 3, have been amplified, supporting Patterson's theory that this is a text 'in progress'.[31]

Conversely, the central section has been at least somewhat truncated in the unique copy in the Lincoln Cathedral manuscript. Thornton seems to have omitted a transitional passage in which the news of the failed rescue of the senators reaches the Emperor, as Malory has it, through a Senator who escapes from the battle and reports to Lucius (between lines 1949 and 1950). Malory himself may have supplied his own linking passage here, but even if his prose is based on a more complete version of the original than Thornton supplies, it seems unlikely that the lost matter would amount to two hundred lines. Similar short passages might have been lost, such as the burial of Holdin and Ligier,[32] accounting for a further proportion of the shortfall of two hundred lines. There is certainly further textual confusion in this section since Lucius seems to die (or suffer life-threatening wounds) twice.[33] It is likely that the battle of Sessye episode has been adapted, perhaps leaving Thornton's or an antecedent exemplar confused or untidy, and not at all impossible that this modification was made as a result of audience collaboration. One point of contention might have been the omission from the original version of the popular figure of Lancelot, whose promotion to apparently killing the Emperor almost deprives Arthur of his prize.[34]

This climactic central section focuses on detailed treatment of battle, which would probably demand slower recitation, particularly by an audience used to or at least interested in the techniques of battle. Perhaps too it might provoke subsequent discussion of the battle tactics described, which would occupy the remaining time slot. Raising the emotional tension by means of metrical heightening would also force the reader to slow down:

31 'Romance of History', p. 212; Hamel suggests the poem was thirty years in composition (*The Morte Arthure: A Critical Edition*, pp. 57–8).

32 See Hamel, *Morte Arthure*, edition, note to 2383. As her note to 2384–85 shows, there is great textual corruption here: 2385 repeats 2380 but now has Cador, who is not dead, buried at 'Cam'.

33 At 2074–79 and 2255. Thornton misplaces 3112–27 (Parts 5 and 6) by including them 44 lines too early.

34 Hamel is unable to resolve the problem of Lancelot's apparently mortal wounding of Lucius (note to 2074); Krishna suggests Lancelot merely penetrates him (*The Alliterative Morte Arthure: A Critical Edition*, New York, 1976, p. 185). Lancelot's very presence in the *Morte* may be an adaptation of an earlier version of the *Morte* itself, based as it is primarily on Wace's *Roman de Brut* and the chronicle tradition in which the romance hero Lancelot does not figure at all.

... But they fitt them fayre,   thes frekk byernez,
Fewters in freely   one feraunte stedes,
Foynes full felly   with flyschande speris,
Freten of orfrayes   feste appon scheldez;
So fele fey es in fyghte   appon þe felde leuyed
That iche a furthe in the firthe   of rede blode rynnys!   (2139–44)

It is surely significant that the run-on alliteration on /f/ which has become stylistically salient ceases just when the poet reaches the desired climax: *rede blode*. Though the extant poem allots only 1160-odd lines to the Roman War, of which only 282 cover the actual battle of Sessye, compared with 822 devoted to the ensuing conquests, the rhetoric of challenge and the virtuoso metrics provide opportunity for dramatic pointing.

In this structural analysis, it is Parts 5 and most of 6 (to 3468, where Arthur meets Cradoke) which form the additions to the basic chronicle source for the *Morte*. Just possibly, in an *ur*-text version, the narrative moved immediately to Arthur's recall to Britain after the disposal of the Emperor's body, that is, from line 2385 to a point near 3479 where he accosts Cradoke.[35] In such a five-part narrative Part 4 would show Arthur's triumph followed immediately by reversal, matching his swift collapse in the chronicles. Might the sieges of Metz and Como and the capitulation of Milan have been prompted by audience demand for further conquests? The romance material in the Priamus episode could have had its origin in demand for further enhancement of that hero of the English, Gawain. The Dream of Fortune is a possible answer to fireside debate about why Arthur's fortunes foundered. If these two parts, 5 and 6 were both later stages in the compositional process, then the poet shows remarkable adroitness in extending the original structure in order to enhance its meaning.

When analyzed, these sections provide a symmetrical framework for the poem. The seven parts here identified present a distinct narrative rationale: enhancing its narrative, each section contains at least one descriptive or confrontational highlight. Examples are: the feast (176–219) and the council (249–406) in Part 1, Arthur's dream of the dragon and bear in 2 (760–813), Gawain's exchange with the Emperor in 3 (1302–52), booty and preparation of coffins in Part 4 (2282–305),[36] the armed knight and *locus amoenus* in 5 (2501–24, 2670–77), the Dream of Fortune in 6 and Arthur's laments and ceremonious end in 7 (3956–68, 4262–341). Such passages form a change in pace from the physical combat which motivates each section except the first –

---

35   The conclusion of Part 6 taken with Part 7 forms 850-odd lines; with the 436 lines of Part 4 this gives a total 1286 lines, or the equivalent of two 600+ line sections, matching the length of Parts 1 and 2, with Part 5 probably beginning near the present 3598 (voyage to Britain) or at 3712, Gawain's attack and death.

36   This account is very brief compared with Geoffrey's emphasis and may have been abbreviated.

where there is only a retrospective list of conquests – but this whets the audience's appetite for fighting and operates like the equivalent of the shots during the credits-run at the start of a movie: no one taking their seat belatedly need fear they have missed much. Such mixed fare would suit a mixed gentry audience of extended family and higher-ranking servants; any visiting dignitaries, accustomed to prelections in French, would not be offended by the *Morte* which is both an adaptation of Wace's French and a mélange of other French works.[37]

This disposition of parts highlights the parallel construction often noted by critics: the dream of the Dragon in Part 2 balances the Dream of Fortune in Part 6, and the courage of Cador in Part 3 is matched by that of Gawain in Part 5. Arthur's nephew Mordrede, who will not take responsibility, in 2, contrasts in Part 6 Gawain's 'son' Florent (2735), who does exercise authority, and his ward Chasteleyne, bold even to death; Arthur redresses Uther's disgrace (521,1310) and Idrus puts Arthur before his father's need (4142–54). The symmetry is reflected in small details and large blocks: triumphant, Arthur hunts at Caerleon in Part 1 (61); his coming desolation is announced in 6 by Cradoke, who was keeper of Caerleon (3512) and just before the end, Guinevere enters a nunnery there (3916); Arthur kills a giant in Part 2, an Emperor in Part 4 and dies himself in Part 7. The panoply of Christmas and New Year celebrations at the start of the poem is repeated in the elaborate funeral rites for Arthur in the following winter.[38] Other near-symmetrical pointings include the oft-noted parallel *locus amoenus* passages, which form a prelude to the fight with the giant and the fight with Priamus in Parts 2 and 5; they form a subtext which contrasts an idealized nature (Priamus's restorative elixir in 5 and the dream setting in 6) with nature debased and in the raw (the Giant who exposes his nakedness). A further *locus amoenus* in 3230–49 before the siege of Como in Part 6 forms an ominous parallel: the peaceful peasants at Como will suffer just as the giant at Mont St Michel has ravaged the local populace in Part 2. The natural world and nature transcended in Parts 2, 5, 6 contrast the inescapability of human death: the nine worthies die simply because all men do; this Arthur is no *rex futurus*.

The function of death in the text is pointed by the structure: Kay and Gawain die in Parts 4 and 7, the middle and end of the poem. Arthur is absent from the action for much of Parts 3 and 5, but is represented by his men, who act as his surrogates. The interdependence of leader and men is paramount in the text and is compromised by independent action and personal grief. Arthur's role is enhanced in Parts 1 and 2 and 7 and 8: we see him first as the conquering leader

---

37   Patterson, 'Romance of History', pp. 217–21.
38   Ritzke-Rutherford, 'Macrostructure', p. 91; some of the exact symmetries she notes are admittedly lost in this sectioning: Arthur's single combat with the giant is not exactly matched with his fight with Mordrede (p. 94).

who fights on behalf of his people in epic mode; military success assures him personal greatness and a role in history but his own life is inevitably transient. On the Wheel of Fortune Arthur is the first of the third, Christian, order in history, but he has also taken over the places of Alexander, first of the pagans, David, last of the biblical heroes and Charlemagne, his successor in the Christian order: his career resembles Alexander's, his personal life resembles David's,[39] and his connection with Alexander and Charlemagne is secured in the narrative intertexts in the Priamus episode drawn from the *Fuerres de Gadres* (linked to the *Roman d'Alexandre*) and the *Fierabras* (a Charlemagne romance).[40] Arthur in martial success annexes even the literary past of the heroes of French romance.

The death of leaders is foregrounded in the poem: while nature is self-renewing, even for great men death is absolute, and the supernatural dream of Fortune in Part 6 signals this. In the *Morte* Avalon is merely a manor: Arthur is buried and will not return. The poem forms a half-circle which moves from challenge to attainment to inevitable demise, and Arthur is one more instance of greatness that must unavoidably end. Inevitably, he has erred, but he is not explicitly punished for committing carnage in unjust war.[41] Critical debate on his culpability reflects the way the poem is constructed to provoke audience discussion.

But not all modern responses are apt;[42] the medieval respect for *wyrchipe*, the public acclaim of a conqueror (Arthur's title in the *Morte*) is shown in the Syre of Melane's capitulation without fight and his promise of enormous tribute, which has political point if Benson's date of 1400 for the *Morte* is correct: Milan was the centre of weapon production (perhaps for this reason known to the poet and his audience; could they have been associated with the Great Wardrobe?) and the Visconti were hugely powerful tyrants. Such a conquest

---

39 R. A. Shoaf, 'The *Alliterative Morte Arthure*: the story of Britain's David', *Journal of English and Germanic Philology* 81 (1982), 204–26. Hardman shows that the *Morte* 'fits well with the establishing of universal power', placed by Thornton immediately after his copy of the *Prose Alexander* 'which represents a reading of the text as a history of conquest and the establishment of empire' ('Reading the Spaces', p. 255).

40 Priamus's own ancestry also spans both pagan, Jewish and Christian systems (2602–07) and his own namesake ancestor figures in the closing episode (4344).

41 Ritzke-Rutherford, 'Macrostructure', p. 93; M. Hamel, 'The Dream of a King: the *Alliterative Morte Arthure* and Dante', *Chaucer Review* 14 (1980), 307. For demonstration of Boccaccio's condemnation of Arthur's pride, and Lydgate's exculpation of him, see E. D. Kennedy, 'Generic Intertextuality in the English *Alliterative Morte Arthure*: the Italian Connection', in N. J. Lacy (ed.) *Text and Intertext in Medieval Arthurian Literature*, New York, 1996, pp. 41–56.

42 W. Parks, 'The Flyting Contract and Adversarial Patterning in the *Alliterative Morte Arthure*', in D. G. Allen and R. A. White (eds) *Traditions and Innovations: Essays on British Literature of the Middle Ages and the Renaissance*, eds D. G. Allen and Robert A. White, Newark, 1990, pp. 59–74.

would be power indeed, and far from being condemned for unjust war, Arthur would earn the audience's amused admiration.[43] The collapse of his plans is not presented as punishment.

Competition and conquest motivate the narrative, and Arthur succeeds until mere fate, the result of misjudging Mordrede, intervenes: Fortune tosses all men to death, and the greatest fall most conspicuously. The *Morte* is subtler than this, however: Arthur is no mere exemplary figure. In failure, he is invested with greater personality and becomes more sympathetic in loss and disaster than in success. Like an epic hero, he fulfils the vow he made in Part 1:

> I sall at Lammesse take leue,   to lenge at my large
> In Lorayne or Lumberdye,   whethire me leue thynkys
> Merke vnto Meloyne   and myne doun þe wallez
> Bathe of Petyrsande and of Pys   and of þe Pounte Tremble;
> In þe vale of Viterbe   vetaile my knyghttes ...   (349–53)

Modern sensibilities are shocked by the violence necessary to gain this success, responding to the text's invitation to consider the losers' fate and the suffering of non-combatants: *The pyne of the pople was peté, for to here* (3043). Yet the Duchess of Lorraine's plea: *send vs some socoure* (3052) is met in Arthur's textbook-behaviour in raising Metz (*hade lely conquerid*, 3068). Arthur is merciful, but conquest inevitably brings suffering, and this double viewpoint offers invitation to debate. All the nine worthies are celebrated as martial heroes, and like Alexander, David, and proleptically, Charlemagne, Arthur is one more example of how men change the world by conquest, but are in their turn moved on.[44]

The audience is given more direction to ponder the implications of power in Arthur's own emotional weakness in defeat. The death of his men now provokes him to tears like those of the women bereaved and made homeless by his own conquests: *I may helples one hethe house be myn one,/Alls a wafull wedowe þat wanttes hir beryn* (4284–85). His status is diminished and feminized, and now the men he once led instruct him: *It es no wirchipe, iwysse, to wrynge thyn hondes/To wepe als a woman it es no witt holden* (3977–78).[45] Arthur's threnody over Gawain's corpse contrasts with his resolute revenge

---

43   D. Wallace, *Chaucerian Polity: Absolutist Lineages and Associational Forms in England and Italy*, Stanford, 1997, pp. 39–43.

44   Patterson, 'Romance of History', pp. 227–30.

45   For A. C. Bartlett, Arthur's unstable masculinity typifies the challenge of women in late medieval society ('Cracking the Penile Code: Reading Gender and Conquest in the *Alliterative Morte Arthure*', *Arthuriana* 8:2 (1998), 56–76); Jeff Westover also thinks Arthur's masculinity is challenged ('Arthur's End: the King's Emasculation in the *Alliterative Morte Arthure*', *Chaucer Review* 32 (1998), 310–24); equally provocatively, Rondolone thinks Arthur's confusion reflects the clash of the God-centred literate world-view with the hero-centred oral-epic (*Wyrchipe*, 235).

for Kay (2198, 2264) and Bedivere (2241–42) in Part 4, but his keenly depicted suffering brings him and his emotions into closer focus than when he was the successful commander ordering troops. Such engagement of our sympathy provokes critical debate, as it is designed to. In grief and disaster Arthur ceases to be a type of the great man, and becomes an individual, who makes a good end that is itself debatable: the spiritual estate of the soldier is always problematic.

Unlike the linear chronicle accounts of kings' reigns from accession to death, the structure of the *Morte* rises to a pinnacle in Part 4 and then falls, echoing the dominant motif of Fortune's wheel. Performance-length division suggests that the *Morte* is a seven-part construct that has not come down to us quite intact, which provides salutary warning, like the chronicles, of the vulnerability human greatness to the eroding force of politics and physical debility, or, in shorthand, 'Fortune'.

FEASTING IN MIDDLE ENGLISH ALLITERATIVE POETRY

RALPH HANNA

I AM EXPANDING here on an earlier discussion, in which I discussed in passing the fictiveness of festive descriptions in alliterative poems.[1] I hope this elaboration on earlier work will indicate our communal debts to Ron Waldron (my effort will surely teach him nothing he has not long known). For, from his thesis onward, Ron has spent long years showing us the necessity for a broad consideration of alliterative 'themes' and the community of alliterative diction and interest which surmounts the boundaries of the individual work.

> When folk are fested and fed, fayn wald þai here
> Sum farand þinge eftir fode to faynen þare hertis.
>
> *(Wars of Alexander* 1–2)[2]

> Elenge is þe halle, ech day in þe wike,
> Ther þe lord ne þe lady likeþ noȝt to sitte.
> Now haþ ech riche a rule to eten by hymselue.
>
> *(Piers Plowman* B 10.97–99)[3]

---

1 'Alliterative Poetry', in D. Wallace (ed.) *The Cambridge History of Medieval English Literature*, Cambridge, 1999, pp. 488–512; see especially pp. 501–4.

2 I cite Middle English alliterative poems from the following texts: R. Hanna III (ed.) *The Awntyrs of Arthure at the Terne Wathelyn*, Manchester, 1974; G. A. Panton and D. Donaldson (eds) *The Geste Historiale of the Destruction of Troy*, Early English Text Society [hereafter EETS] o.s. 39, 56, London, 1869–74; T. Turville-Petre (ed.) *St Erkenwald, The Parlement of the Thre Ages* and *Wynnere and Wastoure* in *Alliterative Poetry of the Later Middle Ages: An Anthology*, London, 1989, pp. 101–19, pp. 67–100, pp. 38–66; M. Andrew and R. A. Waldron (eds) *The Poems of the Pearl Manuscript*, Berkeley, 1982; M. Hamel (ed.) *Morte Arthure*, New York, 1984; G. Kane (gen. ed.) *Piers Plowman* (3 vols), London, 1960–1997; H. N. Duggan and T. Turville-Petre (eds) *The Wars of Alexander*, EETS s.s. 10, Oxford, 1989.

3 Cf. Langland's willingness to indulge such a view as that enunciated in *Wars*:
   Leriþ it þus lewide men, for lettrid it knowiþ …
   … preche it in þin harpe
   þer þou art mery at mete, ȝif men bidde þe ȝedde. *(Piers Plowman* A 1.125, 137–38)

These contemporary alliterative poems share a common perception of feasting – and deviate from one another in their sense of the degree to which it is socially realised. For both, the great hall of the lord's house is/should be a place of community; in the case of *The Wars*, this is most fully imagined as participation in literary experience, joyous listening to an historical *geste* (*a farand þinge ...*/ [that befell] *Or þai ware fourmed on fold or þaire fadirs oþir*) – like the poem which the passage introduces. In Study's diatribe from *Piers Plowman*, that community has been shattered by the discovery of privacy, and even hall-joys, when they occur, have been subjected to new and perverse transformations:

> Ac if þei carpen of crist, þise clerkes and þise lewed,
> At mete in hir murþe whan Mynstrals beþ stille,
> Than telleþ þei of a Trinite how two slowe þe þridde ....
> Thus þei dryuele at hir deys þe deitee to knowe,
> And gnawen god in þe gorge whanne hir guttes fullen.
>
> (*Piers* B 10.52–54, 57–58)

At table, lords behave just as if they were in chamber, not hall, by making the minstrels shut up and by participating in private conversation. But the conversation itself is revelatory. Its perversity does not simply reflect its improper sense of company, argument instead of conversation, nor simply its ignorant theologising, laymen attempting to escape their proper social status, the hierarchy which a feast should express, and subjecting to a *balled reson* (B 10.55), choplogic, the greatest mysteries of the faith. The trinitarian discussion disaggregates the most powerful social symbol of differences reconciled (and through the second person, the corporate body of Christians), the Trinity itself.

Both these passages participate in an ancient topos of alliterative poetry, indeed of European epic generally. In English, the description of the first feast in Heorot surely provides the *locus classicus*:

> He [Hrothgar] beot ne aleh, beagas dælde,
> sinc æt symle. Sele hlifade
> heah and horngeap; heaðowylma bad,
> laðan liges; ne wæs hit lenge þa gen,
> þæt se ecghete aþumsweoran
> æfter wælniðe wæcnan scolde.
>   Ða se ellengæst earfoðlice
> þrage geþolode, se þe in þystrum bad,
> þæt he dogora gehwam dream gehyrde
> hludne in healle; þær wæs hearpan sweg,
> swutol sang scopes. Sægde se þe cuþe
> frumsceaft fira feorran reccan,
> cwæð þæt se Ælmihtiga eorðan worhte,

wlitebeorhtne wang, swa wæter bebugeð,
gesette sigehreþig sunnan and monan
leoman to leohte landbuendum ...   (*Beowulf* 80–95)[4]

While one cannot underplay the foreboding that is part of the passage, one should equally insist upon its productive reciprocities. King, scop and God all operate similarly, albeit in differentiated spheres of creativity – building the greatest of halls, improvising a poem to the harp, making the world itself. Moreover, each actor creates, not out of self-indulgent fatuity, but from a sense of reciprocity, to express a bond to others: Hrothgar so that he can fulfil his oath and social responsibilities, reward his partners in conquest, his *heorþgeneatas* (*beagas dælde, sinc æt symle*); the scop to contribute to the generalised joy associated with that act; God to create a happy and fulfilling environment for mankind (*landbuendum*; cf. *teode/firum foldan*, *Cædmon's Hymn* 8b–9a).[5]

Yet the foreboding remains – and will come to pass. The feast, while expressing social and cosmic harmony, is equally compromised by the promise of its opposite: those sworn to one another will leave the hall in flames, presumably brought to enmity by just those treasures which here are seen as the devices of social bonding. Likewise, the scop's *swutol sang* – 'clarifying' in its evocation of racial memory, 'clear as a bell' in its aural effects – is the *dream hludne* which attracts the monster's attention and inadvertently destroys the civility it intends to foster:

Þa wæs eaðfynde þe him elles hwær
gerumlicor ræste sohte,
bed æfter burum ...
... oð þæt idel stod
husa selest.   (138–40a, 145b–46a)

And God at moments protects his creation by instituting social difference, decreeing a class forbidden to enjoy his gifts and driving these newly identified enemies from them (*forscrifen hæfde* 106b). Such a *wonsæli wer* (105) as Grendel cannot inhabit the formed world of human enjoyment (*eorðan* ... *swa wæter bebugeð*), only a wilderness where the differentiations associated with creation are in danger of constant collapse (*moras* ... *fen ond fæsten* 103b–4a).[6] The absence of an abiding providence allows the exile, in his animosity, the same vengeful possibilities enacted by the *aþumsweoran*.

Of course, this uncreating impulse has its own poetry as well:

---

4   Cited from F. Klaeber (ed.) *Beowulf and the Fight at Finnsburg*, Lexington, 1950.
5   Except for *Beowulf* (for which see note 4 above), I cite all Old English poetry from G. P. Krapp and E. van K. Dobbie (eds) *The Anglo-Saxon Poetic Records* (6 vols), New York, 1931–42.
6   Which in contrast to the differentiated created world, I would translate, 'marshy places with firm bits'.

Iþde swa þisne eardgeard ælda scyppend
oð þæt burgwara breahtma lease,
eald enta geweorc idlu stodon.   (*The Wanderer* 85–87)

The gesture towards Roman ruins, emblem of the passage of worldly kingdoms and greatness, may be antique, but Middle English alliterative poetry
sometimes includes much the same detail. For example, *Winner and Waster*
juxtaposes:

When wawes waxen schall wilde and walles bene doun
And hares appon herthestones schall hurcle in hire fourne ...

with

Whylome were lordes in londe þat loued in thaire hertis
To here makers of myrthes þat matirs couthe fynde.   (12–13, 19–20)

All these examples bespeak the deep melancholy and elegiac tone which
permeates European historical epic. The topos begins (like everything else) with
Homer, in the *Odyssey*. There the hero, enjoying the perfect civility of the
Phaikian feast, hears the great minstrel Demodokos, who sings both of gods
(whom he may treat satirically) and of men, Troy (book 8); Odysseus's tears
presage his own account, the recitation of personally experienced epic loss and
struggle (books 9–12).[7] Virgil's imitation occurs at the head of the *Aeneid*: the
hero weeps before the visual images of Troy, decorative features of the temple in
Carthage (1.452–93). Here the *arx* has already been constructed, the foundation
story fulfilled and denatured by nostalgia, while Aeneas must endure yet further
torments to found his own city. And like Odysseus, the hero offers his personal
account, in book 2. Throughout the tradition, what can be applauded as commu-
nity-forming and glorified in song is precisely and only what is most at risk, most
subject to abuse, loss, failure. *Sunt lacrimae rerum et mentem mortalia tangunt.*
    Middle English alliterative poetry, most pervasively an historical poetry,
re-enacts these same topics. The basic contrastive pattern I have been developing appears perhaps most explicitly in *St Erkenwald* and is most lavishly discussed in *Cleanness*. The central figure of the first poem, the forgotten pagan
justice, describes his state:

Quat wan we with oure wele-dede þat wroghten ay riȝt,
Quen we are dampnyd dulfully into þe depe lake,
And exilid fro þat soper so þat solempne fest,
Þer richely hit arne refetyd þat after right hungride?   (301–04)

Earthly struggles for justice are bound by the very processes of history; in
spite of his virtuous action, the justice remains yet another lamenting exile, a
sinner. (In this case, the cycles of God's providential history themselves decree

---

7   For an appreciation of hall-joy, cf. Odysseus's speech at the opening of book 9.

he must be such, since he lived before the Conversion of England.) In contrast, heaven itself, God's hall, is conceived as *solempne fest*. Perhaps presciently, *St Erkenwald* here evokes a topic descended from Old English, yet another transitional context, in which (pagan) literary diction and (Christian) religious sentiment fuse;[8] in *The Dream of the Rood*, for example, the speaker hopes the cross:

> me þonne gebringe þær is blis mycel,
> dream on heofenum, þær is dryhtnes folc,
> geseted to symle, þær is singal blis;
> ond me þonne asette þær ic siþþan mot
> wunian on wuldre, well mid þam halgum
> dreames brucan.[9]   (139–44a)

As Turville-Petre's note to *St Erkenwald* 304 indicates, such a conceptualisation is predicated on the gospels, Jesus's words at Luke 22: 29–30. And *Cleanness*, as countless studies have indicated, recasts feasting in strictly biblical terms. Here the *Gawain*-poet retells at length (33–192) the parable of the wedding feast from Matthew 22: 1–14; this version, as opposed to the truncated account at Luke 14: 16–24, attracts him because of the materials, absent from Luke, describing the guest expelled for wearing a soiled garment. While the parable retains its biblical force – accepting the lord's invitation/having a clean garment means being accepted into the Kingdom (see 161ff) – the poet, as is his wont, elaborately develops the literal sense as well.[10] The socially maladept detail of wearing one's workclothes to high table achieves force only in the material social context of an elaborately disposed banquet, as one would find in a medieval hall (see 89–92, for example). And the poet's presentation is far from some empty 'late medieval realisation of detail', for dining and the associated ethics of the courteous life bind the poem's diverse episodes thematically.

The perfect heavenly Lord's feast appears in *Cleanness* only tangentially. There is but one direct reference (176): *se þy sauior and his sete ryche*, perhaps even to be construed as God enthroned, not on the high dais at table. But certainly in the parable, one is to understand that the host is God. This identification explains Langland's agitation in *Piers Plowman* B about lordly absence. If

---

8   H. Magennis, *Images of Community in Old English Poetry*, Cambridge, 1996, provides a useful conspectus of references, both to passages in the poetry and to past treatments, but is short on analysis.

9   Also cited by J. Nicholls, *The Matter of Courtesy: Medieval Courtesy Books and the Gawain-Poet*, Cambridge, 1985, in a provocative discussion of feasting, pp. 18–21.

10 Langland also cites Matthew 22: 14 in Scripture's sermon at B 11.107–14, a hellfire and brimstone threat of damnation, but in the culmination of his entire discussion (11.189–96), begun more than a passus earlier, he 'concords' Luke's version, relying particularly on 14: 12–15, the verses immediately preceding the parable proper.

alliterative poetry is supposed to do a supernal work, it is because of the range of homologies already evident from my reading of *Beowulf*. Presence is important: the lord's presence signs divine beneficence, and underwrites the truthful character of the minstrel's utterance.

But *Piers Plowman* needs to be seen as discussing something less than a fact, less than a historicisable shift in the nature of dining arrangements. Or if it is such, Langland's complaint resembles views like those deconstructed in Raymond Williams's account of idealised English rural society, *The Country and the City*.[11] Williams could find no historical moment at which rural social integration, the pastoral myth, was a verifiable fact; there was, in his argument, no moment at which one could not have lamented a fall from a previously whole state. The feast as a moment of social cohesion is (as the example of *Beowulf* would suggest) equally a figment. As Grendel's presence indicates, the providentially guided communal identity allegedly forged in feasts has always already been lost, and most alliterative poets do not share Langland's objections to lordly absence.[12]

Moreover, one can trace this complaint historically. It also appears before Langland in Robert Manning and earlier still in Grosseteste. But perhaps contemporary with, or even before, Grosseteste, it had been made by the Dominican Bartholomew the Englishman in his encyclopedia *De proprietatibus rerum*:[13]

> Soper hatte *cena* in latyn and haþ þat name of *cenon*, þat is comynge for komynge of ham þat sopid togedres. In olde tyme men vsid to ete togedres in opun place, lest singulerite schulde brede lecherie. But *cena* may be iseide of *cenos*, þat is schadue, for now for scarsite men sopiþ in hidinge and in priue place. So seiþ Papias. And more verreiliche *cenas* of *synos*, þat is an hound, for lak and defaute of loue and charite. Eueryche takeþ vpon hym to ete his owne soper, *prima Corinthiorum 9°*.[14]

---

11 New York, 1973.

12 Merely a handful of examples: *Cleanness* 129, 1586–90; *Sir Gawain and the Green Knight* 830–34; *Morte Arthure* 407–13, 1664–67.

13 See B. A. Henisch, *Fast and Feast: Food in Medieval Society*, Pennsylvania State University Park, 1976, *passim*. The Trevisa/Bartholomew citation I owe to Derek Brewer, 'Feasts in England and English Literature in the Fourteenth Century', in D. Altenburg, J. Jarnut and H.-H. Steinhoff (eds) *Feste und Feiern im Mittelalter*, Sigmaringen, 1991, pp. 13–28. This last volume includes several other relevant studies: E. Brewer, 'Feasts and the Role of Women in Malory's *Le Morte Darthur*', pp. 441–8; J. O. Fichte, 'Das Fest also Testsituation in der mittelenglischen Artusromanze', pp. 449–59; and R. Newhauser, 'Court Festivities in *Sir Gawain and the Green Knight*: Paradigm and Transformation', pp. 461–8.

14 M. C. Seymour *et al.* (eds) *On the Properties of Things: John Trevisa's Translation of Bartholomaeus Anglicus De Proprietatibus Rerum: A critical text*, Oxford, 1975, 330/7–14.

The regression only continues. Bartholomew cites Papias, an eleventh-century grammarian; Papias himself is only embroidering upon Isidore (*Etymologies* 20.2.14); and ultimately a biblical text describing the primitive church draws attention to solitary feasting. Rather than any identifying some social newfangledness, Langland's complaint is very ancient indeed, and many examples may simply be quotational, inherited.

But although the poet of *Cleanness* needs no present lord for a successful feast, he does require a divine presence, in human respect for purity. Here the antitype to gospel parable is Balthazar's feast; read as a parable, this account offers a trenchant commentary on the purely human ability to compose, comprehend, and learn from the history which is the subject matter of alliterative poetry. If feasting is a powerful social image through its alignment of divine beneficence, patronal power, and historical poetry, *Cleanness* may be taken as an analysis of the failure of the creating word, in the face of human indifference to the divine.

Balthazar attempts to create what Roger Lass once provocatively described as 'man's heaven',[15] an image of insuperable power expressed as supreme festive merriment. Central to his project are the captured vessels of the Jerusalem temple, virtually a replay of Old English *sincþege* (see 1437ff): detached from divine presence, these, Balthazar thinks, can be resacralised as an expression of his creative power, capable of converting queans to queens (1352, 1370). In this, he of course errs; the holy vessel soiled by drinking is but an emblem of the human backsliding into sin (cf. 1145). As the *Gawain*-poet indicates, Balthazar's behaviour is merely foolishness (1425, 1500, 1518); belief in self-creation, in an absence of reciprocal festive homologies, destabilises, rather than validates (just as does promoting whores), the social integrity of the feast.

But Balthazar's failure is ultimately exposed as that of the bad audience for alliterative poetry. For what the hand writes on the wall, illuminated by the still functioning sacral menorah (see 1532), is in fact the plot of alliterative history, the translation of kingdoms. In his impurity, the king finds this writing, with its promise of the fall of princes, horrifying yet incomprehensible. And the text itself proves a challenge to scholarly decipherment as well; it cannot be read out by conventional clerical means (1551–81).[16] In fact, only Daniel, an intact divine temple, the inheritor of Jerusalem prophets, reads appropriately and assigns spiritual values to an otherwise incomprehensible text (1597–1618, 1623–40). The melancholy of the account deepens through its being intercalated with the story of Nebuchadnezzar, a king who attended to such readings, who changed his life through penance and who dies in his sacral glory. In his pride, Balthazar believes one can put off the inevitability of death until

---

15 'Man's Heaven: The Symbolism of Gawain's Shield', *Mediaeval Studies* 28 (1966), pp. 354–60.

16 The same topic appears prominently in *St Erkenwald*, at 51–56, 101–04, 150–58.

tomorrow; failing to perceive the immediacy of the message, he dies shockingly overnight.

A narrative like this demonstrates that David Lawton is surely right in identifying the central concern of Middle English alliterative poetry as the penitential mode.[17] In *Piers*, the fundamental problem with feasting turns out to be that *singulerite* ('singularity') on which Bartholomew comments, the failure of social cohesion. Dinner table retreats and theology proceeds instead of listening to a sacral word, Langland's ideal biblical *geste*, the story of Tobit (B 10.33, 88, 90). This apocryphal tall tale is culturally important because Tobit provides the example of enacting the magically necessary *seventh* work of corporeal mercy, the burial of the dead (based on Tobit 2: 21). Consequently, he represents by synecdoche an emphasis upon this entire complex of pious activity (cf. Tobit 2: 15–21, verses which stimulated the conventional identification). The first such 'work' is derived from Matthew 25: 35, Jesus's words to the righteous, *Esurivi enim, et dedistis mihi manducare*, and thus speaks to the social responsibility to share one's food with others, especially starving social inferiors.[18]

Inevitably in the poems, the greatest celebratory moments are marked as insufficient. They speak to social blindness, not solidarity, and the Balthazar-like monarchs who indulge in them, whatever their worldly nobility, need to comprehend the futility of human efforts in the post-providential world of history. Inevitably, poetic injunctions are directed toward the creation of penitential self-consciousness, the late medieval translation of troubled Virgilian *pietas*:

> And than kayre to the courte that I come fro,
> With ladys full louely to lappyn in myn armes,
> And clyp thaym and kysse thaym and comforthe myn hert;
> And than with damesels dere to daunsen in thaire chambirs,
> Riche romance to rede and rekken the sothe
> Off kempes and of conquerours, of kynges full noblee,
> How thay wirchipe and welthe wanne in thaire lyues.
> With renkes in ryotte to reuelle in haulle
> With coundythes and carolles and compaynyes sere
> And chese me to the chesse that chefe es of gamnes.
>
> (*Parliament of the Three Ages* 246–55)

Youth's wild partying and self-indulgence (which never seems to extend to eating) is split between the two domestic spheres. Part is private chamber

---

17 'The Unity of Middle English Alliterative Poetry', *Speculum* 58 (1983), 72–94.
18 The primary contrastive scene in *Piers Plowman* B/C is provided by the simultaneous dinner-hall appearances of Patience and the fraternal doctor of divinity in B 13/C 15. Note especially B 13.76–80.

action, part public in hall. Significantly, he does not hear oral stories at a feast but reads – and that in the context of extremely private flirtation (cf. 174–81, perhaps especially 176) and without a privileged Daniel-like expositor/poet. What he reads is *romance*, here defined as tales of unremitting triumph. But as the poem progresses, *romance* turns to history – which is loss, not *wirchipe and welthe* – and Youth must learn that what awaits him is Elde's penitential awareness: *amendes ʒoure mysse whills ʒe are men here* (640).

Or consider the *Alliterative Morte Arthure*. In the height of his pride in Viterbo, Arthur, now unconscious of his reduction to being but *The kyng myghtty of myrthe* (3197):

> Reuell[es] with riche wyne, riotes hymselfen
> This roy with his ryall men of þe Rownde Table
> With myrthis and melodye and many kyn gamnes;
> Was neuer meriere men made on this erthe.   (3172–5)

He throws yet one more ostentatious feast in his tent to overawe the Roman ambassadors (3193–201), an echo of the sumptuous display with which he began the poem. But by line 3400, after his disastrous dream (another message of a terrifying transience, indecipherable by its recipient), his philosophers are instructing him about his tyranny and urging him, *Schryfe the of thy schame and schape for thyn ende.*

Or (a final example), consider the ghost's efforts to instruct Guinevere in *The Awntyrs of Arthure*. The spirit compactly demands that the glorious queen, lecherous and prideful, attend to those whom she has ignored, or face a future of hellfire and gnawing toads:

> Þe praier of þe poer may purchas þe pes,
> Of þase þat ʒellis at thi ʒete
> Whan þou art set in þi sete,
> With al merthes at mete
> And dayntes on des.   (178–82)[19]

Indeed alliterative poetry always situates itself so as to call attention to these melancholy lessons of history. As a particularly overwrought example, *The Destruction of Troy* deserves a brief glance. The poem quite overtly belongs in a scholar's study, not in a hall as an oral composition. It is 'writerly', its lengthy prologue consumed with assessing the relative veracity of historical accounts, which, even if the product of eyewitnesses, survive as texts for consultation, not public performance. Moreover, the poet closely translates learned Latin. And the poem includes a variety of far from inevitable literary features only capable of full appreciation in a written form – multiple book

---

19   See further 231–34, 251–60, as well as the outcome of Arthur's feast (beginning at 339–41).

divisions, a contents table, an elaborate acrostic predicated on the first letters of each book.

But equally, *Troy* parades its orality. At the ends and openings of books especially, the poet relies upon the fiction of a present traditional hall audience:

> ye hastely shall here, and ye houe stille ...

> Every wegh þat will wete of þere werkes more
> Listen a litle and leng here a while;
> Let vs karpe of thies kynges or we cayre ferre ...

> Herkinys now a hondqwile of a hegh cas.   (3531, 4547–9, 7346)

And, although it has been omitted from the surviving copy, the contents table promises to tell at the poem's end *the nome of the knight þat causet it to be made and the nome of hym that translatid it out of latyn into englysshe* (p. lxx). These revelations, as the scribal treatment implies, would be meaningless outside the familial situation in which a specific lord is a valuable centre of communal activity.

The written is, of course, the form of absence, of deferral and of fall into the world of temporality and of loss. And insofar as they are *history*, alliterative poems cannot dispense with learned source materials. Yet they are equally underwritten (and rendered elegiac, rather than ironic) by a nostalgia for presence, for the wholeness of origins. As we have seen, from *Beowulf* onwards, feasting, with its assumptions of lord, God, and poet as analogous creators, adumbrates that theme.

To redress a balance, I return at the end to Langland. He may well misrepresent the history of privacy, but he is also the alliterative poet who worries most – and most sophisticatedly – about the status of his poetry, and of 'minstrelsy' in general.[20] At his most daring, Langland reconstructs an alliterative hall community, but one not predicated on traditional poetic figures, generally decried as *fooles sages, flatereris, and lieris* (B 13.422). (One might think this a comment on poets like that of *Troy* and of *William of Palerne*, modern versions of Balthazar's sycophantic clerks, who feel constrained to write patrons into their texts.)

Langland's idealised minstrelsy is almost entirely metaphorical:

> Forþi I rede yow riche, reueles whan ye makeþ,
> For to solace youre soules swiche minstrales to haue:
> The pouere for a fool sage sittyng at þi table,
> And a lered man to lere þee what our lord suffred

---

20   I have taken up some of these issues elsewhere; see 'Will's Work', in S. Justice and K. Kerby-Fulton (eds) *Written Work: Langland, Labor and Authorship*, Philadelphia, 1997, pp. 23–66, especially pp. 44–53.

> For to saue þi soule from sathan þyn enemy,
> And fiþele þee wiþout flaterynge of good friday þe geste,
> And a blynd man for a bourdeour, or a bedrede womman
> To crie a largesse bifore oure lord, youre good los to shewe.
> Thise þre maner minstrales makeþ a man to lauȝe,
> And in his deeþ deyinge þei don hym gret confort.   (B 13.441–50)

Only one of the minstrels, the learned man, actually says anything in this scene. His *geste* is, of course, the gospel, the 'clean' sacral text which ensures salvific community in *Cleanness*. But Langland's learned man shares with his remaining recommended minstrel companions a single feature, that he is *pouere*. As Langland reminds his readers elsewhere:

> Why I meue þis matere is moost for þe pouere,
> For in hir liknesse oure lord lome haþ ben yknowe ...
> And in þe apparaille of a pouere man and pilgrymes liknesse
> Many tyme god haþ ben met among nedy peple,
> Ther neuere segge hym seiȝ in secte of þe riche.
>
> (B 11.231–32, 243–45)

The lord at his table can be redeemed by a single unprepossessing figure because the poor are, in some sense, Jesus's human image. The guest/minstrel reinstitutes presence, potentially without any poetic language being uttered; the poor enact gospel ideals, and this purely gestural *geste* is salvific. Moreover, they sanctify the lord who entertains them, for through his charitable social acts, through returning to the communal impulse supposedly inherent in the feast, he may merit a *largesse*, an ironic inversion of the technical term for a handout to the poor, God's redemptive gift of inclusion in the Great Feast.

WORD GAMES: GLOSSING *PIERS PLOWMAN*

GEORGE KANE

RONALD WALDRON has always stressed the importance of reading texts exactly. In these notes I describe some problems of glossing *Piers Plowman* which have been troublesome either to myself or to others who have been bold enough to record their notion of what the words in question mean in their particular context. Most involve a choice between homographs; a few are rare, or uniquely instanced.

I

B II 98 *breden*

Among the properties in the marriage settlement of Meed and False is a life of sloth which includes to

> breden as Burgh swyn and bedden hem esily
> Til Sleuþe and sleep sliken his sydes.

The word has been glossed 'breed, engender'[1] and 'breed, grow fat?' and translated 'copulate'.[2] However engaging the notion may be of town pigs being sexually liberated and their country cousins strait-laced, *Middle English Dictionary* (MED) *breden* v. (3) does not support it. We have here another word, MED *breden* v. (2) 1.(a) 'to spread out, extend' etc., or in the *Palladius* instruction there on how to build a farm cart, 'becomes wider, broadens'. When it comes to that, pigs, like most mammals, mate seasonally. To the contextual point, medieval town pigs lived an easy life in pens with plenty of kitchen-leftover swill while their country cousins had to forage in the woods

---

1   W. W. Skeat, *The Vision of William Concerning Piers the Plowman in Three Parallel Texts* (2 vols), Oxford, 1886, II, p. 322.
2   A. V. C. Schmidt (ed.) *William Langland: The Vision of Piers Plowman*, 2nd edn, London, 1995 (henceforth *Vision*), p. 31; A. V. C. Schmidt, *William Langland: Piers Plowman, a New Translation of the B-text*, Oxford, 1992 (henceforth *New Translation*), p. 17.

most of the year under the care of swineherds and came back to the village only to be fattened for slaughter.

B III 67–68, C III 71–72 *cost*

Advertising your benefaction in a stained-glass window is forbidden because it amounts to committing the sin of pride, says the moralist,

> For god knoweþ þi conscience and þi kynde wille
> And þi cost and þi coueitise and who þe catel ouȝte.

Skeat did not gloss *cost*; it has since been glossed 'expense'[3] and translated 'the precise details of the cost'.[4] At first sight that seems apt. But in this moral situation the amount of the donor's expenditure is not primarily material; the sin lies in his state of mind, which cannot be hidden from God, his 'inmost thought and true intention'. The word is MED *cost* n. (1) where indeed this instance appears under 2.(a) and means 'natural disposition'.

C I 149 *semede*

Lady Holychurch, teaching the Dreamer that Love, by which she means the Deity, is the best of treasures, tells him how

> heuene holde hit ne myghte, so heuy hit semede
> Til hit hadde of erthe yȝoten hitsilue,

assumed human form. In that account *semede*, 'appeared, gave the impression of being', makes bad sense. For one thing, in the doctrine behind the trope the weight was real, anything but an appearance. For another, the modal *ne myghte*, meaning uncompromisingly 'was unable to, could not', rejects it. For a third the translation 'seemed' would raise the contextually absurd question 'to whom?' This is MED *semen* v.(3) 2.(a), and *so heuy hit* ~ means 'it was of such weight'.

B IV 138–44 *mette*

This is the principle of absolute justice by which Reason would rule if he *were kyng with coroune to kepen a Reaume*:

> *Nullum malum* þe man mette wiþ *inpunitum*
> And bad *Nullum bonum* be *irremuneratum.*

It is represented as a conundrum, a problem of grammar and sense for the King's confessor and others to construe. The principle is hidden in the word order, but unmistakable when the negatives have been factored out: *omne*

---

3 D. Pearsall (ed.) *Piers Plowman by William Langland … the C-text* (henceforth *C-text*), Berkeley and Los Angeles, 1979, p. 392.
4 Schmidt, *New Translation*, p. 25.

malum punitum, omne bonum remuneratum. Of course Meed buys the confessors and they ignore it. Modern interpretation has erred in taking *þe man* to be in apposition to *Nullum malum* and *mette* to be a part of MED *meten* v.(4)1.(b) and to mean 'experience' or some such sense.[5] But this entails translating *Nullum malum* as 'innocence' and *Nullum bonum* as 'wickedness'; ingenious, no doubt, but it deprives the principle of the absoluteness which is its import.[6] It also ignores the larger, cultural context, which identifies *þe man* as *iudex iustus* of Innocent's *De Miseria Humane Condicionis*, as any self-respecting fourteenth-century clerk would know, and further as the Deity by echoes of Ps 7.12 and Heb 4.13, in whom the principle of absolute justice is inherent.[7] With this in mind taking *mette* to be a part of MED *meten* v.(1) 'measure' etc., much illustrated from moral contexts, is indicated. One looks for a use to match that in 140 and finds it in 3.(b) *W.Bible* (1) (Bod 959) 2 Kings 8.2 *Dauyþ ... smoot Moab, and he mat hem with a litil corde euenynge to erþe, forsoþe he metede two litle cordes, oon to slen & an ooþer to quykenen*: *with* here has the sense 'by means of', governing the instrument of measure. I shall gloss this 'measured against, matched with'.

In each of these instances the set of homographs to which it belongs is relatively small: *breden* two or three, *semede* three, *cost(e* four, *meten* five. Context and requirement of syntax quickly single out a competing pair.

II

By contrast a very large set of homographs is constituted by the letter-group *lo+two minims+e*, where the minims can have the modern values *n* or *u* or *v* or *w*. If I have counted right there are eighteen such. Since the number may surprise, here they are in the order of their MED headwords.

lof n.(1) 'praise'; n.(4) 'a spar';

lone n.(1) 'something lent or owing'; n.(2) 'concealment, shelter'; adj. 'single, sole, isolated';

loue n.(1) 'hill, mountain'; n.(2) 'fire, flame'; n.(3) 'low place'; adj. and adv. 'low';

louen v.(1) 'lower, make low'; v.(2) 'burn, blaze'; v.(3) 'low (of cattle)';

v.(4) 'praise, commend';

5   J. F. Goodridge (trans.) *William Langland: Piers Plowman*, Harmondsworth, 1975, pp. 59, 271; Schmidt, *New Translation*, p. 39; and cf. Skeat, *Vision of William*, vol. II, p. 59.

6   Schmidt, *Vision*, p. 59.

7   R. E. Lewis (ed.) *Lotario dei Segni: De Miseria Humane Condicionis*, Athens (Georgia), 1978, pp. 229, 302–3.

love n.(1) 'love'; n.(2) 'remainder, relict'; n.(3) 'palm of the hand';

loven v.(1) 'love'; v.(2) 'praise, honour'.

Some, but no means a majority, of *Piers Plowman* scribes, in late fourteenth- and earlier fifteenth-century manuscripts using anglicana formata, signalled their reading of the immediate exemplar by ligature to differentiate *u* and *n* or by using *v* or *w*. Eleven of the words in the list occur in *Piers Plowman*. Here are some instances which seem to, or ought to have been found, troublesome.

C Pr 103 *loue*

This is Conscience in righteous anger with clergy who have charge of pilgrimage centres and tolerate, indeed, encourage, ignorant pilgrims in idolatry and exploit it for their own profit.

> I leue, by oure lord, for loue of ȝoure coueytise
> That al þe world be þe wors.

The indignation is unmistakable, but the expression *loue of coueytise* makes no sense if we translate *loue* 'love'. I take the word here to be MED n.(2) 'flame, fire'.

A IV 36/ B IV 49 *loue/looue*

Among the charges in Peace's appeal against Wrong before Reason sitting in judgement in the King's Court is that

> wrong aȝen his wil hadde his wyf take
>
> And ... rauisshide rose, reynaldis loue
> And margerete of hire maydenhed maugre hire chekis.

The word *loue/looue* has been translated 'girl' and 'who was to marry R.', and glossed 'sweetheart'.[8] Its other possible sense here is 'relict, widow', MED *love* n.(2).(c). This is how it was unmistakably read by scribes in two unrelated copies of the B-text of *Piers Plowman* where the spelling *looue* is intended to differentiate the pronunciation of the stem vowel as [ ]:]. If we translate *loue/looue* here as 'relict, widow' Wrong's alleged offences are both more various and presented in ascending scale of criminality. He seduced the wife of Peace, committing adultery with her against not her will but that of Peace (A 35, B 38).[9] He abducted the widow Rose to acquire the disposal of her remarriage for his financial advantage: and, worst of all, he committed the violent crime of sexual assault and rape. That is how the appeal would, in this

---

8   Goodridge, *Piers Plowman*, p. 56; Schmidt, *New Translation*, p. 36; Schmidt, *Vision*, p. 55.
9   For sexual senses of *taken* see MED s.v. 3(a) and OED s.v. *take* 14b, especially a1400 *Punishm.Adultery*, and *Piers Plowman* B VIII 83.

particular, be most effective. So it goes in C, where two of the three lines are revised and read

> How wrong wilfully hadde his wyf forleyn
> And how he raueschede Rose the ryche wydewe.   (IV 46, 47)

It could be argued that these revisions were intended to create such an effect. But this is present already in A and B if we take *loue* to mean 'widow'. The two B scribes were determined to register their opinion to that effect. And certainly it recommends itself as the easier explanation. As like as not the revisions register the poet's irritation with misreadings. There are other instances of B and C revision which look like that.

C VIII 194–96 *loue*

> There was no lad þat lyuede þat ne lowede hym to Peres
> To be his holde hewe thow he hadde no more
> But lyflode for his labour and his loue at nones.

Here *loue* has been transcribed *lone*[10] and glossed 'gift from a superior'.[11] MED does not support this gloss: all but one of the instances in *lon(e* n.(1), 2 are of situations where the recipient is answerable to God for a conferment. The background, of a change of heart induced by the ravages of Hunger, discourages reading *lone at nones* as some sort of bonus at lunchtime. And the willingness of the lad to work for his keep loses its sharp contrast with the bad attitude of the Bretoner and Wastour. I transcribe *loue*, taking the word to mean 'praise'. My next instance supports that reading.

C XIV 215 *loue*

The Dreamer is in dialogue with Ymaginatif, his reflective faculty, about how Trajan's case shows the force of divine justice to be such that it constitutes a fourth possible means of salvation to add to the baptisms of font and blood and fire because

> Ne wolde neuere trewe god but trewe treuthe were alloued   (212)

'God would never will it otherwise than that genuine righteousness be rewarded'; and to that is attached an expectation

> to haue þat treuthe deserueth:
> *Quia super pauca fuisti fidelis* etc.
> And þat is loue and large huyre, yf þe lord be trewe,
> And a cortesye more þen couenant was.

---

10   Skeat, *Vision of William*, vol. I, p. 211; Pearsall, *C-text*, p. 154.
11   Pearsall, *C-text*, p. 401.

That is *loue*, and a generous wage, and a bonus above the agreed amount of the latter. I have not found any specialized sense in MED's instances under *love* n.(1) to suit the context here better than 'praise, approval' (MED *lof* n.(1)); that sense is already strong in *alloued* 'valued', implying grace. Behind it is Mat. 25.21 *Euge serve bone et fidelis*, implied in the quoted Latin.

B XI 171–175 *loue*

Here, earlier in the history of the poem, Trajan himself is proclaiming the principal doctrine of Christianity as it applies to a particular human activity, the acquisition of knowledge.

> Lawe wiþouten loue, ... ley þer a bene!
> Or any Science vnder sonne, þe seuene artʒ and alle –
> But þei ben lerned for oure lordes loue, lost is al þe tyme,
> For no cause to cacche siluer þerby, ne to be called a maister,
> But al for loue of oure lord and þe bet to loue þe peple.

The only true value, he says, from which all genuine values derive, is *loue* (171), *caritas*, MED *love* n.1(c). Time spent acquiring legal erudition or academic distinction and rank is wasted if directed to making money or achieving eminence; the effort is valuable only if made *for oure lordeʒ loue, þe loue of oure lord*, and *þe bet to loue þe peple*. In the last expression *loue* means fulfilment of the commandment of charity in its practical senses, free legal aid and effective pastoral care and giving of alms.[12] But in the first two expressions it concerns a point of moral theology: human achievement is at best worthless, at worst sinfully proud, unless directed to the honour and glory of God by an act of will. So I translate *loue* in those expressions as 'glorification, worship'. The homograph is another word, MED *lof* n.(1)(a).

So much for nouns in this set. Of verbs *Piers Plowman* contains three by MED identification: *louen* v.(4) (Anglo-French *loer, loier, l(o)uer, louher, lower*), 'praise'; *loven* v.(1) (Old English *lufian*) 'love'; and *loven* v.(2) (Old English *lofian*) 'praise'. To what extent *Piers Plowman* scribes, or for that matter its poet, distinguished the first and third of these seems not determinable. Among MED's presumed instances of *lofian* derivatives, spellings with *-f-* are rare, usually early, and those with *-v-* somewhat more frequent, but fewer than those with *-u-*; there are even several with *-w-*. The reason for MED's assignment of words to one or another of the two is not entirely clear. In *Piers Plowman* lexicography it seems sensible to treat them as a semantic group.

---

12 Cf. *to loue and to lene* B IX 204, X 360, XI 180, C X 192, 'to express caritas in solicitude for the poor'. On legal aid for the poor see A VIII 47: *princes and prelates* should pay for this: so B VII 43ff, C IX 44ff.

Eleven instances stand out in the set of 248 homographs spelled *lo+two minims+ e(n* in the three Athlone *Piers* texts, because they occur in contexts that impose a primary sense of appraisal > approval/acceptance/commendation, whereas if they are translated 'love', of which Middle English usage was, except for theological discourse, not much different from ours today, they constitute an extreme trope, a kind of visual paronomasia. Whether Langland intended such effect is not determinable, since we do not know how he spelled the words. The determinant must be that the lines where they occur make better sense, or indeed make sense, if they are taken to be parts of MED *louen* v.(4) or *loven* v.(2). For reasons of space I shall limit myself to listing them after the meanings I find in them.

'applauded': *Litel is he louid or lete by þat suche a lessoun techiþ*
(A XI 29, B X 37, C XI 32)

'acclaimed': *ryche and pore hym louede [Resoun for his ryhtful speche]*
(C IV 153)

'approve of': *Crist ... lene þee lede þi lond so leaute þee louye*
(B Pr 125–6, C Pr 149–150)

'respect': *I counseille þee for cristes sake clergie þat þow louye*
(B XII 92)

alle he lered to be lele, and ech a craft loue ooþer (B/C XIX/XXI 250)

'respects and takes note of': *He ... loueþ noȝt Salomons sawes*
(B IX 95–96)

'respect, honour in practice': *þerfore merueileth me ... Why [man] ne loueth thy lore and leueth ('lives') as þou techest* (C XIII 192–93); *To make men louye mesure þat monkes ben and freres* (C XVII 52)

'think (more) highly of': *for it lat best be loue I loue it þe betere*
(A XI 142, B X 190)

'hold in regard, respect': *þe matere þat she meued, if lewed men it knewe, þe lasse, as I leue, louyen þei wolde The bileue of oure lord þat lettred men techeþ* (B XI 109, C XII 43)

'value, accept the concept of': *'Loue lawe* (sc. a religion) *withoute leutee? allouable was hit neuere!'* (C XVII 130)

'set store by, consider important': *how þey myhte lerne leest goed spene .... þat loueth lordes now and leten hit a dowel* (C XI 75–76)

So much for homographs: identifying the apt one for a given context in that list is a matter of how one has read Langland's text and one's idea of his style formed in the course of reading his poem. I suppose that any one of my meanings above is in those circumstances debatable.

III

Another class of problem, of another order and luckily less frequent, is glossing words little or uniquely attested in Middle English and in *Piers Plowman*. I will conclude with illustration of four of these.

B XVIII 9 *ofrauȝte*

Will is reporting his magnificent Palm Sunday dream with its climax *of cristes passion and penaunce þe peple þat ofrauȝte*. Skeat glossed *ofrauȝte* 'reached, extended to' with support from Middle English instances;[13] this sense of *ofrechen* is confirmed by further instances in the *Oxford English Dictionary* (henceforth OED) and MED. That it does not serve in the *Piers Plowman* context appears from the published translations, 'penance which he suffered for all the people',[14] and 'passion that Christ endured to redeem us all'.[15] Both intrude meaning: *þe peple* does not, here, signify 'all' or 'us all'. Yet the doctrine is sound, and this ought to be easy. So it is, if one looks in the Supplement to Bosworth-Toller,[16] where *ofræcan* appears with one instance, from Liebermann's *Gesetze*, very conveniently in both Latin and English and with an unmistakable sense 'obtain', here 'got possession of'. Who then are *þe peple?*: those in Abraham's lap whom *þe pouke ... haþ attached, populus in tenebris* (B XVI 261, XVIII 323). Skeat of course did not have the Supplement, from which one is able to establish a new sense of Middle English *ofrechen* as well as clear meaning in this passage.

B XIV 194 *decourreþ*

The allegory here is about a *patente*, an open letter of *Acquitaunce* (190), 'release', authorized in *Conuertimini ad me et salvi eritis* (180, Isaiah 45.22) intended for God's *prisoners ... in þe put of meschief* (174). To be valid this *patente* must be copied on parchment – here the allegory is signalled – consisting of *pouerte* and *pure pacience* and *parfit bileue* (192–93). The text goes on

> Of pompe and of pride þe parchemyn decourreþ
> And principalliche of alle peple but þei be poore of herte.

This is the sole instance of *decorren* given in MED which, following Skeat who followed Maetzner, derives it from Old French *decorre, decorir*, and adapts the meaning of that presumed etymon to make it mean here 'departs from, has nothing to do with'.[17] The *Anglo-Norman Dictionary* (henceforth

---

13 Skeat, *Vision of William*, vol. II, p. 407, followed by Schmidt, *Vision*, p. 535.
14 Goodridge, *Piers Plowman*, p. 217.
15 Schmidt, *New Translation*, p. 210.
16 J. Bosworth, T. Toller and A. Campbell, *An Anglo-Saxon Dictionary, with Supplements*, Oxford, 1898–1972.
17 Skeat, *Vision of William*, vol. II, p. 340.

AND) headword is *decure*, *-or(r)e*, *-oure* etc.; it is glossed 'to run down (from); (of liquids) to run away; to stream with (tears); (of wax) to melt; (of leaves) to fall; to weaken'. MED glosses *decourreþ* 'to flow away; ~ of fig. depart from sthing, avoid, shun'. If it here means 'departs from pomp and pride (has nothing to do with them)'[18] or 'departs'[19] the allegory has shifted violently, a *substance* of a particular sort becoming an active *agent* capable of making distinctions. Luckily there is another possible etymon for *decourreþ*, namely Latin *decoriare*, which maintains the allegory of preparing the parchment: the kind of skin, calf or sheep, having been chosen, it must be prepared: 'Scrape the parchment clean of' says the imperative plural, in the spirit of a fourteenth-century injunction *Pellis de carne, de pelle caro removetur; Tu de carne tua carnea vota trahe.*[20] A similar moral allegory based on the preparation of parchment appears in *Cleanness* 1134.[21]

C III 448–9 *panelon*

In the golden age to come when Reason is king access to the law will not be paid for by the plaintiff or defendant: the venality of lawyers will be checked.

> Shal no seriaunt for þat seruice werie a selk houe
> Ne no pelure on his panelon for pledyng at þe barre.

Skeat took this word, with its ambiguous pair of minims, to be *paueylon*[22] and glossed it '(lawyer's) coif', under the entry *Pauilon* 'pavilion, tent'.[23] A modern editor of C transcribes the word *paueloun* and adds 'or hood' to Skeat's gloss.[24] MED, following Skeat, takes the word to be *paviloun* of which its first meaning, well instanced, is 'tent' etc., and its second, with only this instance, glossed '?a garment worn by lawyers ?a coif'. In AND *panelon* is variously glossed 'piece (of tapestry etc.)' and 'housing, horse-cloth' (sc. saddle-blanket). There is no suggestion of a head-dress. The corresponding line in A reads *Ne no ray robe wiþ riche pelure*, 'nor any robe of (expensive) striped fabric trimmed with expensive fur' (III 271); B reads *cloke* for *panelon* (III 296). The etymon of *panelon* is not Old French *papillon* 'butterfly', as Skeat was led to believe. It was formed on Anglo-French *panel*, one use of which appears in Middle English '*panel*, list of jurors': B III 317, C III 470 (where one copy reads *panyloun*). Such lists survive on strips of membrane.

---

18 Skeat, *loc. cit.*
19 Schmidt, *Vision*, pp. 237 and 521. Goodridge goes even further here with 'slips away from' (*Piers Plowman*, p. 172).
20 W. Wattenbach, *Das Schriftwesen im Mittelalter*, Graz, 1958, pp. 209–10.
21 M. Andrew and R. A. Waldron (eds) *The Poems of the Pearl Manuscript*, Berkeley and Los Angeles, 1979, p. 159, line 1134 and note.
22 Skeat, *Vision of William*, vol. I, p. 97.
23 Skeat, *Vision of William*, vol. II, p. 411 s.v. Pauilon.
24 Pearsall, *C-text*, pp. 84 and 405.

The Middle English equivalent, *liste* MED n.(2), was undergoing a similar, probably analogical, semantic development in the fifteenth century. On a robe the 'strip' would be ornamental 'facing' (OED vbl. sb. 4), edging, down the front. This appears in *Sir Gawain and the Green Knight* where the hero's robes have a *pane* (154) and *panez* (855) of fur. Davis glosses the word 'fur edging, facing'.[25]

C XIX 244, 248 *atymye*

The manuscripts variously spell this word *atemy(e* and *ate(y)me*, or substitute *atteyne* (by alteration), *achyue*, *tymy* and *haue tyme*. It appears in MED as *atemien* with a single instance from the eleventh-century *Trinity Homilies*, glossed 'to subject oneself, be humble'. It seems to derive from Old English *ātemian* 'control, restrain, tame'. All instances in Bosworth-Toller and its Supplement are of transitive use. Both the *Trinity Homilies* and *Piers Plowman* examples, with marked infinitive adjunct, appear to be intransitive, and to have a reflexive implication in their contexts. The MED gloss will not do for the *Piers* uses. Skeat glosses the word (*atemye* in his text) 'attain' and appears to think them the same word.[26] That use is rejected by the context, where in both occurrences the necessary sense is 'hold back from, refrain from, check the impulse to'.

This is how the sense of the passage (234–250a) goes. Dives, whose wealth was honestly acquired, was damned because he lavished it on himself and did not give to the poor. Yet his honesty implies that he could well have controlled the impulse to live in the grand style (*wel myhte atymye to*). Today's magnates, not heeding what happened to Dives and moreover rich by dishonest means, even so lack the will (*ȝut wollen nat atymye*) to refrain from living like lords and to escape the punishment for their dishonesty by giving their ill-gotten gains lavishly (*to wasten hit* 250) to the poor, thus taking advantage of the escape clause *Facite vobis amicos de mammona iniquitatis* as indicated by Holy Writ (249, 250a).

The moral argument here is awkwardly shaped. I like to think that Langland would have improved it if the revision had not broken off: it is the last substantial addition but for some slapstick with the demons in XVIII>XX, though not necessarily the latest, in the poem. But it is unmistakable. Scribal difficulty was not about this, but with the unusual spelling in the group ancestor of the X family. Modern difficulty has been with the use of *atymye* with the marked infinitive rather than with *from* and a gerund object. Such use occurs in *Piers*

---

25 J. R. R. Tolkien and E. V. Gordon (eds) *Sir Gawain and the Green Knight*, 2nd edn revised by N. Davis, Oxford, 1967, pp. 80–1, note to line 154; see also line 855 of the text.

26 Skeat, *Vision of William*, vol. II, p. 246; Pearsall (*C-text* p. 387) follows his gloss and suggests a transcription *atyinye*.

Plowman with *be waer* C XI 78, *lette* B X 271, XI 137–8, C XII 72–3, XIV 177, *leue* B VII 155–6, *spare* B III, 51–2, X 103, XI 101–2 and XVI 64–5, and is not peculiar to Langland.[27]

---

27 MED *spare* v.2(c), *ware* a.3. The usage can vary, as with MED *absteinen* v.2 where it has the sense 'to restrain oneself, refrain'; cf. the instances *Mandev.* and *SSecr*.

UNTYING THE KNOT:
READING *SIR GAWAIN AND THE GREEN KNIGHT*

SUSAN POWELL

AS AN UNDERGRADUATE AT King's College London in the late 1960s, I was fortunate to be taught *Sir Gawain and the Green Knight* by Ron Waldron. The edition we used was that of Sir Israel Gollancz,[1] who had held the medieval chair at King's from 1903 to 1930. It was not user-friendly, but we hardly expected things to be so in those days. By 1970, when I was undertaking my postgraduate research, Ron (now my supervisor) had brought out his own edition of the poem, stunningly bereft of thorns and yoghs and altogether much more accessible.[2] This was to be followed before the end of the decade by his edition with Malcolm Andrew of the poems of the whole manuscript, radically titled *The Poems of the Pearl Manuscript*.[3] In my own teaching of *Sir Gawain and the Green Knight*, as of other medieval texts, I am indebted to the example of unostentatious scholarship which Ron offers both as a teacher and as an author and editor. This essay is a small tribute to him.

I

It is well known, and much discussed, that the poet of *Sir Gawain and the Green Knight* refers to the pentangle worn by Gawain on his shield and on his cote-armour, as *þe endeles knot* (line 630).[4] One of the many meanings of

---

1 Sir I. Gollancz (ed.) *Sir Gawain and the Green Knight, with introductory essays by Mabel Day and Mary S. Serjeantson*, Early English Text Society, o.s. 210, London, 1940 (for 1938).

2 R. A. Waldron (ed.) *Sir Gawain and the Green Knight*, York Medieval Texts, London, 1970.

3 M. Andrew and R. A. Waldron (eds) *The Poems of the Pearl Manuscript*, London, 1978. All quotations will be from this edition.

4 While acknowledging my specific debt to Ron Waldron, I do not aim (and cannot hope) to acknowledge the by now often unconscious debts I owe to other scholars whose readings of *Sir Gawain and the Green Knight* have influenced me over the past thirty years. On the specific subject of this essay, I have, however, found the following

'knot' in Middle English is 'an intellectual knot to be untied, a theological or philosophical problem; a riddle, mystery' (MED *knotte* n., 2.(a)), and it is my contention in this paper that a proper investigation of the significance of the word 'knot' is essential in attempting to untie the knot of *Sir Gawain and the Green Knight*.

The pentangle is central to an understanding of the poem. The poet impresses us with his determination to intrude the pentangle description into the arming scene at the beginning of Fitt 2 (*I am in tent yow to telle, þof tary hyt me schulde*, line 624), and he provides unmissable clues which alert us to the centrality of the pentangle in the context of the poem as a whole.

> Then þay schewed hym þe schelde, þat was of schyr goulez
> Wyth þe pentangel depaynt of pure golde hwez;
> He braydez hit by þe bauderyk, aboute þe hals kestes.
> Þat bisemed þe segge semlyly fayre
> And quy þe pentangel apendez to þat prynce noble
> I am in tent yow to telle, þof tary hyt me schulde.
> Hit is a syngne þat Salamon set sumquyle
> In bytoknyng of trawþe, bi tytle þat hit habbez;
> For hit is a figure þat haldez fyue poyntez
> And vche lyne vmbelappez and loukez in oþer
> And ayquere hit is endelez (and Englych hit callen
> Oueral, as I here, 'þe endeles knot').
> Forþy hit acordez to þis knyȝt and to his cler armez,
> For ay faythful in fyue and sere fyue syþez,
> Gawan watz for gode knawen and, as golde pured,
> Voyded of vche vylany, wyth vertuez ennourned
>   In mote.
>   Forþy þe pentangel nwe
>   He ber in schelde and cote,

books and articles (presented chronologically) of great help and have used their scholarship freely: V. F. Hopper, *Medieval Number Symbolism: Its Sources, Meaning, and Influence on Thought and Expression*, New York, 1938; E. R. Curtius, *European Literature and the Latin Middle Ages*, London, 1953, especially pp. 501–9; D. R. Howard, 'Structure and Symmetry in Sir Gawain', *Speculum* 39 (1964), 425–33; A. Kent Hieatt, 'Sir Gawain: pentangle, luf-lace, numerical structure', in *Silent Poetry: Essays in Numerological Analysis*, ed. Alastair Fowler, London, 1970; Allan Metcalf, 'Gawain's Number', in *Essays in the Numerical Criticism of Medieval Literature*, ed. C. D. Eckhardt, Lewisburg, 1980; Ross G. Arthur, *Medieval Sign Theory and Sir Gawain and the Green Knight*, Toronto, 1987; R. A. Shoaf, 'The Syngne of Surfet and the Surfeit of Signs in *Sir Gawain and the Green Knight*', in *The Passing of Arthur: New Essays in Arthurian Tradition*, eds Christopher Baswell and William Sharpe, New York, 1988.

> As tulk of tale most trwe
> And gentylest kny3t of lote.   (lines 619–39)

Painted on the red shield (and also, we are told at line 637, on Gawain's cote-armour) is the gold pentangle, a symbol devised by Solomon to signify truth (*in bytoknyng of trawþe*, line 626). Pentangle, which is from the Greek, means five angles (*hit is a figure þat haldez fyve poyntez*, line 627, with a pun on points meaning both angles and characteristics), and the pentangle is suitable for Gawain as one who was always faithful in five things and each one five times (*ay faythful in fyue and sere fyue syþez*, line 632). Critics have rightly made much of the significance of numerology in medieval and Renaissance texts in general,[5] and those who have written on the *Gawain*-poet have argued that his artistic intentions are reflected in the number symbolism he imposes on his poems. The importance of the pentangle in *Sir Gawain and the Green Knight* is reinforced in the poem by the poet's quasi-magical use of the number five.

The arming of Gawain, which contains within it the description of the five-angled pentangle (each of the fives multiplied by five), begins at the twenty-fifth stanza of the poem (five multiplied by five). Each stanza ends with five lines, the 'bob and wheel' which in this form is unique in the whole of medieval literature. The first line of the poem (*Siþen þe sege and þe assaut watz sesed at Troye*, line 1) is repeated in the final stanza so that the poem comes full circle (*After þe segge and þe asaute watz sesed at Troye*, line 2525). It is clearly deliberate that this repetition comes in line 2525, with the double repetition of five multiplied by five. Significantly, only the five lines of the bob and wheel remain to the poem at that point. The fives which inform the poem as a whole alert us as readers to the significance of the pentangle.

In the second stanza of his description of the pentangle, the poet explores the meaning of its five times fiveness in relation to Gawain:

> Fyrst he watz funden fautlez in his fyue wyttez.
> And efte fayled neuer þe freke in his fyue fyngres.
> And alle his afyaunce vpon folde watz in þe fyue woundez
> Þat Cryst ka3t on þe croys, as þe Crede tellez.
> And quereseoeuer þys mon in melly watz stad,
> His þro þo3t watz in þat, þur3 alle oþer þyngez,
> Þat alle his forsnes he fong at þe fyue joyez
> Þat þe hende Heuen Quene had of hir Chylde.
> (At þis cause þe kny3t comlyche hade

---

5   Numerology is sanctioned in Christian culture by the Book of the Wisdom of Solomon, xi, 20: *Omnia in mensura, et numero, et pondere disposuisti*, i.e. 'thou hast ordered all things by measure and number and weight', translated in *The New English Bible: The Apocrypha*, Cambridge, 1970.

In þe inore half of his schelde hir ymage depaynted,
Þat quen he blusched þerto his belde neuer payred.)
Þe fyft fyue þat I fynde þat þe frek vsed
Watz fraunchyse and felaȝschyp forbe al þyng,
His clannes and his cortaysye croked were neuer,
And pité, þat passez alle poyntez – þyse pure fyue
Were harder happed on þat haþel þen on any oþer.
Now alle þese fyue syþez for soþe were fetled on þis knyȝt
And vchone halched in oþer, þat non ende hade,
And fyched vpon fyue poyntez þat fayld neuer,
Ne samned neuer in no syde, ne sundred nouþer,
Withouten ende at any noke I oquere fynde,
Whereeuer þe gomen bygan or glod to an ende.
Þerfore on his schene schelde schapen watz þe knot,
Ryally wyth red golde vpon rede gowlez,
Þat is þe pure 'pentaungel' wyth þe peple called
   With lore.
  Now grayþed is Gawan gay
  And laȝt his launce ryȝt þore
  And gef hem alle goud day –
  He wende for euermore. (lines 640–69)

Gawain was faultless first in his five senses, secondly in his five fingers, thirdly in the five wounds of Christ, fourthly in the five joys of Mary, and fifthly in five knightly virtues: a noble and generous nature, loyalty to his companions, moral purity, *cortaysye* (line 653, with everything that implies of behaviour appropriate to the court), and piety/compassion. Unlike the previous four, this fifth combination of fives is not recorded elsewhere and may be assumed to be the poet's own choice of virtues to demonstrate the quintessence of Gawain.[6]

I use the word 'quintessence' carefully. As an alchemical term which depends on the number five, it suits a discussion of the pentangle, which is itself quasi-magical. At lines 625–26, it is described as a sign devised by Solomon. As king of Israel (c.970–c.933 BC), Solomon's reputation rested on his proverbial wisdom,[7] his building of the Temple at Jerusalem, and his apostasy

---

6 On these various pentads, see, in particular, R. W. Ackerman, 'Gawain's Shield: Penitential Doctrine in *Gawain and the Green Knight*', *Anglia* 76 (1958), 254–65; R. H. Green, 'Gawain's Shield and the Quest for Perfection', *A Journal of English Literary History* 29 (1962), 121–39; and T. Silverstein (ed.) *Sir Gawain and the Green Knight: A New Critical Edition*, Chicago, 1984, p. 134 (*sub* lines 651–53).

7 Hence, the attribution to him of several books of the Old Testament (Proverbs, Ecclesiastes, Song of Solomon, the Book of Wisdom).

in old age through the influence of his wives.[8] From classical times he was known as a magician, and by the Middle Ages he appears as such in Christian culture.[9] This is the reputation he clearly has to the *Gawain*-poet, where his symbol, the pentangle, is a sign of truth (line 626).

In fact, the association of Solomon with Christian truth is not unassailable, and his reputation is essentially an ambivalent one.[10] The pentangle too is ambivalent as a Christian symbol: it finds a context in black, as well as white, magic. It became associated with Solomon during the Middle Ages, an association which perhaps takes its origin in the details of the dimensions of the Temple.[11] According to Bede, whose interpretation was incorporated into the *Glossa Ordinaria*, the pentagonal posts of the entrance to the Holy of Holies represent the body with its five senses.[12] Various five-lettered words were attached to its five points from time to time: in Christian culture the names JESUS and MARIA occur in relation to it, as does the word SALUS: so too the first and last letters of the Greek alphabet, ALPHA and OMEGA.[13] The pentangle of *Sir Gawain and the Green Knight* has most obvious connections with the latter through their biblical use (in the 'magical' Book of Revelation) as a metaphor of the Godhead: 'I am Alpha and Omega, the beginning and the ending, saith the Lord, which is, and which was, and which is to come, the Almighty' (Revelation i, 8). The pentangle too is *endelez* (line 629):

> Withouten ende at any noke I oquere fynde,
> Whereeuer þe gomen bygan or glod to an ende.   (lines 660–61)

The association of five angles with an essentially circular device is perhaps odd, but the number five, intrinsic to the pentangle, is known as a circular number because it repeats itself in the last digit when multiplied by itself ($5 \times 5 = 25$, $25 \times 25 = 625$, etc.). The circular numbers are the numbers of perfection

---

8   The reputation derives from 1 Kings, i–xi.

9   L. Thorndike, *A History of Magic and Experimental Science during the first Thirteen Centuries of our Era* (8 vols), London, 1923, vol. 2, pp. 279–81.

10   Solomon has not in general been felt to play a significant role in the poem, but the inconsistencies of his reputation may cast light on much-discussed problems such as the ambivalent nature of the Green Knight/Bertilak or the excoriation of women by Gawain.

11   1 Kings, vi, 31: *Et in ingressu oraculi fecit ostiola de lignis olivarum, postesque angulorum quinque*, i.e. 'At the entrance of the inner shrine he made a double door of wild olive: the pilasters and the door-posts were pentagonal', translated in *The New English Bible: The Old Testament*, Cambridge, 1970. An early medieval reference to the pentangle in relation to Solomon is a rejection of it by William of Auvergne, bishop of Paris (Thorndike, *Magic and Experimental Science*, vol. 2, pp. 279–80).

12   Green, 'Gawain's Shield', p. 133.

13   There is a useful brief discussion of the pentangle in Silverstein, *Sir Gawain*, pp. 129–31 (*sub* line 619ff).

– 10 and 100 being the supreme circular numbers.[14] But 5 is also the number of the flesh by virtue of the five senses. It would fit well with the *Gawain*-poet's explanation of the pentangle to assume that he saw in it a symbol representative of man's aspiration to the perfection of the Godhead. The particular path by which Gawain aspires to this perfection is through the various rigorous tests he encounters as a Round Table knight.

II

It is only amongst the learned that the pentangle is known by its Latin name (lines 664–65).[15] Its common name, by which, the poet assures us, the device is known everywhere in England, is the *endeles knot* (lines 629–30). At line 662 he refers to it again as a *knot*, and yet 'knot' is hardly the first word that would spring to mind in relation to the pentangle. The one thing one would tend to think it was not is a knot. What the poet stresses is that it is not knotted but continuous and without end:

> And vche lyne vmbelappez and loukez in oþer
> And ayquere hit is endelez ...   (lines 628–29)

If we are aware of anything knotted in the poem, it is not the pentangle but the girdle which Gawain accepts from the Lady in Fitt 3. The verb *to knit* (OE *cnyttan*, to knit) is cognate with the noun *knot* (OE *cnotta*, knot). It occurs in the first lines in which Gawain encounters the girdle:

> ' ... I schal gif yow my girdel, þat gaynes yow lasse.'
> Ho laȝt a lace lyȝtly þat leke vmbe hir sydez,
> *Knit* vpon hir kyrtel, vnder þe clere mantyle ...   (lines 1829–31)[16]

I think it is reasonable to assume here that *knit* means 'knotted', rather than merely 'fastened' (which is another possible meaning).[17] A knot capable of being easily loosed would be the natural fastening of a girdle. Certainly, when it is next worn, by Gawain himself, it is tied with a loose knot (perhaps a 'bow', as we would say today), as becomes clear when he tears it off and flings it at the Green Knight in disgust:

---

14 Although the numerological key to *Pearl* is the number 12, not the number 5, that poem also advertises the poet's interest in the concept of circularity/endlessness through the image of the pearl itself and through the linking words between the last line of one stanza and the first of the next (and so between the last line of the poem and its very first line).

15 The word is rare in the English vernacular: apart from references in *Gawain* (MED *pent-angel*), it is not recorded until 1646 (OED *pentangle* n., 1.).

16 Italicisation of the text is always my own.

17 MED *knitten* v., 1.(a) to fasten (a rope, thread, etc.) by a knot ... , 2.(a) to fasten (sth. with a thread, rope, etc.); tie (sth. to sth. else).

> Þenne he kaȝt to þe *knot* and þe kest lawsez,
> Brayde broþely þe belt to þe burne seluen ... (lines 2376–77)[18]

From that point he undertakes to wear the girdle as a sign of his sin (*in syngne of my surfet*, line 2433), and indeed on his way back to Camelot he wears it over the now-healed wound in his neck, again fastened with a knot:

> Þe hurt watz hole þat he hade hent in his nek
> And þe blykkande belt he bere þeraboute,
> Abelef, as a bauderyk, bounden bi his syde,
> Loken vnder his lyfte arme, þe lace, with a *knot*,
> In tokenyng he watz tane in tech of a faute.   (lines 2484–88)

What is of course of interest is the implicit contrast between the knotted and unknotted girdle and the *endeles knot* of the pentangle, which can never be undone and has neither beginning nor end:

> Withouten ende at any noke I oquere fynde,
> Whereeuer þe gomen bygan or glod to an ende.   (lines 660–61)

If the poet had not told us himself, it would not be difficult to guess that the pentangle is *in bytoknyng of trawþe* (line 626) and the girdle is þe *token of vntrawþe*, the sign of untruth (line 2509).

III

Solomon, we are told, established the pentangle as a symbol of truth by its very name (*in bytoknyng of trawþe, bi tytle þat hit habbez*, line 626). There is nothing in the title *pentangle* that suggests its suitability as a symbol of truth. The name must be the English one, the endless knot. It is an endless knot which suggests *trawþe*, whereas it is a loose knot which suggests *vntrawþe*. Indeed, a further meaning of the word *knot* in the Middle Ages is 'a bond between persons; an agreement' (MED *knotte* n., 3.(c)).[19] Gawain's sin at the end of the poem consists in his breaking the bond between himself and Bertilak. He does not break the bond with the Green Knight in the Beheading Game, and he has no intention of doing so, but in another significant game in the poem (which seems significant neither to us nor to Gawain at the time), the Exchange of Winnings Game, he breaks the agreement that he will give up to Bertilak whatever he has gained during the course of the day. Instead, he conceals the girdle.

Trawþe is what characterises Gawain: it is blazoned on his shield and cote-

---

18 Silverstein (*Sir Gawain*, p. 164, *sub* line 2376) argues convincingly that the meaning of *kest* here is 'not merely a fastening, but more precisely a bow or tie', in other words, a knot.

19 Cf. MED *knitten* v., 7.(a) To establish (a covenant, marriage, peace, etc.) ... (b) to bind (sb.) in an agreement.

armour through the sign of the pentangle. The rules of the two games played on/with Gawain by the Green Knight/Bertilak are taken very seriously, indeed legalistically, in the poem, and in each game Gawain is made to go through a careful ceremony which binds him to its rules.[20] In each case he is made to swear on his honour, a phrase which employs the loaded word *trawþe* (*bi þi trawþe*, line 394; *with trawþe*, line 1108), and in the final Fitt it becomes clear that it is Gawain's word of honour that has been tested throughout the poem:

> Fyrst I mansed þe muryly with a mynt one
> And roue þe wyth no rof-sore. With ryʒt I þe profered
> For þe forwarde þat we fest in þe fyrst nyʒt;
> And þou trystyly þe trawþe and *trwly* me haldez:
> Al þe gayne þow me gef, as god mon schulde.
> Þat oþer munt for þe morne, mon, I þe profered:
> Þou kyssedes my clere wyf, þe cossez me raʒtez.
> For boþe two here I þe bede bot two bare myntes
>   Boute scaþe.
> *Trwe* mon *trwe* restore;
> Þenne þar mon drede no waþe.
> At þe þrid þou fayled þore,
> And þerfor þat tappe ta þe.   (lines 2345–57)[21]

However much the Green Knight/Bertilak may insist on Gawain's comparative integrity (*As perle bi þe quite pese is of prys more,/ So is Gawayn, in god fayth, bi oþer gay knyʒtez*, lines 2364–65), and however much he may assure him, in the very last words that he speaks to him, that he loves him *for þy grete trauþe* (line 2470), Gawain wears the girdle from then on, over his cote-armour and so over the pentangle, as *þe token of vntrawþe þat I am tan inne* (line 2509).

IV

The symbol of *vntrawþe*, the girdle, has therefore by the end of the poem been superimposed on the symbol of *trawþe*, the pentangle. The girdle is *loken vnder his lyfte arme, þe lace, with a knot* (line 2487). The verb *to lock* (OE *lōcan*, to lock) appears to be a synonym for *knit* and is used of the way in which both Gawain and the Lady wear the girdle (cf. *[it] leke vmbe hir [the Lady's] sydez*, line 1830). It is an odd word to choose, and the MED suggests the

---

20 See Robert J. Blanch and Julian N. Wasserman, 'Medieval Contracts and Covenants: the Legal Coloring of *Sir Gawain and the Green Knight*', *Neophilologus* 68 (1984), 598–610.

21 The Green Knight/Bertilak goes on to point out that Gawain, in taking the girdle and not returning it, lacked *lewté* (line 2366), and Gawain himself accepts that he has forsaken what should be natural to him, the *larges and lewté* which belong to knighthood (line 2381). *Lewté* acts here as a less pregnant but alliteratively convenient synonym for *trawþe*, as *vnleute* does for *vntrawþe* at line 2499.

meaning 'to be joined or fastened' (MED *louken* v.(1), 4 (b)). However, that meaning is not recorded anywhere else in Middle English literature, and I would suggest that the poet is deliberately extending his metaphor of the lock (as he does of the knot) into contexts where their very oddness is intended to alert us to his careful symbolism.

We have, in fact, come across the word *lock* in two earlier contexts which are pertinent here. First, in relation to the pentangle, where each line overlaps and locks into the next (*vche lyne vmbelappez and loukez in oþer*, line 628), and, in the same Fitt but in a seemingly different context, of the ribbon fastened and wound round the handle of the axe used in the Beheading Game:

> A lace lapped aboute, þat *louked* at þe hede
> And so after þe halme halched ful ofte ...   (lines 217–18)

In the overlapping and locking, therefore, the pentangle is rather like the axe lace, which is also lapped around and locked at the head, as well as like the girdle which is locked around the Lady's (and later around Gawain's) sides. But in one respect it is very different: the endless knot of the pentangle cannot be untied, whereas the material of both the axe handle and the Lady's girdle is knotted and can be untied. All three are said to be 'locked', but, unlike the pentangle, the lace of the axe handle and of the girdle can be unlocked.

The association of integrity (*trawþe*) with what is locked is dominant in the poem. Indeed, the verb *lock* alliterates with the adjective *lel*, meaning 'loyal, true', in a familiar line right at the start of the poem, where the poet asserts that he will narrate it:

> As hit is stad and stoken
> In stori stif and stronge,
> With lel letteres loken,
> In londe so hatz ben longe.   (lines 33–36)

The oddness of these lines has perhaps been lost to us since the general acceptance that they refer to the poet's use of alliterative verse, but it is tempting in the context of the discussion above to use the collocation of *lel* and *loken* to read the lines as an assertion that the poem, like the *pentangle* (*in bytoknyng of trawþe*, line 626, where *vche lyne vmbelappez and loukez in oþer*, line 628) is a magical device incorporating a secret truth waiting to be unlocked.

V

There are several interesting points of resemblance between the axe lace and the girdle.[22] Both, of course, turn out to be the possessions of the same shape-shifting challenger, the Green Knight/Bertilak. Both are offered as gifts at New

---

22   Their relationship is discussed in a very illuminating way by Kent Hieatt, although the latter part of his argument seems to me more tendentious.

Year entertainments, a traditional time of gift-giving. Both are offered in the context of a game, the one clearly sinister, the other clearly innocuous.[23] Both axe-lace and girdle have gold tassels, but, more importantly, both are green, like the Green Knight himself, and are therefore associated with Celtic myth and the world of faery, as well as with love, the devil, and the huntsman.[24] The green girdle and the axe with its green ribbon both have magical powers which enable the owner to escape death. Gawain uses the axe to behead the Green Knight, who miraculously survives the beheading; in the case of the girdle, he is explicitly told of its powers by the Lady:

> 'Now forsake ȝe þis silke,' sayde þe burde þenne,
> 'For hit is symple in hitself? ...
> ... quat gome so is gorde with þis grene lace,
> While he hit hade hemely halched aboute
> Þer is no haþel vnder heuen tohewe hym þat myȝt,
> For he myȝt not be slayn for slyȝt vpon erþe.'   (lines 1846–54)

The term *grene lace* (line 1851) is an interesting one. Both the ribbon on the axe handle and the Lady's girdle are described as *lace* (lines 217, 2226 of the axe, lines 1830, 1851, 2030, 2487, 2505 of the girdle). 'Lace' to us today would mean the sort of openwork, created at one time by hand, which edges delicate fabric. This is not a medieval meaning (OED *lace* n., 6, where the first recorded date is 1555). The word *lace* in the Middle Ages describes cord or ribbon used for various purposes – to fasten clothing, to hang objects from, to tie something or someone up (MED *las* n., 1a, 1b, 1c, 1d). It survives only in our word *shoelace*.

But lace also has the meaning 'a net, noose, or snare' (MED *las* n., 4, OED 1), a significant hunting metaphor applied frequently in Middle English texts to the bondage of love. The phrase *luflace* occurs twice in *Sir Gawain and the Green Knight*, used of the girdle after Gawain has accepted it from the Lady (lines 1874, 2438). The *lace* is a trap for Gawain. The trap is fastened with a knot – and another potential meaning of the word *knot* in the Middle Ages is synonymous with this

---

23   The Beheading Game is explicitly introduced as a *gomen* (line 273), merely *a Crystemas gomen* (line 283). Rather differently, the Exchange of Winnings Game is assumed by Gawain to be a game (*And þat yow lyst for to layke lef hit me þynkes*, line 1111), an assumption ironically endorsed by the poet (*To bed ȝet er þay ȝede, /Recorded couenauntez ofte; /Þe olde lorde of þat leude /Cowþe wel halde layk alofte*, lines 1122–25). Intrinsic to the Exchange of Winnings Game are the hunting game played by Bertilak (*Þus laykez þis lorde*, line 1178) and the wooing game played by the Lady (*þe lel layk of luf*, line 1513) at which Gawain and the Lady *laȝed and layked longe* (line 1554).

24   In relation to the green-clad yeoman who becomes sworn brother to the summoner in Chaucer's Friar's Tale, there is a useful note (with brief bibliography) on the significance of the colour green in L. Benson (ed.) *The Riverside Chaucer*, Oxford, 1988, p. 875 (*sub* lines 1380–83).

meaning of *lace*: a bond, a fetter (MED *knotte*, n., 3(a)). Indeed, *knot*, meaning bond or fetter, is often used in magical contexts such as this one, where the bond is the binding of a magic spell.[25] In taking the lace and wearing it around his body, Gawain places himself, literally and figuratively, within the magic circle of the knotted girdle and so within the supernatural power of Bertilak.

VI

So far, I have tried to demonstrate that the *knot* is crucial to the poem, both actually and symbolically. *Trawþe* is represented as an endless knot; *vntrawþe* exists in what can be knotted and unknotted, the axe lace and the girdle with which Gawain is trapped. To break one's word, as Gawain ultimately does, is to break the knot.[26] I want to return now to a puzzle in relation to the word *knot* – why should the pentangle be called an endless knot in the first place? Why *knot*? Surely the one thing that the poet demonstrates is that it is not a knot. If there were evidence that the term was used of the pentangle throughout the whole of England (as the poet says it is), then perhaps we would be content with the title, however inexplicable, but no other use of the phrase 'endless knot' appears to have been recorded in Middle English literature. There must be some significance in the term itself in relation to the pentangle.

A painting in the National Gallery in London started off the ensuing line of investigation. Paolo Uccello's *Rout of San Romano* shows the military leader Niccolò da Tolentino leading the Florentines against the Sienese in an impromptu battle of 1432. His banner shows a device which appears to be a garland twisted into knots at four points, identified as the *groppo di Salamone*, the knot of Solomon.[27] This knot of Solomon differs crucially from the *Gawain*-poet's knot of Solomon. For a start, it appears not to be endless but

---

25 In this context it is worth noting that the noun *kest*, which can mean 'knot' (see note 18 above), is cognate with the verb *to cast*, as in 'to cast a spell'. Today's meaning of the word *spell* is not recorded until 1579 (OED *spell* n.1, 3.a).

26 The metaphor of breaking is intrinsic to the vocabulary of allegiance (OED *break* v., III, 15).

27 The painting and a detail of the knots of Solomon on Niccolò's banner are reproduced as Plates 1 and 2. The panel is one of three commissioned by Cosimo de' Medici in 1434–35 to celebrate the victory. John Pope-Hennessy notes: 'The identity of the first scene is established by a banner with the device of Niccolò da Tolentino, the "groppo di Salamone" (Solomon's knot)' (*Paolo Uccello*, London, 1969, pp. 152–3). For other instances of the *groppo/nodo di Salamone*, see Silverstein, *Sir Gawain*, pp. 132–3 (*sub* lines 628–30), where it is noted that the early Italian dictionaries define *nodo* (= knot) as *vn certo lavoro ... a guisa di nodo, di cui non apparisce ne il capo ne il fine*, i.e. 'a certain device ... in the form of a knot, in which neither the beginning nor the end is apparent'. Silverstein's own conclusion, however, is that 'there is no evidence ... connecting it specifically with the pentangle' (p. 133). On the Compagnia del Nodo, see further below.

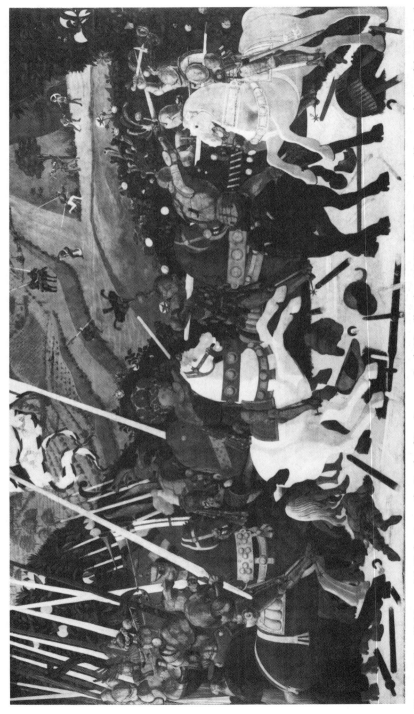

Plate 1   *Niccolò Mauruzi da Tolentino at the Battle of San Romano*, Paolo Uccello, about 1397–1475. Reproduced by permission of the National Gallery, London.

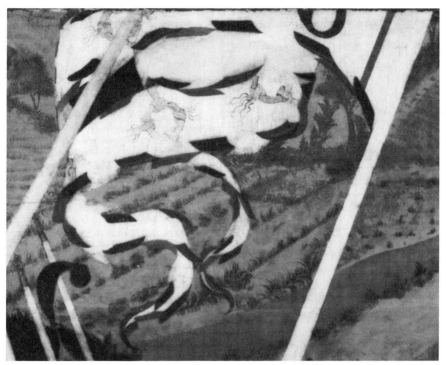

Plate 2   Detail of the knot of Solomon on the banner of Niccolò da Tolentino, from *Niccolò Mauruzi da Tolentino at the Battle of San Romano*, Paolo Uccello, about 1397–1475.   Reproduced by permission of the National Gallery, London.

tied in knots with loose ends, and secondly it is knotted at four, not five points. Nevertheless, the knot as a heraldic device seemed to merit further exploration.

Tolentino's device of the knot of Solomon may have had its origin in the Company of the Holy Spirit of Right Desire, or the Company of the Knot (*Compagnia del Nodo*), which appears to have flourished only briefly in fourteenth-century Italy.[28] The parallels between this knot and Gawain's knot are not, however, close,[29] and the device may in fact have been in wide use.

28   For the Company of the Knot, see D'A. J. D. Boulton, *The Knights of the Crown: the Monarchical Orders of Knighthood in Later Medieval Europe, 1325–1520*, Woodbridge, 1987, pp. 241–9.

29   The knot, which was around 20 inches long and tied like a love-knot, would be untied when certain feats of arms and piety had been accomplished. After visiting the Holy Sepulchre at Jerusalem (where a knot would be left as a votive offering), the original knot would be retied. It would carry the motto *Il a plecu a Dieu* ('it has pleased God') and would display a ray of the Holy Spirit.

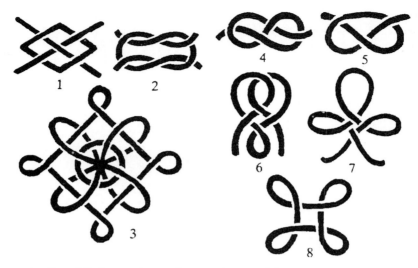

Figure 1   Heraldic knots: 1. Harrington, 2. Bourchier, 3. Lacy, 4. Cavendish, 5. Stafford, 6. Heneage, 7. Hungerford, 8. Bowen. Reproduced from Stephen Friar, *Heraldry*, Stroud, 1992, p. 226, by kind permission of the artist, Andrew Jamieson.

Certainly, the knot is a common heraldic badge and is associated with several families,[30] although no known knot resembles the description of the pentangle. If we think of the pentangle, not as a one-dimensional geometric device, but as an elaborately twisted cord, it makes an effective parallel to the axelace and girdle, the girdle clearly a knotted silken cord (line 1846) and the axelace seemingly the same. In other words, the poet's understanding of the pentangle may have encompassed not only the five-angled figure often illustrated in our editions of the poem, but also a device closer to our present-day perception of a knot. It may be too that heraldic terminology informs other lexical items in the poem.

VII

When Gawain first wore the girdle, setting out to find the Green Chapel on the final morning, he wore it wrapped twice round his hips, rather like a military

---

30   See, for example, the definition in S. Friar, *Heraldry*, Stroud, 1992, p. 226 and the illustration of knots reproduced here. OED records this heraldic use only from an *Encyclopaedia of Heraldry* of 1828–40 (OED *knot* n.1, 2b.), and MED does not record a specifically heraldic definition at all (but cf. MED *knotte* n., 4. (a): 'an ornamental knob on armor, a bed, garment, etc.; a button; ?also, a tassel, a tuft'). However, a knot is the badge of the Bourchiers, the Bowens, the Heneages, the Ormonds, the Staffords, the Wakes, and other medieval families.

belt. But on his journey back to Camelot, it has taken on a different significance, and he wears it differently, slung from shoulder to side diagonally across his body:

> *Abelef as a bauderyk*, bounden bi his syde,
> *Loken* vnder his lyfte arme, þe *lace*, with a *knot*,
> In tokenyng he watz tane in tech of a faute.   (lines 2486–88)

It is worn diagonally (using the heraldic term *abelef*),[31] like a baldric (MED *bauderik* n. 1. 'A sash or girdle, worn over the shoulder or around the waist, for carrying a sword, a hunting horn, a pouch; a baldric; also an ornamental sash or girdle').[32] It is locked at his side, fastened under his left arm with a knot, as a sign of his sin. Wearing it like this superimposes over the pentangle on Gawain's cote-armour the diagonal band known in heraldry as a *bend* (MED *bend(e* n.(1), 4. *Her.* 'A broad diagonal band or stripe placed over a coat-of-arms, banner, shield, etc.').[33] That we are meant to see it this way is clear from the poet's own use of the word *bend*:

> 'Lo! lorde,' quoþ þe leude, and þe *lace* hondeled,
> 'Þis is þe *bende* of þis blame I bere in my nek,
> Þis is þe laþe and þe losse þat I laȝt haue
> Of couardise and couetyse þat I haf caȝt þare.
> Þis is þe token of vntrawþe þat I am tan inne,
> And I mot nedez hit were wyle I may last ...'   (lines 2505–10)

The *bend* is then taken up by the whole court and becomes part of their accoutrement:

---

31 The phrase is used again at line 2517 (*bende abelef*). See MED *abelef* adv., where the sole references are to *Sir Gawain and the Green Knight*. For the heraldic term *belic/belif/belive*, etc. see Gerard J. Brault, *Early Blazon: Heraldic Terminology in the Twelfth and Thirteenth Centuries with special reference to Arthurian Literature*, Oxford, 1972, p. 120, col. 1, and for *bende de belic*, see p. 124, col. 2. Another heraldic term (*goulez*) is used of the red of the shield on which the gold pentangle is painted (lines 619, 663).

32 The semantic overlap becomes quite dense here, since *girdle* can itself mean 'baldric' (MED *girdel* 2a. (a)), while lace can similarly be used to refer to 'a cord used to suspend a hanging object' (MED *lās* 1c. (a)).

33 The figure of a knight reproduced as Figure 2 (page 70) shows the *bend* worn on both the shield and the surcoat (cote-armour). MED does not recognise the word as having heraldic significance in the poem but instead defines it: '3. (a) An ornamental lace, ribbon, sash, etc., on a garment; a stripe or band on a garment or bedspread'. For heraldic details, see Brault, *Early Blazon*, p. 80 and figure 60. The poet makes plain that the bend runs from the right shoulder down to the left armpit, i.e. that it is a *bend dexter*. A diagonal line the other way is a *bend sinister*, often assumed (erroneously) to be a mark of illegitimacy. For a diagram of a bend, see Friar, *Heraldry*, p. 182, and for further information, see T. Woodcock and J. M. Robinson, *The Oxford Guide to Heraldry*, Oxford, 1990, pp. 59–60.

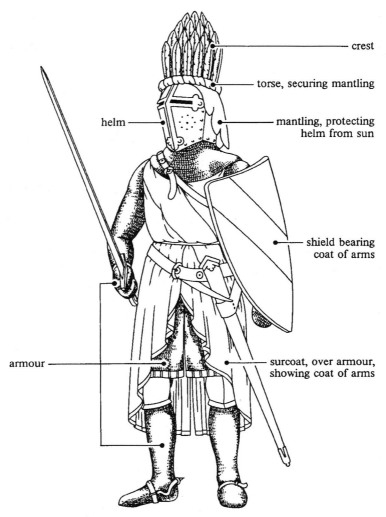

- crest
- torse, securing mantling
- helm
- mantling, protecting helm from sun
- shield bearing coat of arms
- armour
- surcoat, over armour, showing coat of arms

Figure 2   Figure of a knight, showing the *bend* worn on both the shield and the surcoat (cote-armour). Reproduced from Y. E. Weir, *A Guide to the Heraldry in York Minster*, York, 1986, p. 6. Drawing by P. Eurich: reproduced by kind permission of the Dean and Chapter of York.

Þe kynge comfortez þe kny3t, and alle þe court als
La3en loude þerat, and luflyly acorden
Þat lordes and ledes þat longed to the Table,
Vche burne of þe broþerhede, a bauderyk schulde haue,
A *bende abelef* hym aboute of a bry3t grene,
And þat for sake of þat segge, in swete to were ...   (lines 2513–18)

70

Worn crosswise across his body, the *bend* is now symbolic of Gawain, as the pentangle, no longer mentioned, was previously symbolic of him. It is an heraldic device which, for him, marks out his *vntrawþe*, as previously the pentangle was the blazon of his *trawþe*.

VIII

It is inherently likely that heraldry played a role in the poet's conception of the poem. Gawain is, of course, a knight of the fellowship of the Round Table, which was imitated by Edward III in the founding of the Order of the Garter 1347–50,[34] and by other English and European kings and noblemen in the founding of other medieval orders of chivalry.[35] The author of *Sir Gawain and the Green Knight* was most likely himself a knight.[36]

Gawain's arms are well documented in medieval literature: there is more than one version, but a golden eagle is the most frequent device.[37] The fact that it is only in *Sir Gawain and the Green Knight* that he is associated with the pentangle is clearly significant,[38] as is the remarkable emphasis on the colour green in the poem.[39] Inevitably, scholars have searched for a chivalric order which combines the pentangle and the colour green.[40]

The poem ends, of course, with the Garter motto (*Hony soyt qui mal pence*). This appears, however, to have been added in a later hand, and the connections between the Order of the Garter and the details of the poem are hard to maintain.[41] The Percy Folio ballad, *The Grene Knight*, has a Gawain who is given a

---

34 See Boulton, *Knights of the Crown*, pp. 96–166.

35 Boulton, *Knights of the Crown*, is invaluable for details of the monarchical orders of chivalry from 1325 on. For details of the military orders before that date, see note 48 below.

36 See, for example, the arguments of Clifford J. Peterson, 'The *Pearl*-Poet and John Massey of Cotton, Cheshire', *Review of English Studies* 25 (1974), 257–66, and Michael J. Bennett, *Community, Class and Careerism: Cheshire and Lancashire Society in the Age of Sir Gawain and the Green Knight*, Cambridge, 1983.

37 Brault, *Early Blazon*, pp. 38–43.

38 It is not always accepted that *nwe* (*Forþy þe pentangel nwe/ He ber in schelde and cote*, lines 636–39) means a newly assumed blazon, but this is in fact just what it appears to be.

39 The colour green is firmly associated with both the Green Knight (in whose initial description the word occurs no fewer than fifteen times, lines 150–236) and with Bertilak (through the green girdle and through his implied hunting outfit).

40 Green Knights appear to be less common in Arthurian literature than knights of other colours (Brault, *Early Blazon*, p. 35).

41 For an early argument, see Isaac Jackson, '*Sir Gawain and the Green Knight* considered as a "Garter" Poem', *Anglia* 37 (1913), 393–423. Jackson is concerned to show the Garter connections of the poem and its association with the Black Prince, but his interpretation of the pentangle is similar to my own: 'I cannot see much point in calling a rigid, formal figure like the pentangle "a knot"' (p. 422). On the badge and

white, rather than a green, lace: the poet explains that this is why knights of the Order of the Bath wear a white lace.[42] Scholars have found other, but never entirely satisfactory, connections with orders such as the Ordre de l'Etoile founded in 1351 by Jean le Bon,[43] or the Order of the Collar founded in 1362 by Count Amedeo VI of Saxony.[44] A more recent identification of the poem's patron as Henry of Grosmont notes associations in the poem with the Order of the Band founded in 1330 by Alfonso XI, as well as with the Order of the Garter.[45] As I have noted above, the Company of the Knot would seem to offer a source for the pentangle of the poem, but the parallel is not exact. In fact, elements of several contemporary orders of chivalry appear to surface in the poem.

It may anyway seem reductive to attempt to pin the poet down to one particular order of knighthood. Yet it seems to me that the poet does have a secret, a knot to be untied, which is encrypted, not only in the word *knot*, but also in *bend* and *lace*, and which suggests that he was strongly influenced by the example of the chivalric orders. The testing of a knight is, of course, the essence of the poem, and in several ways the stages of Gawain's treatment at the hands of the Green Knight/Bertilak accord with the rituals involved in the making of a knight in the Middle Ages: the testing of the squire, the elaborate ceremony which initiates him into knighthood, the role of the Church as well as the State in that ceremony.[46]

Of course, Gawain is already a knight, so that what we have in the poem, perhaps, is rather a refined test and ritual leading to a higher rank of knighthood than that already held by the knight. In the Order of the Bath, for example, which was founded by Henry V on the eve of his coronation in 1413, a

insignia of the Order, see Boulton, *Knights of the Crown*, pp. 152–61. A comment of Boulton is of some interest in that it illustrates the misunderstanding occasioned by the use of the word *lace* today: a story 'which maintained that the garter of the Order was inspired by a bit of lace given by Richard I to certain of his knights to wear around their legs during his attacks on Cyprus and Acre ... can be dismissed as a late invention without any foundation' (p. 155). The story was recorded by the compiler of the Black Book of the Order in 1534.

42　See J. R. Hulbert, '*Syr Gawayn and the Grene Knyȝt*', *Modern Philology* 13 (1915–16), 433–62, 689–730.

43　H. L. Savage, *The Gawain-Poet: Studies in his Personality and Background*, Chapel Hill, 1956, Appendix E, pp. 158–68.

44　Hulbert, '*Syr Gawayn*', pp. 139–40.

45　W. G. Cooke and D'A. J. D. Boulton, '*Sir Gawain and the Green Knight*: A Poem for Henry of Grosmont?', *Medium Aevum* 68 (1999), 42–54. On the Order of the Band, see Boulton, *Knights of the Crown*, pp. 46–95.

46　The customary chapel vigil, followed by confession and mass, and the dubbing of the knight by the accolade (a light blow on the neck with a sword) may be compared with episodes in Fitt 4 of the poem, where, at the Green Chapel, Bertilak strikes Gawain on the neck with his axe, hears his confession, and absolves him of sin (lines 2309–14, 2385–94).

white lace is worn on the left shoulder, only to be removed by a noble lady when the knight has further distinguished himself.[47] Or it may be that Gawain is to be initiated into a new order, one more arcane, sophisticated, and privileged than that of the Round Table, and here a comparison might be made with the Order of the Charity of the Temple of Solomon, where one who had already been dubbed a knight would demonstrate through his chastity, humility, and obedience that he was worthy to be received into the religious and military order of the Knights Templar.[48]

IX

The court to which Gawain returns sees him as having successfully passed his test, and they wear the sign of that test, the girdle, as a mark of honour:

> For þat watz acorded þe renoun of þe Rounde Table,
> And he honoured þat hit hade, euermore after ...   (lines 2519–20)

Gawain himself wears it for quite other reasons. He alone knows that his sin is attached to him in a way that cannot be shrugged off. We were told earlier in the poem that the five points of chivalry were *harder happed on þat haþel þen on any oþer* (line 655). What is now firmly fastened in Gawain is his sin. The knot of the green bend he now wears can be untied, but his sin can never be unloosed. In his mind it has taken on the endless qualities of the pentangle:

> 'Lo! lorde,' quoþ þe leude, and þe lace hondeled,
> 'Þis is þe *bende* of þis blame I bere in my nek,
> Þis is þe laþe and þe losse þat I laȝt haue
> Of couardise and couetyse þat I haf caȝt þare.
> Þis is þe token of vntrawþe þat I am tan inne,
> And I mot nedez hit were wyle I may last;

47   See A. Wagner, N. Barker and A. Payne, *Medieval Pageant: Writhe's Garter Book: The Ceremony of the Bath and the Earldom of Salisbury Roll*, London, 1993, pp. 3–5, Appendix B (especially p. 74), and Plates pp. 105–28.
48   There is no detailed history of the Templars in England. Recent studies include E. Burman, *The Templars: Knights of God*, London, 1986; Alan Forey, *The Military Orders from the Twelfth to the Early Fourteenth Centuries*, Basingstoke and London, 1992; and Helen Nicholson, *Templars, Hospitallers and Teutonic Knights: Images of the Military Orders, 1128–1291*, Leicester, 1993. Despite their close association with Solomon's Temple in Jerusalem, there appears to be surprisingly little evidence of the Templars' interest in Solomon (although one should perhaps not expect too much evidence of a secret society such as the Templars were). In this context, the connection between the Templars and Freemasonry is of some interest, and the chief symbol in the third degree of freemasonry (the master mason) is the pentangle of Solomon, whose points are the five points of fellowship (Jeremiah How, *The Freemason's Manual*, 3rd edn, London, 1881, pp. 142–4). See too D. Knoop and G. P. Jones, *The Genesis of Freemasonry*, Manchester, 1947.

For mon may hyden his harme, bot vnhap ne may hit,
For þer hit onez is tachched twynne wil hit neuer.'   (lines 2505–12)

It is usual to accept that Gawain's opinion of himself is out of kilter with that of Bertilak, as well as with that of the court. It seems to me, however, that Gawain has indeed failed the test. As Bertilak points out, he has not been *trwe* (*Trwe mon trwe restore*, line 2354, *lewté, yow wonted*, line 2366); he has ultimately failed Bertilak's test (*At þe þrid þou fayled þore*, line 2356, *yow lakked a lyttel*, line 2366); and his reputation can only be compared with that of other Round Table knights (*as perle bi quite pese ... bi oþer gay knyʒtez*, lines 2364–65). He has not passed the test to be admitted into the more arcane order of knighthood to which the shapeshifting Bertilak belongs. For that reason, the pentangle is overlaid by the *bend*, the endless knot overlaid by the knotted girdle.

X

In this essay I may appear to have raised more questions than I have answered. I have not solved (nor even, I am sure, recognised) all the clues that the *Gawain*-poet offers his reader. The aim of my essay is to argue that such clues exist and to suggest what sort of clues they are. *Sir Gawain and the Green Knight* is a knotty problem, a game that has been set up by its author with a *knot*, a central puzzle that informs the whole. The pun on *knot* is, I think, intentional, and the *knot* (= problem) centres around the *knot* (= pentangle). It can be unknotted only painstakingly and perhaps now only partially. It may be that it will always to some extent remain an *endeles knot*.

TWO NOTES ON LAƷAMON'S *BRUT*

JANE ROBERTS

I

READERS of Laȝamon's *Brut* have, for a century and a half, turned to Madden's glossary for help when difficulties are encountered, and will continue to do so until the publication of the third volume of the Early English Text Society (EETS) edition.[1] Recently, through light cast upon the Caligula text by a flurry of interesting translations, it is clear that there are still cruces to solve.[2] Here, as an amusement for Ron Waldron, I should like to share with him my thoughts about a couple of passages which, according to the most recent translations, remain opaque. Yet in each case, as I reread Laȝamon's words, interpretations sprang immediately to mind. The evidence to support my understanding of these passages was not to be found in either the *Middle English Dictionary* (MED) or the *Oxford English Dictionary* (OED). Consultation, however, of Old English dictionaries yielded some interesting parallel forms, bearing out the point Gillespy made long ago that Laȝamon's 'extended and astonishingly pure English vocabulary at once establishes a presumption in favor of wide reading in his own language'.[3] Laȝamon, living at a time when English was changing rapidly both in structure and vocabulary, drew upon words that were, even as he used them, very likely being displaced.[4]

---

1 F. Madden (ed.) *Laȝamons Brut, or Chronicle of Britain; a poetical semi-Saxon paraphrase of the Brut of Wace*, London, 1847; G. L. Brook and R. F. Leslie (eds) *Laȝamon: Brut*, EETS, o.s. 250, 277. London, New York, Toronto, 1963, 1978.

2 D. G. Bzdyl (trans.) *Layamon's Brut: a history of the Britons*, Binghamton, New York, 1989; R. Allen (trans.) *Lawman: Brut*, J. M. Dent & Sons Ltd, 1992; W. R. J. Barron and S. C. Weinberg (eds and trans.) *Laȝamon: Brut or Hystoria Brutonum*, Harlow, 1995.

3 F. L. Gillespy, 'Layamon's Brut: A Comparative Study in Narrative Art', *University of California Publications in Modern Philology* 3 (1916), p. 504.

4 See also J. Roberts, 'Laȝamon's Plain Words', in *Middle English Miscellany. From vocabulary to linguistic variation*, ed. J. Fisiak, Poznan 1996, pp. 107–22, where I argue that Laȝamon's choice of words reflects the everyday usage of his age.

II

First, the clause *al hit him aloðede* (14966) seems generally to puzzle its readers. The context is the defeat of the last great pagan Anglo-Saxon leader in the northern part of England. Cadwan of North Wales (Geoffrey's Venedotia or Gwynedd) and Mergadud of South Wales (Geoffrey's Demetia or Dyfed), together with Baldric of Cornwall, summoned a great army to attack Ælfric (the historical Ethelfrith) of Northumbria.[5] The battle was *vnimete* (14950), with huge casualties: ten thousand Britons died, among them Baldric, and seventeen thousand Angles and Saxons. Ælfric, sorely wounded, retreated with a much diminished force into Northumbria. Cadwan and Margadud called an assembly, summoning all minded to live as part of the people of this country. As well as the Britons, English and 'Saxish' (14953–54) attended, and they declared Cadwan their leader:

> Cadwan and Margadud: and heore mon-weorede.
> buȝen uorh mid heom: al Brut-leoden.
> to Leirchestre foren: and þa burh nomen.
> Þa hehten heo an hiȝinge: cumen to hus-tinge.
> al þat wolde libben: inne þissere leoden.
> Þer comen Ænglisce: þer comen Sexise.
> þer heo makeden to kinge: Cadwan þene kene.   (14959–65)

Before turning to Ælfric's state of health, Laȝamon adds a line that has puzzled all who read the poem:

> al hit him aloðede: þat he on lokede.
> þa weoren Æluriches wunden ...   (14966–67)

There is no Otho text here to consult. Equally, Wace provides no help:

> Dunc se sunt Bretun assemblé,
> A Leïrcestre sunt alé ;
> Cadwan, ki savant ert e pruz,
> Firent rei par le los de tuz.
> Cil add tuz mandez e sumuns
> Serjanz, chevaliers e baruns.
> Engleis, ki les cuntez teneient
> E reis apeler se feseient,
> Sunt tuit a sa merci venu
> E si hume sunt devenu.
> Puis dist qu'il passera le Humbre

---

5 Wace was responsible for the substitution of the English names North and South Wales.

Se gent plus fiere ne l'encumbre,
Northumberlande destruira
E la gent tute en chacera ;
Lu rei Elfrid ... (1359–73)

The form *aloðede* occurs only here in the *Brut*. Madden translates the clauses in which it stands 'all it to him bowed, that he on looked' (III. 203) and in his glossary he explains the form as 'submitted'. Bzdyl's 'all he looked upon submitted to him' follows Madden.[6] The MED editors take this form under the headword *alōthen* 'to become odious to (sb), disgust (sb.)', an interpretation followed by Allen and by Barron and Weinberg in their translations, with 'Everything he gazed at made him disgusted' and 'all that he beheld was displeasing to him' respectively. Barron and Weinberg draw attention to their uneasy acceptance of the MED explanation, noting that 'the meaning of 14966 in its context remains unclear'.[7]

Not only is the line unclear as generally interpreted, it is bewildering. If Cadwan is leader, why should he be displeased? Rather, he is a leader who surveys all he rules and is glad. If the form is thought of as *aleoðede* (*eo* and *o* can interchange in the Caligula *Brut*), the translation 'Everything pleased him' seems feasible. Cadwan is in the frame of mind represented by *(i)liðe*, an adjective found frequently in the *Brut* and glossed 'gracious, mild, calm, pleasant, obedient' by Madden. The verb should be related to Madden's glossary entry for *leoðien*, for which he gives the meanings 'to set free, loose, assuage'. La3amon's use of the verb to mean 'to loosen'[8] and 'to release, set free'[9] is clear enough, but the two most recent translations diverge interestingly in their interpretation of line 6008 *Þe wind gon aliðen· 7 þat weder leoðede*. Barron and Weinberg stick close to Madden's glossary with their 'The wind abated and the storm subsided', whereas Allen's 'The wind began abating, and the weather then grew mild' indicates her understanding of the verb's range. The Old English *(ge)liþigian*, which has a similar range of reference, includes 'to make glad' among its meanings. It is noteworthy that the Otho redactor retains none of these *(a)lið(i)en* forms. For *leoðien* (2384) he has *griþie*, for *leoðe* (10939) and *leoðien* (11650) he has respectively *slake* and *slakie*, and his line corresponding to 6008 runs *Þe wind gan a-legge· an þat weder softi*.

III

With a second phrase that gives pause to the recent translators of La3amon's *Brut*, again my explanation springs from evidence recorded in Old English

---

6 Bzdyl, *Layamon*, p. 264.
7 Barron and Weinberg, *La3amon*, p. 839.
8 Madden, *Brut*, II. 497, II. 558 = Brook and Leslie, *La3amon*, lines 10939, 11650.
9 Madden, *Brut*, I. 203 = Brook and Leslie, *La3amon*, line 2384.

dictionary resources. Laȝamon uses the words *to ȝiueles þingen* (11280) in a passage in which he departs significantly from his source. No words in Wace's *Brut* correspond exactly with the phrase *to ȝiueles þingen*, but it is helpful to examine the fuller context for arriving at an understanding of it. Wace, following his account of the conquest of Ireland, turns his attention to the submission of the northern world:[10]

> Quant Artur out cunquis Irlande,
> Trespassez est jesqu'en Islande ;
> La terre prist tute e cunquist
> E a sei tute la suzmist ;
> Par tut volt aver seinnurie.
> Gonvais, ki ert reis d'Orchenie,
> E Doldani, reis de Godlande,
> E Rummaret de Wenelande
> Orent tost la nuvele oïe,
> E chescuns i aveit s'espie,
> Que Artur sur els passereit
> E tuz les isles destruereit.
> N'aveit suz ciel d'armes sun per,
> Ne ki tel gent peüst mener.
> Pur poür que sur els n'alast
> Ne que lur terres ne guastast,
> Senz esforcement, de lur gré,
> Sunt en Islande a lui alé.
> De lur aveirs tant li porterent,
> Tant pramistrent e tant dunerent,
> Pais firent, si hume devindrent,
> Lur eritages de lui tindrent.
> Treü unt pramis e numé,
> Ostage en ad chescuns duné ;
> Par tant sunt tuit en pais remés,
> E Artur est venuz es nés ;
> En Engleterre est revenuz
> E a grant joie receüz.   (9703–30)

Laȝamon's version of this incident runs to well over a hundred lines, with lines 11210–316 of his *Brut* corresponding to the lines 9703–27 cited above from Wace. This represents a considerable expansion, even for that area of Laȝamon's poem which is, according to Le Saux, very freely related to

---

10   I. Arnold (ed.) *Le Roman de Brut de Wace*, Société des Anciens Textes Français, Paris, I. 1938, II. 1940.

Wace.[11] Indeed the first king named here by Laзamon does not appear in Wace.

Most appropriately, for this whole episode is set in Iceland, a king of Iceland, Ælcus, is the first of Laзamon's group of northern kings to welcome Arthur. He offers fealty, and his son Esscol, son of *þas kinges dohter of Rusie*, as Arthur's *aзene mon* or 'own man' (11225–26). Ælcus also, of his own accord, states that he will make a yearly payment of seven thousand pounds and that he will give counsel when called upon. Hardly surprisingly:

> Arður wes wunsum: þer he hafde his iwillen.
> ꝺ he wes wod sturne: wið his wiðer-iwinnen.
> Arður þa liðe word iherde: of an leod-kinge.
> al þat he зirnde: al he him зette.   (11234–67)

In their turn, the kings of Orkney and Jutland come to Arthur to offer allegiance. Alarmed by news that Arthur plans to visit Orkney *mid muchele scip-ferde* (11244), Gonwais arrives, promising a yearly supply of sixty shiploads of fish to London at his own expense (*mid his aзere costninge* (11251)). Next Arthur sends properly drawn-up papers (*writen gode* (11259)) to King Doldanim of Gutlond, ordering Doldanim to come immediately with his two sons to offer allegiance. Should he not come, Arthur threatens to send an invading force. The threat brings Doldanim quickly to Iceland, well provided with fine clothing, hounds, hawks, excellent horses and a great deal of gold and silver. With admirable economy, Laзamon completes his account of Doldanim's submission in an eleven-line speech. Doldanim, after greeting Arthur and presenting his sons, places them under Arthur's authority (*Ich tache þe mine leofen sunen* (11277)). He is careful to declare that these are sons of his queen, a woman of royal race won out of Russia. As Ælcus had pledged, he too promises to send seven thousand pounds of yearly tribute:

> And ic wulle sende: gauel of mine londe.
> æuer-ælche зere: to зiueles þingen.
> ich wulle senden þe in-to Lundene. seouen þusend punden;   (11279–81)

Allen and, more recently, Barron and Weinberg note their uncertainty as to the meaning of the phrase *to зiueles þingen*, making shift respectively with 'as items of tribute' and 'as a sign of tribute' in their translations of lines 11279–81.[12] Yet, taking *зiueles* as the miswriting of *gaueles* results in clumsy tautology.

---

11   Françoise Le Saux, *Laзamon's Brut: The Poem and its Sources*. Arthurian Studies 19, Cambridge, 1989, p. 31

12   See Allen, *Lawman*, p. 479, and Barron and Weinberg, *Laзamon*, p. 835. Bzdyl, *Layamon*, p. 212, deals more radically with the problem: 'and I will also send seven thousand pounds a year as tribute to you in London'.

The speeches of submission made by Ælcus and Doldanim, although they begin and end similarly, with opening formulaic greetings and closing promises of true service, are carefully differentiated. Doldanim, like Ælcus of Iceland, offers tribute (*gauel*), in his case seven thousand pounds, and, although his two sons also have a Russian mother, this mother was taken *mid ræflac: ut of Rusie* (11278). These are both powerful leaders, with wide possessions and wealth. Sandwiched between their professions of loyalty, Gonwais, apparently a brave fighting man, is a different kettle of fish. His profession of loyalty is reported, and his offered tribute is in kind rather than gold and silver. Gonwais rules a kingdom of thirty-two islands, and his followers are *ut-laʒen* – reivers or pirates.[13] Only his comparatively unpolished leavetaking is given in direct speech:

> Lauerd haue wel godne dæi. ich wulle cumen: wenne ich mai.
> for nu þu art mi lauer<d> leouest alre kingen.   (11256–57)

Once Arthur has received Doldanim's act of fealty, *Brut-lond ⁊ Scot-lond./ Gutlond ⁊ Irlond, Orcaneie ⁊ Island* (11287–88) are under his rule, and he sends to *Winent-londe* (11285) – some have argued to Vinland, but Wendland seems a less controversial identification.[14] In effect, in elaborating on the willing capitulation of the northern kings as related by Geoffrey, Wace and Laʒamon have each added a king: Laʒamon's Ælcus of Iceland and Wace's equally spurious Rumareth of Wendland, an area between the south of the Baltic and the Vistula.[15] Greatly *afered* (11294), just as the other three were, Rumareth journeys to Iceland, places himself at the feet of Arthur and makes his formal speech of submission, which ends: *þas ʒeuen ich finde þe wulle: æue[r]-alche ʒere* (11315). In Wace's words, these northern kings were to come to Iceland *Senz esforcement, de lur gré* (9719). Laʒamon's extended account is of the submission of four kings, Alchus, Gonwais, Doldanim and Rumareth, who voluntarily sue for peace and offer gifts rather than face war. From this point Arthur reigns supreme in the northern world, and these submissions mark the beginning of twelve years of peaceful rule.

Madden made two attempts to explain Doldanim's phrase *to ʒiueles þingen*, first translating it by 'as thing bestowed(?)' (II. 526) and later suggesting emendation to *gaueles* for 'thing of tribute'. That he remained dissatisfied is clear from his glossary entry, where he marks *ʒifeles* as faulty and places a

---

13   See Laʒamon (Caligula MS) line 12170, and compare *Le Roman de Brut* line 10310 *utlage*.
14   See *Le Roman de Brut*, II. 809, where Arnold records this suggestion with a degree of scepticism.
15   For this identification of Wendland I look to J. Bately, *The Old English Orosius*, EETS, s.s. 6, London, New York and Toronto, 1980, p. 178. J. S. P. Tatlock, *The Legendary History of Britain*, Berkeley, 1950, p. 473 footnote, suggests two parallels for the king's name: St Romaricus, an abbot, and the Raumaricii mentioned by Jordanes.

question mark beside the meaning 'tribute'.[16] The first of Madden's alternative readings seems the more appropriate to Laꝫamon's account of Arthur's visit to Iceland, for it is striking how all four northern kings emphasise that they are offering gifts. This point is made in Rumareth's final words. Ælcus, it must be admitted, is *afæred* (11219) when he speaks, but he makes it clear that he will *ꝫiuen* (11228) his gifts yearly, and Gonwais's reported words indicate that the provision of sixty ships is offered at his own expense. Moreover, the gifts proffered by these four leaders go unquestioned, as was not the case with Arthur's reaction to the unreliably extravagant promises of Gilomar of Ireland, made after the conquest of Ireland and just before Arthur's journey to Iceland. It would seem likely therefore that Doldanim is making a courtly point, and emphasising that his yearly payment is a deed of gift rather than an extraction of tribute. The form *ꝫiueles*, in a line held together by two alliterating elements that begin with *ꝫ*-, is best seen as a late reflex of Old English *gifl*.

It is clear that *gifl*- forms held connotations of generosity in Old English. I should like, therefore, to propose that Laꝫamon's *to ꝫifles þingen* is to be understood as 'by way of gift'. A cognate noun in *-nes* occurs twice in a long and carefully worded sentence on the need for humility in Alfred's *Pastoral Care*:

Him wære ðonne micel ðearf ðæt hie leten Godes ege hie geeaðmedan. & eac him is micel ðearf ðæt hie geornlice geðencen ðæt hie to unweorðlice ne dælen ðæt him befæsð bið, ðylæs hie awuht sellen ðæm ðe hie nanwuht ne sceoldon, oððe nan wuht ðæm ðe hie hwæthwugu sceoldon, oððe eft fela ðam ðe hie lytel sceoldon, oððe lytel ðæm ðe hie micel sceoldon, ðylæs hie unnytlice forweorpen ðæt ðæt hie sellen for hira hrædhydignesse, oððe him eft hefiglice ofðynce ðæs ðe hie sealdon, & [hi] scylen selfe beon biddende, & forðy weorðen geunrotsode, oððe hie eft her wilnigen ðara leana ðæs ðe hie on ælmessan sellað, ðylæs sio gidsung ðæs lænan lofes adwæsce ðæt leoht ðære giofolnesse, oððe eft sio giofolness sie gemenged wið unrotnesse, oþþe [he] eft for ðæm giefu*m*, ðe him ðonne ðynceð ðæt he suiðe wel atogen hæbbe, his mod suiður fægnige & blissige ðonne hit gemetlic oððe gedafenlic sie.[17]

The noun is confirmed by its later appearance in an Aldhelm gloss.[18]

---

16 Madden, *Brut*, III. 501, III. 655. In their textual notes Barron and Weinberg, *Laꝫamon*, relate *ꝫiueles* to the MED entry for *gǎvel* 'tribute', noting the MED identification of *gæfel* and *gevel* as variant spellings and suggesting the possible influence of Middle English *gife* 'gift'.

17 Henry Sweet, *King Alfred's West-Saxon Version of Gregory's Pastoral Care*, EETS, o.s. 45, 50, London, 1871–2, II. 321, lines 11–25.

18 See L. Goossens, *The Old English Glosses of MS. Brussels, Royal Library 1650*, Brussels Verhandelingen van de koninklijke Akademie voor Wetenschappen, Letteren en schone Kunsten van Belgie, Klasse der Letteren, 36 (Brussels), p. 310, no. 2501, where the words *gifelnysse mid gecweme duðedgyfe / l sylene* clearly remain above gratuita . . . / munificenti((ā)).

Alfred's *Pastoral Care* also has an example of the adjective *gifol* in some such sense as 'generous, liberal': *Ne beo ge oðrum monnum sua gifole ðæt hit weorðe eow selfum to gesuince.*[19] The better attested compounds *rumgifel* and *rumgifelnys*, where in each case the first element suggests an accommodation to the Latin words *largus* and *largitas* they sometimes gloss, lend clear support to the currency of the meaning 'generosity' among the word senses appropriate to *gifl-* forms.[20]

The instances of the Old English noun form *gifl* that I have found provide less clear support for the interpretation 'generosity, largesse'. All seem, in some way, to refer to gifts or offerings, very often to be eaten. So much is clear from a passage in the *Fortunes of Men*, in which part of the taming of a *wildne fugel* is with *lytlum gieflum*,[21] and from the occurrence of *geofola* against *buccilla* in a gloss.[22] When used in collocation with *wyrma*, there is the implication that mortal bodies will be eaten by worms, twice in the poem entitled *Soul and Body*[23] and once in a Vercelli homily.[24] *Gifl* is used twice of the fruit given by Eve to Adam: in *The Phoenix* it is simply *þæt gyfl* taken against God's command,[25] whereas in *Guthlac B* it is described with greater elaboration, as the *deaðberende gyfl/ þæt ða sinhiwan to swylte teah*, given to Adam *þurh deofles searo*.[26] The *Guthlac B* poet also uses *gifl* to refer to the eucharist in his description of the dying saint as *husle gereorded,/ eaðmod þy æþelan gyfle*.[27] The saint is both refreshed by the eucharist and humble through the efficacy of that noble morsel of food. Even more startlingly, the word is used in the *Seasons for Fasting* of the *wiste* given Elias in the desert: *and se gestrangud wearð*

19   Henry Sweet, *King Alfred's West-Saxon Version*, p. 325, lines 8–9. Comparable is the gloss *gefol wif* for *mulier gratioso*: see Julius Zupitza, 'Kentische glossen des neunten jahrhunderts', *Zeitschrift fur Deutsches Alterthum* 21 (1877), 26 and footnote. Note also the use of *gifol* in such compounds as *rŭmgifol* 'abundant, generous' and *rŭmgifolnes* 'abundance, generosity'.

20   Interestingly *rumgifel* and *rumgifelnes* are not, from the evidence to be found in Antoinette DiPaolo Healey and Richard L. Venezky (eds), *A Microfiche Concordance to Old English*, Toronto, 1980, words found in Old English poetry.

21   G. P. Krapp and E. V. K. Dobbie, *The Exeter Book,* The Anglo-Saxon Poetic Records 3, New York, 1935, *Fortunes of Men*, lines 85ff.

22   R. T. Oliphant, *The Harley Latin-Old English Glossary, edited from British Museum MS Harley 3376*, Janua Linguarum, series practica 20, The Hague, 1966, p. 36 (B 408).

23   G. P. Krapp, *The Vercelli Book,* The Anglo-Saxon Poetic Records 2, New York 1932, *Soul and Body I*, line 22, *ðu huru wyrma gyfl* and *Bið þonne wyrma gifel,/ æt on eorþan* (lines 124–25), and the parallel phrases of *Soul and Body II* in Krapp and Dobbie, *The Exeter Book*, lines 22 and 119–20.

24   See D. G. Scragg, *The Vercelli Homilies and Related Texts*, EETS, o.s. 300, Oxford, 1992, p. 98, line 208 : *ðu eorðan lamb ⁊ dust ⁊ wyrma gifel.*

25   Krapp and Dobbie, *The Exeter Book*, *The Phoenix*, line 410.

26   Krapp and Dobbie, *The Exeter Book*, *Guthlac B*, lines 850–51.

27   Krapp and Dobbie, *The Exeter Book*, *Guthlac B*, lines 1300–01.

styþum gyfle/ to gefæstenne feowertig daga/ and nihta samod.[28] In particular, these last two instances carry with them strong associations of generosity, referring as they do to a gift of food given to save mankind from death. Overall the instances of the noun *gifl* indicate that it has affinities with both the adjective *gifol* and the noun *gifolnes* and that it may have had as its most generalised sense the meaning 'generous gift'.

Contextually the word relates most typically to food, and, even with the grim phrase *wyrma gifl*, to food that is received as a gift. I should like here to admit that this is a noun that is under represented in the *Thesaurus of Old English*.[29] I remember that Lynne Grundy and I put aside the relevant slips on one more than one occasion during final editing, uncertain as to how many entries the form should support, let alone where they should be placed. Ron Waldron, in his masterly account of semantic fields and systems, points out:

> Some uses of language depend very heavily on evoking the same associations in everyone. Much poetry, for example, would not work unless the poet could rely on a fairly large area of agreement in the kind of subsidiary associations we attach to words.[30]

Looking back, I realise that for certain uses of *gifl* in Old English poetry we were unable to separate out association from connotation. This Laƥamon passage brought the word *gifl* back to mind, and I hunted for it in the *Thesaurus of Old English* with increasing dismay, finding the simplex only at Category 04.01.02.04, where the entry *geofola/giefl* was among the forms listed as having the meaning 'small quantity of food'. This meaning of *gifl* is clearly supported by the compounds *æfengifl* and *underngifl*.[31] The sense 'generous gift' requires representation in the thesaurus structure, and *gifl* should therefore be inserted into Category 10.03 Giving, to stand among the forms listed against 'A gift, present'. It could also be inserted in Category 10.03.08 Bountifulness, munificence, where, interestingly, both *gifolnes* and *rūmgifulnes* are to be found among the forms listed.

One curiosity remains in Laƥamon's account of the submission of the four northern kings. The first to submit to Arthur is Ælcus, king of Iceland, his name apparently plucked out of the air, for Madden tells us that the names of

---

28 E. V. K. Dobbie, *The Anglo-Saxon Minor Poems*, The Anglo-Saxon Poetic Records 6, New York 1942, *Seasons for Fasting*, lines 121ff.

29 J. Roberts and C. Kay with L. Grundy, *A Thesaurus of Old English*, King's College London Medieval Series 11, London, 1995.

30 R. A. Waldron, *Sense and Sense Development*, 2nd edn, London, 1979, p. 99.

31 There are seven occurrences of *æfengifl* in Old English; *underngifl* occurs once only, contrasting with and linked to *æfengifl*.

Ælcus and his son Esscol 'do not exist in historians'.[32] Laȝamon later names the king of Iceland differently, as Maluerus:

> To tellen þat folc of Kairliun: ne mihte hit na mon idon.
> Þer wes Gillomar þe king: Irisce monnen deorling.
> Maluerus king of Islonde: Doldanet king. of Gutlonde.
> Kin[g] Kailin of Frislonde: Æscil king of Denelonde.
> Þer wes Loð þe kene: þe king wes bi Norðe.
> and Gonwæis Orcaneie king: ut-laȝen deor-ling.   (12165–70)

This name is obviously related to the Malvaisus of the source passage in Wace:

> Assez out a la curt baruns
> Dunt jo sai dire les nuns :
> Gillomar i fu, reis d'Irlande,
> E Malvaisus, li reis d'Islande,
> E Doldanïed de Gollande,
> Ki n'unt pas plenté, de viande.
> Aschil i fu, reis des Daneis,
> E Loth, ki ert reis des Norreis,
> E Gonvais, li reis d'Orchenie,
> Ki maint utlage out en baillie.   (10301–10)

It is not my purpose here to explore the names Laȝamon gives Icelandic kings, but I cannot resist the idle speculation that this later occurrence of the name *Aschil* among Arthur's host for a king of Danes might have triggered off the curiously named *Esscol* as he invented names for the king of Iceland and his son. Again Laȝamon and Wace differ in their list of northern kings, if less strikingly. Here Laȝamon includes a leader from *Frislonde* (12168), just as he does in Vortiger's speech designed to scare King Constance (lines 6640–61), where he fleshes out Wace's reference to the likely incursions of Danes and Norwegians, also adding the kings of *Rusie* and *Gutlonde*. With such added details Laȝamon gives a wider if even more anachronistic view of the northern world than either Geoffrey of Monmouth or Wace.[33]

IV

With both these readings, for *ȝiueles* and *aloðede*, I depend on the continuity of the language from Anglo-Saxon England through into Laȝamon's time, finding in him inherited ways of thought, and the new translations have helped to push me to reading his *Brut* more carefully. In the absence of the third

---

32 Madden, *Brut*, III. 382.
33 R. Allen, '*Eorles* and *Beornes*: Contextualizing Lawman's *Brut*', *Arthuriana* 8:3 (1998), 4–22, points out that the Frisian references could have been designed to appeal to William de Frise, whom she identifies as Laȝamon's patron.

volume of the EETS edition, we still depend on Madden's glossary and apparatus, and the new translations are important for incorporating reassessments of his translation and of his editorial decisions. The translations can disagree with one another, for example at line 13311 *and lut þer of-nomen: ah monie heo of-sloȝen*. Barron and Weinberg translate 'capturing a few, but slaying many'. Allen, who follows Madden in reading *þer-of nomen*, translates the line by 'Taking very few of them captive there, but killing very many'. Whether or not the verb is *of-nomen* or *nomen*, her wording does not block the retrieval of litotes – nor does Madden's 'and few there captured, but many they slew'.[34] Here Barron and Weinberg sanitise the *Brut*, failing to recognise that in earlier English *lyt* very often sparked off statements bleak in their exploitation of grim irony. Laȝamon was not just widely read in his own language: he had the ability to exploit its inherited vocabulary and stylistic conventions as suited his purpose. In this paper I have attempted to explain two cruces in Laȝamon by turning to Old English evidence which provides clues to a new understanding of these passages. His *Brut*, it seems to me, is positioned linguistically between late Old English and other newer Middle English styles that were absorbing French words with astonishing rapidity, and for some of the difficulties presented by his *Brut* we should therefore look back to lexicographical resources for Old English, to take account of words that were demonstrably dropping out of use during the twelfth century.

---

34 See Madden, *Brut*, III. 61, where his translation 'and few there [they] captured, but [and] many they slew' serves for both versions, with Otho variants indicated in square brackets. The Otho text here reads *(a)nd feue hii þar nemen: and manye hii of-slowen*.

SEMANTICS AND METRICAL FORM IN
SIR GAWAIN AND THE GREEN KNIGHT

JEREMY J. SMITH

True Ease in Writing comes from Art, not Chance,
As those move easiest who have learn'd to dance.
'Tis not enough no Harshness gives Offence,
The *Sound* must seem an *Eccho* to the *Sense*.
Soft is the Strain when *Zephyr* gently blows,
And the *smooth Stream* in *smoother Numbers* flows;
But when loud Surges lash the sounding Shore,
The *hoarse, rough Verse* shou'd like the *Torrent* roar.
Alexander Pope, *Essay on Criticism*, 362–9[1]

I

THE PRESENT PAPER attempts to bring together two fields where Ron Waldron has made a major contribution to scholarship: alliterative poetry from the Middle English period, and semantics.[2] This paper is organised as follows: after this short introduction, two pairs of lines from the late-fourteenth-century poem *Sir Gawain and the Green Knight* are analysed, and various interpretations are discussed. In both pairs, related sets of lexemes appear, and the semantic and formal properties of these lexemes in early English are discussed. The paper then correlates the discussion of these lexemes with a broader argument on the function of alliteration, with special reference to possible phonaesthetic properties in alliterating lexemes. Although the paper concentrates on *Sir Gawain and the Green Knight*, it is hoped that the discussion has some wider relevance for the understanding of the relationship between form and meaning in alliterative verse.

---

1   J. Butt (ed.) *The Poems of Alexander Pope*, London, 1963, p. 155.
2   See R. A. Waldron, *Sense and Sense Development*, 2nd edn, London, 1979.

II

The following two pairs of lines appear in the third Fitt of *Sir Gawain and the Green Knight*:

> (A) And as in slomeryng he slode, sleȝly he herde
> A littel dyn at his dor and der[n]ly vpon …

(lines 1182–83; all quotations are taken from Andrew and Waldron's edition, but, for reasons which will become apparent below, the emendation *dernly* for MS *derfly* is adopted here)[3]

> (B) 'God moroun, Sir Gawayn,' sayde þat gay lady,
> 'ȝe ar a sleper vnslyȝe, þat mon may slyde hider …'

(lines 1208–09[4]). It is at once clear that the two pairs of lines, which appear in close proximity, 'echo' each other. Not only do both (A) and (B) manifest alliteration on *sl-*, but also the collocational sets of alliterating words in both are, semantically, closely related: *slomeryng, sleȝly* and *slode* in (A) beside (B)'s *sleper, vnslyȝe* and *slyde*.

The context for these lines may be briefly stated. The Lady of the Castle has come to tempt the hero, who *lurkkez* under the bed-clothes, trying to relax in preparation for his coming ordeal at the Green Chapel where he is to receive a return blow as part of his earlier bargain with the Green Knight.

Translation of these lines into present-day English is not straightforward. In (A), one difficulty of interpretation lies in the placing of *sleȝly*. W. R. J. Barron[5] translates the lines as 'And as he drifted in and out of sleep, he half heard a little noise at his door, and heard it stealthily open', *vpon* being used verbally with the meaning 'open'. In this interpretation, *sleȝly* is taken to modify Gawain's action (*herde*). Barron discusses this interpretation in a footnote.[6] He suggests there that the form is to be interpreted either in a 'derived sense', i.e. 'quietly, faintly, half-consciously', or that the form is a scribal error for *sleȝtly* 'without much care or attention, carelessly, lightly' – even though such forms are not recorded before the sixteenth century in the *Oxford English Dictionary* (henceforth OED) (see OED *slightly* adv., 2). However, these interpretations seem somewhat forced. The range of meanings for *sleighli* and derivatives recorded in the *Middle English Dictionary* (henceforth MED) include 'wisely', 'dexterously', 'cautiously' etc., all of which would seem to require definite consciousness with regard to action; it seems inappropriate in an interpretation of this passage to ascribe such

---

3 M. Andrew and R. A. Waldron (eds) *The Poems of the Pearl Manuscript*, London, 1978, p. 251.
4 Andrew and Waldron, *Poems*, p. 252.
5 W. R. J. Barron (ed.) *Sir Gawain and the Green Knight*, Manchester, 1974, p. 91.
6 Barron, *Sir Gawain*, p. 175.

consciousness to Gawain. It seems therefore best to interpret *sleʒly* as relating to the Lady's actions.

This latter interpretation is adopted in N. Davis's revision of the edition by J. R. R. Tolkien and E. V. Gordon.[7] Davis gives '(made) warily' for *sleʒly* in his Glossary, although he does not explicitly integrate the word into his translation of the line: '(He heard) a little noise at his door, and (heard it) stealthily open.'[8] The implication of Davis's gloss is that *sleʒly* should be seen as an adverb qualifying the nature of the door-opening, not Gawain's behaviour. This interpretation seems justifiable given the range of available contemporary meanings just quoted in the citation from MED. Such an interpretation is made explicit by Andrew and Waldron in their translation of the line: 'And as he drifted in sleep (dozed) he heard a little stealthy sound at his door and (heard it) quickly open'; they point out that '*sleʒly* is to be loosely construed with the next line, rather than with *herde*'.

Another problem is presented by the form *der[n]ly* (manuscript *derfly*). Davis gives the emended form; his primary reason for emendation is that the 'recorded uses of *derf* imply boldness or vigour, unsuitable here'.[9] The precise form which is substituted is based on the following reconstruction: the original form **dernly* was misinterpreted (as commonly happens) as **deruly*, and *f* was then (as is also common) substituted for *u* to produce the manuscript-form *derfly*. However, the range of meanings recorded in MED for the adverb *derfli* and its derivatives includes not only 'boldly', 'fearlessly', 'fiercely', 'cruelly' and 'painfully', but also 'promptly'. Given this last meaning, Andrew and Waldron prefer the manuscript reading; their retention of the manuscript-form is thus for them justifiable as a difficult reading in terms of the Middle English evidence.

Despite Andrew and Waldron's cogent argument, however, the emendation suggested by Barron and Davis has been adopted in this paper. The reasons for adoption of this emendation here are two. First, *dernly* is a well-established (indeed, notorious) item in the Middle English vocabulary of 'courtly love',[10] and thus especially suitable in the context of Gawain's relationship with the Lady. Secondly, the form finds an echo later in the stanza in line 1188: [the Lady] *droʒ the dor after hir ful dernly and stylle*. Such cohesive 'echoing' is a salient feature of the poet's technique, which will be discussed further below. We might therefore translate passage (1) as follows: 'And as he dozed, he heard a little noise (made) warily at his door, and (heard it) stealthily open.'

---

7   J. R. R. Tolkien and E. V. Gordon (eds) *Sir Gawain and the Green Knight*, 2nd edn revised by N. Davis, Oxford, 1967.

8   Tolkien, Gordon and Davis, *Sir Gawain*, p. 108.

9   Ibid.

10   E. T. Donaldson, 'The Idiom of Popular Poetry in the Miller's Tale', in *Speaking of Chaucer*, London, 1970, pp. 13–29.

The interpretation of (B) is, on the face of it, more straightforward. Barron's translation seems fairly uncontroversial: "'Good morning, Sir Gawain," said that fair lady, "you are a careless sleeper, that one can steal in here.'"[11] But of course, as is commonplace in *Sir Gawain and the Green Knight*, the connotations of words are as important as their denotations, and hard to capture in a translation. For instance – and this interpretation is relevant for its antonym in passage (A) – *vnslyʒe* may be fairly translated as 'careless'. However, there are also connotations of 'lack of treachery' and 'lack of wisdom' recorded in the semantic make-up of the Middle English word which have important resonances in the wider context of the poem and its themes.

III

The semantic and formal properties of the *sl-* lexemes in passages (A) and (B) will now be addressed.

(1) *'slide'*: In Old English, *slīdan* is a word with a wide range of meanings, and with the publication of the *Thesaurus of Old English*[12] scholars are now able to classify these meanings in quite precise ways. The *Thesaurus* places *slīdan* in the following categories: 05.07 'Ending of existence, end of world' ('to fail, come to an end'); 05.12.01.04.01.04 'To stumble, trip, strike (with the foot)' ('to slip, stumble'); 05.12.05.06.01 'To travel smoothly, slide, glide'; 06.01.07.05 'Error, being astray'; 08.01.03.06.01 'Affliction, misfortune, calamity' (see Appendix).

In Middle English, the same range of figurative and non-figurative usages are recorded: 'fall', 'fall into sin', with derived forms (e.g. *slydynge*) used as adjectives meaning 'deceitful', 'delusive', 'unstable'. Perhaps the most famous occurrence of the form in medieval literature is the phrase *slydynge of corage*, used by Chaucer in *Troilus and Criseyde* (V.825) to describe Criseyde, and generally glossed 'inconstant of spirit'. Chaucer also uses the form with this sense in his translation of Boethius (I, metre 5), the text most closely related in date and in spirit to *Troilus*. Chaucer also gives the word to the Canon Yeoman to describe, scathingly, his master's alchemy: *that slidynge science (Canterbury Tales* G.732).[13] Similar usages – which may of course be imitations of Chaucer – appear in, e.g., Lydgate, *Fall of Princes* (III.4434), *Stories ... preue ther power is nat abidyng,/ But ... slydyng and fallible.*[14]

---

11 Barron, *Sir Gawain*, p. 91.
12 J. Roberts and C. Kay, with L. Grundy, *A Thesaurus of Old English*, London, 1995.
13 See R. W. V. Elliott, *Chaucer's English*, London, 1974, pp. 324–5.
14 Much more precise categorisations of Middle English vocabulary will be possible when the *Historical Thesaurus of English* is published, probably c.2001/2002, supported by an envisaged supplementary *Middle English Thesaurus*. See Roberts and Kay, *Thesaurus*, xv–xxxv, and references there cited; see also M. L. Samuels,

(2) *'sleep'/'slumber'*: The range of meanings covered in Old English by *slæp-* and *slūma/slūmere* is rather more restricted. Most forms simply fall into *Thesaurus* category 02.05.04 'Sleepiness, drowsiness, sleep', although some related forms with *slāp-* fall into category 11.06 'Disinclination to act, listlessness'. In Middle English texts, the semantic component 'lethargic, slothful' can be detected in addition to those present in Old English; thus in the *Parson's Tale* (I.705) the collocations indicate a clearly negative connotation to the form: *Thanne cometh sompnolence, that is, sloggy slombrynge, which maketh a man be hevy and dul in body and in soule; and thus synne comth of Slouthe.*

(3) *'sly'*: It is not possible to use the *Thesaurus* for the 'sly' lexeme found in *Sir Gawain and the Green Knight* since the word is derived from Norse *slægr*, and is thus not in the extant Old English lexicon. The Norse form is usually glossed 'clever', 'crafty', and the range of meanings in Middle English is similar. Thus the phrase *slye reflexiouns* (*Squire's Tale*, F.230) refers to the efficiency of the astrological technology being practised, and does not seem to have any negative connotation, whereas when the Host describes the Canon's Yeoman's duplicitous master as *so crafty and so sly* (G.655) he seems to intend no compliment. In present-day English, of course, the connotations of 'sly' are entirely negative.

The collocation of reflexes of the present-day English lexemes 'slide', 'sly' and 'sleep' is recorded elsewhere in Middle English literature, commonly in alliterative verse but occasionally elsewhere. Thus MED includes the following quotations: *He slod slizli adoun aslepe ful harde* (*William of Palerne* 792); *He hente owte and hurte anoþer ... Sleyghly in at the slotte slytes hym thorowe, That the slydande spere of his hande sleppes* (*Morte Arthure* 2975); *Byneþe þe erþe ... Is a water rennyng dep þat makes þy werk slyden o slep* (Mannyng, *Chronicle Pt. 1*, 8150); *For-werre slidus he on slepe; No lengur myȝte he wake* (*Avowing of Arthur* 271); *Aunters ben olde ... And slydyn vppon shlepe by slomeryng of Age* (*Destruction of Troy* 6); *þan slade he slizly a-way* (*Wars of Alexander* 2870); *He shulde slyde forth sleghly & vnslayn worthe* (*Destruction of Troy* 789). Similar collocations are used elsewhere in the poems of MS Cotton Nero A.x: *Hatz þou ... no gouernour ne god on to calle þat þou þus slydes on slepe when þou slayn worþes?* (*Patience* 200); *He slydez on a sloumbe-slep sloghe vnder leues* (*Patience* 466); *I slode vpon a slepyng-slaȝte* (*Pearl* 59).

Part of the reason for the frequency of this collocation is that, evidently, some Middle English poets placed restrictions on permissible alliterations. For instance, an analysis of the text of the *Alliterative Morte Arthure* shows that in

Linguistic Evolution, Cambridge, 1972, p. 180, and also forthcoming work by Jane Roberts and Louise Sylvester.

almost all cases *sl*-words alliterated only with *sl*-words, and indeed lines alliterating on *sl-* frequently cluster together in that poem, presumably for the purposes of stylistic foregrounding. There was therefore a consequent effect on
choice of forms available for alliteration. This effect is illustrated simply
enough if we compare the numbers of *sl*-words in present-day English with *s*-
words in general; whereas in (for instance) *The Chambers Dictionary* (1998) *s*-
words occupy 232 pages, *sl*-words occupy a mere 7. There is a comparable distribution in Middle English.[15]

Now the *Gawain*-poet, unlike the author of the *Alliterative Morte Arthure*,
quite freely alliterates *sl*-words with those with simple initial *s-*, which gives
him many more lexical collocations to choose from. But this comparative freedom means that, when he chooses to restrict his alliterating lexemes to *sl*-clus-
ters, such a choice has a literary salience not found in the *Morte Arthure*. That
the *Gawain*-poet chooses first to set up a pattern of alliteration on *sl-* and then
repeat that precise pattern a few lines later, with broadly the same lexemes,
may reasonably be assumed to be something which would have been especially foregrounded for contemporaries.

IV

In discussions of medieval English verse, it is usual to emphasise the formal
characteristics of the verse-form in question: the patterns of stress in relation to
alliteration, for instance, or the formal patterning of rhyme. But such a
restriction to surface characteristics has always seemed to me both limited and
limiting. After all, the function of metre in verse has traditionally been taken as
to do with the interplay of metrical norm and rhythmical deviation with the
intention of making the modulation between norm and deviation salient in
terms of meaning – something which poets often emphasise by accompanying
their metrical choices with other stylistic effects.

The process may be simply illustrated by a line such as Pope's *Puffs, Powders, Patches, Bibles, Billet-doux* (*The Rape of the Lock*, 138).[16] In this line,
the substitution of a stressed syllable (*Puffs*) where an unstressed syllable

---

15 A useful research project would be to compare patterns in a range of Middle English
    alliterative poems – something made comparatively easy with the increasing
    accessibility of machine-readable texts. A pilot examination of a random selection of
    available Middle English alliterative poems other than those cited above reveals that *sl*-
    almost always alliterates only on *sl-* in *The Parlement of the Thre Ages*. *Sl-* alliterates
    with other *s*-words in *Piers Plowman* (B-text), *The Siege of Jerusalem* and *The
    Simonie*, although there are lines in all these texts where *sl-* alliterates only with itself
    and where some foregrounding may be suspected. In *Wynnere and Wastoure* and *The
    Awntyrs of Arthure*, *sl-* is a rare cluster, alliterating with *sl-* and with *s-*. Consonant
    clustering in the *Alliterative Morte Arthure* is further discussed by Dr Allen (see p. 25
    above).

16 Butt, *The Poems of Alexander Pope*, p. 222.

would be the norm in iambic pentameter is further foregrounded by the alliterative sequence which then follows. Of course, this is not the only way in which salience is achieved in this line. The sudden shift from a voiceless to a voiced plosive in the middle of the line throws ironic emphasis initially on the contrast between *Bibles* and the cosmetic accoutrements (*Puffs, Powders, Patches*) of Belinda's dressing-table. The ironic effect is then in turn intensified by an equation being set up between holy writ and love letters (*Billet-doux*), signalled by the alliteration connecting the two noun phrases last in the line.[17]

There is no formal handbook of alliterative poetry surviving from the Middle English period. In his *Ane Schort Treatise, conteining some revlis and cautelis to be observit and eschewit in Scottis Poesie* (1585), James VI has interesting things to say about what he calls '*Tumbling* verse' – generally assumed to be alliterative poetry – from a Renaissance perspective, and his discussion of the distinct metrical nature of such poetry (*Tumbling verse flowis not on that fassoun, as utheris dois*)[18] – is, as we shall see, a shrewd observation. But the *Treatise* is indeed *Schort*, and the rules of alliterative verse have in general to be painfully reconstructed from the surviving evidence.

One key principle, however, seems to be accepted by modern scholars: it seems almost certain that, as in other kinds of poetry, a framework of modulation between norm and deviation, linked to literary salience, lies at the heart of alliterative verse-practice. This view has been argued very effectively by (among others) George Kane, who points out that a poet's success derives from the way in which

> his versification exists as part of the meaning of his poetic statements, not merely because the verse is effective in making that meaning more emphatic, clearer, more evidently interrelated, but also because it will engage the reader's auditory interest and confer the combination of physical and intellectual pleasure experienced when pattern and meaning are simultaneously apprehended.[19]

David Lawton makes a similar point. For Lawton, the key to engaging with Langland's style is to identify 'the issues [readers] must take into account in arriving at an understanding of the interaction between pattern and meaning in *Piers Plowman*',[20] and he goes on to show that metre 'is not meaning; but it is one of its prime exponents'.[21]

---

17   I am conscious of an ancient debt to Malcolm Parkes in my discussion of this line.

18   R. Rait (ed.) *A Royal Rhetorician*, London 1900, p. 18.

19   G. Kane, 'Music Neither Unpleasant nor Monotonous', in *Medieval Studies for J. A. W. Bennett*, ed. P. L. Heyworth, Oxford, 1981, pp. 43–63: 46.

20   D. Lawton, 'Alliterative Style', in *A Companion to Piers Plowman*, ed. J. Alford, Berkeley, 1988, pp. 223–249: 227.

21   Lawton, 'Alliterative Style', p. 233.

Although Lawton's paper is for the most part devoted to the study of Langland, his work has significance for the study of alliterative verse in general. Lawton persuasively identifies the role of alliteration in 'long line' alliterative poetry as the organising principle which links *a*- and *b*- verses together, 'and it is in this sense ... that alliteration deserves to be called the *metre* of alliterative poetry, even though – unlike most other metres – it does not *measure*'.[22] Kane and Donaldson[23] establish that the normative alliterative pattern of Langland's verse is of what is generally termed the '*aa/ax*' variety, but that there are numerous deviant patterns (e.g. *aa/aa*, *aaa/ax*, *aa/bb* etc.), including lines with so-called 'supplementary' alliteration.[24] Thus a line such as

> In habite as a hermite vnholy of workes

(Langland, *Piers Plowman B* Prol. 3), which follows the normative pattern *aa/ax*, may be compared with deviant lines such as the opening of the poem:

> In a somer seson whan soft was the sonne

(Langland, *Piers Plowman B* Prol. 1) (*aa/aa*). In the latter line, the extra alliteration may be interpreted as a prominent metrical signal, appropriate at the beginning of a poem and underlined by the quasi-formulaic conventionality of the lexis adopted.

V

It is of course to be expected that Middle English alliterative poets developed a range of techniques of modulation, and the evidence is that various practices emerged at various times and in various places. A characteristic practice, exemplified not just in *Sir Gawain and the Green Knight* but also in other poems of the 'alliterative revival', is the use of sound-symbolism. That sound-symbolism was salient to contemporaries is signalled through its employment by poets not writing in the alliterative tradition but drawing upon familiarity with that tradition for their effects. A frequently quoted example is a passage in Chaucer's *Knight's Tale* (A.2602–19), e.g. *Ther shyveren shaftes upon sheeldes thikke* 2605, which could be scanned as *aa/ax*.

Now sound-symbolism in verse has sometimes attracted rather impressionistic literary criticism, often signalled by the presence of value-laden and somewhat unconvincing adjectives such as 'harsh' or 'rough'. Linguists too have often felt uneasy about sound-symbolism; not only is it a phenomenon

---

22 Ibid., pp. 225–6.
23 G. Kane and E. T. Donaldson (eds) *Piers Plowman: The B-Version*, London, 1975.
24 See further Kane, 'Music', p. 46 for a succinct exposition of principles, and A. T. E. Matonis, 'Middle English alliterative poetry', in *So meny people longages and tonges: philological essays in Scots and mediaeval English presented to Angus McIntosh*, eds M. Benskin and M. L. Samuels, Edinburgh, 1981, pp. 341–54.

which is hard to categorise in terms of linguistic level, but also the notion seems to go against basic Saussurean axioms: 'The bond between the signifier and the signified is arbitrary ... The idea of "sister" is not linked by any inner relationship to the succession of sounds ... which serves as its signifier.'[25]

Although Saussure's statement is universally accepted by serious linguists, there has nevertheless always been an interest in sound-symbolism, even though this interest has rather often been from outside the fashionable main-stream of linguistic enquiry. Perhaps the most important work in this area, from distinct perspectives, was undertaken by Roman Jakobson and J. R. Firth, both scholars who, somewhat against the grain of contemporary linguistic thinking, placed meaning at the centre of their interests.[26]

There are generally accepted to be two kinds of sound-symbolism: ono-matopoeia and phonaesthesia. Onomatopoeia is defined in *The Chambers Dictionary* (1998) as 'the formation of a word in imitation of the sound of the thing meant',[27] which is an excellent definition as far as it goes. A good illustration of onomatopoeia might be the birds in *Sir Gawain and the Green Knight* who *pitosly þer piped for pyne of þe colde* (line 747); *piped* would seem quite an accurate representation of the sound the birds made, and was probably more so in the fourteenth century when the word was pronounced [piːpəd].[28] And yet, as is well known, human languages represent the noises of animals differently: a British cockerel sings *cockadoodledoo*, whereas a German cockerel sings *kikeriki* and a French one *cocorico*.[29] It would seem that onomatopoeic ele-ments are themselves essentially conventional.

Phonaesthesia is a more complex matter. It may be defined as a phenome-non whereby the presence of a particular phonological component seems to correspond regularly – though, disconcertingly, not consistently – to one

25 F. de Saussure, *Course in General Linguistics*, trans. W. Baskin, Glasgow, 1974, p. 67.
26 See R. Jakobson and L. Waugh, *The Sound Shape of Language*, Brighton, 1979; J. R. Firth, *Speech*, Oxford, 1964. A useful if limited introductory account appears in D. Crystal, *The Cambridge Encyclopedia of the English Language*, Cambridge, 1995, pp. 250–3. A more advanced discussion appears in I. E. Reay, 'Sound Symbolism', in *An Encyclopedia of Language and Linguistics*, eds R. Asher and J. M. Y. Simpson, Oxford, 1994, pp. 4064–70, which is based upon Reay's thesis: 'A Lexical Analysis of Metaphor and Phonaestheme', Diss. Ph.D., Glasgow, 1991. Also important is H. Käsmann, 'Das englische Phonästhem *sl-* ', *Anglia* 110 (1992) 307–46. Käsmann draws attention (*inter alia*) to the lengthy history of scholarly interest in the phenomenon, dating back to at least John Wallis's *Grammatica Linguae Anglicanae* (1653); see Käsmann, 'Phonästhem', p. 310. There is also a good discussion in Waldron, *Sense and Sense Development*, pp. 17–18, on which J. J. Smith, *An Historical Study of English*, London, 1996, p. 114 draws.
27 *The Chambers Dictionary*, Edinburgh, 1998, p. 1134.
28 See Waldron, *Sense and Sense Development*, p. 18, who cites O. Jespersen, *Language: Its Nature, Development and Origin*, London, 1922, pp. 396–411.
29 See Waldron, *Sense and Sense Development*, p. 17.

semantic component. For example, as discussed elsewhere,[30] the element ('phonaestheme') *gr*- shared by *grudge, gruff, grumble, gripe, grizzle, grim, grunt* seems to signal a common semantic component of rudeness, ill-temper and/or taciturnity in the meaning of these words. However, forms such as *grin* and *great* would seem in present-day English to be counter-examples – although *grin* had an older meaning 'bare one's teeth in rage' – and the same goes for other phonaesthemes which have been distinguished by scholars. An accessible list of some phonaesthemes has been provided by D. Crystal.[31] The process seems to have been one of extension, whereby 'associations [which] may have been accidental at first … [were] extended to other words of similar meaning';[32] thus the basic principle of the arbitrary nature of signs is retained. As Firth put it, 'The above remarks are not to be interpreted as a theory of inherent sound symbolism. [...] with the doubtful exception of certain sibilant consonants, there would appear to be no inherent phonaesthetic value in any speech sound. It is all a matter of habit.'[33]

One phonaestheme which has been frequently identified by scholars is *sl*-. I. E. Reay has identified at least three sets of meanings associated with this cluster, with sub-groups derived through metaphorical extension etc.:

(i) *sl*- attack – physical or verbal: *slag, slam, slander, slang, slap, slash, slate, slaughter, slay, slight, sling, slog, slug, slosh, slur.*

(ii) *sl*- sliding movement: *slalom, sledge, sleigh, slick, slide, slip, slither, slop, slope, slouch, slump* ...

– *sl*- slimy wet substances: *slime, slop, slosh, sludge, slurry, slush.*

– *sl*- eject or add water: *slake, slobber, sluice, slurp.*

– *sl*- indolence, carelessness: *slack, slattern, sleazy, slob, slut*
[to which I would add *sloth* and perhaps even *sleep(y)*].

– *sl*- cunning, crafty: *sleuth, slippery* (customer), *slick* (operator), *sly* ...

(iii) *sl*- slim, thin: *slender, slim, slit, sliver.*[34]

---

30 Smith, *Historical Study*, p. 114.
31 Crystal, *Encyclopedia*, p. 251.
32 Waldron, *Sense and Sense Development*, p. 17.
33 Firth, *Speech*, p. 187. The role of phonaesthesia in historical linguistics has been highly controversial; see Samuels, *Linguistic Evolution*, pp. 45–8 and references there cited. Nevertheless, it is a topic which is ripe for reappraisal, as work by Reay and Käsmann has indicated; see note 26 above and references there cited. For instance, Prokosch's classic and suggestive anecdote to illustrate the role of ablaut/gradation in the Germanic verb could easily be recouched in terms of phonaesthesia. See further E. Prokosch, *A Comparative Germanic Grammar*, Baltimore, 1938, pp. 120–2, especially note on p. 122.
34 Reay, 'Sound Symbolism', p. 4065. See also Crystal, *Encyclopedia*, p. 251.

An extended classification of *sl*-forms, including forms found in the *English Dialect Dictionary* and the *Scottish National Dictionary*, has been undertaken by H. Käsmann,[35] and his study should be referred to for further information.

Several semantic components of course may well be active in single lexemes – as is suggested by a form such as *slippery*, which has a literal meaning (e.g. 'Caution: This floor is slippery') and a metaphorical one (e.g. 'he's a slippery customer'). Sometimes the metaphorical extension has become the core meaning of the word over time, as seems to be the case with *slick*, which originally meant 'sleek, smooth' and is now primarily, in its adjectival use, a word of abuse meaning 'glibly clever'; cf. the soubriquet *Slick Willie*, applied to US President Clinton by his political opponents.

Reconstructing the phonaesthetic associations of past states of the language is of course somewhat problematic,[36] but it seems certain that phonaesthetic associations have always existed. Thus it is surely no coincidence that the *gr*-phonaestheme is applied to the evil demon (*se grimma gāst*) *Grendel* in *Beowulf*, and this suggests one approach to the problem: through the study of collocations in past states of the language, it is possible to arrive at fairly firm semantic classifications of older lexicons. An analysis of *sl*-words and their associations in Old English is now possible using the *Thesaurus of Old English*, and such an analysis shows a similar pattern to the present-day English semantic configuration (see Appendix).

In the light of phonaesthetic analysis, the use of *sl*- in the two passages from *Sir Gawain and the Green Knight* becomes more precisely illuminated. Given that the *sl*- element is formally foregrounded in the *Gawain*-poet's alliterative practice, it seems logical to go on to assume that the phonaestheme was salient to contemporaries in their appreciation of the lines. Thus the passages

> (A) And as in slomeryng he slode, sleȝly he herde
> A littel dyn at his dor and der[n]ly vpon …

and

> (B) 'God moroun, Sir Gawayn,' sayde þat gay lady,
> 'ȝe ar a sleper vnslyȝe, þat mon may slyde hider …'

may be securely (as opposed to impressionistically) interpreted as containing at least some of the phonaesthetic associations connected with *sl*-: negativity, falling (with all the metaphorical connotations of that action), evil, carelessness, sloth.[37] All these associations are of course central to the

---

35   See Käsmann, 'Phonästhem'; his classification of *sl*-forms appears on pp. 328–36.
36   See Reay, 'Sound Symbolism', and Reay, 'Lexical Analysis'.
37   Käsmann, 'Phonästhem', pp. 328–36, gives the following useful definitions culled

developing thought of the poem; the alliteration therefore relates directly to meaning. The overall effect is to make the state of sleep a metaphor of moral abdication.[38,39]

This interpretation is confirmed when we turn to other quotations from the works of the *Gawain*-poet which demonstrate alliteration on *sl-*: *Slypped on a sloumbe-slepe and sloberande he routes* (*Patience* 186); *Hatz þou ... no gouernour ne god on to calle þat þou þus slydes on slepe when þou slayn worþes?* (*Patience* 200); *He slydez on a sloumbe-slep sloghe vnder leues* (*Patience* 466); *I slode vpon a slepyng-slaȝe* (*Pearl* 59). Two of the quotations from *Patience* are addressed to the prophet Jonah when he is failing to act in accordance with God's commands: again, the associations are ones of negativity, and Jonah's sleep represents an attempt to avoid the moral imperatives placed on him by God. The first quotation describes Jonah's sleep on board the ship he takes to escape the duty laid on him by God – *sloberande* seems pretty negative, and *slypped, sloumbe-slepe* again signal moral failure.[40]

The quotation from *Pearl* is more nuanced, but a possible interpretation of the line, taking into account the phonaesthetic associations of *slode* and *slepyng-slaȝe*, is offered here. It might be argued that the concerns of the poem with transmutation mean that the negative connotations of *slode* and *slepyng-slaȝe* associated with the Dreamer are changed through the dream and the encounter with the Pearl-maiden: the fall therefore indeed becomes fortunate, and sleep is an opportunity for spiritual growth rather than moral abdication.

from OED. The dates when extended meanings are first recorded are of course significant for the meaning of the words at the time of composition of *Sir Gawain and the Green Knight*:

slide v.: OE [*slīdan*] to slide, slip (to lapse morally, err or go wrong a1000; to fall into sin or evil c1230 (?a1200)) ...

sly a.: c1225(c1200) [ON] (wise, prudent etc. ?c1200); crafty, cunning, deceitful c1225 (?c1200) ...

38 The association of sleep with moral danger is of course not restricted to the works of the *Gawain*-poet. Something comparable may be observed in Spenser's *Faerie Queene*; see, e.g., Book I, Canto I, stanzas 33–38.

39 There may even, given the meanings of the lexemes classified in 01.01 in the Appendix (e.g. *slīm* 'slime'), be more distant echoes present of uncleanliness, which is used by the poet elsewhere in his writings as a metaphor of evil (see *Cleanness* 134, and the associated footnote in Andrew and Waldron, *Poems*, p. 117 and references there cited).

40 One might speculate on whether some prefiguration of Jonah's dirty clothes is suggested; see previous note, and also *Patience* 342 and the associated note in Andrew and Waldron, *Poems*, pp. 199–200.

VI

The analysis presented here has, it may be argued, both particular and general implications: particular implications for the interpretation of the passage in question and for our appreciation of the *Gawain*-poet's skill, and general implications for the non-impressionistic interpretation of phonaesthetic phenomena in alliterative poetry. It may also have been observed in the interpretations just offered that the analysis of linguistic detail need not preclude the exercise of literary-critical judgement – something Ron Waldron has always emphasised in both his teaching and his research.

APPENDIX

The following categories may be distinguished in the *Thesaurus of Old English* with regard to *sl*-lexemes. The listing offered here may be compared with the classification of forms offered by Käsmann,[41] noting that (of course) the semantic properties of forms change over time; thus Old English *slingan* may be glossed 'to worm, twist oneself, creep into' whereas present-day English 'sling' means 'throw', 'hurl' (interestingly, the Norse cognate *slyngva* means both 'throw, fling' and 'wind about'). Those forms where a potentially phonaesthetic element seems to be a component of the meaning of the lexeme are marked with an asterisk (*) and distinguished according to Reay's classification as follows: (A) 'hit, attack'(including sudden downward movements), (B) 'sliding movement' (including slimy/wet, eject/add water, and the metaphorical extensions indolence and carelessness, cunning), (C) 'slim, thin'. Problematic forms are marked with a query (?).

It should be noted that the presence or absence of an actual (rather than potential) phonaesthetic semantic component is a matter of judgement rather than certainty, and the categorisation offered here is therefore tentative. It will also be noticed that many categories are inflated in size since they contain compounded words (see for instance 02.07); but it will also be observed that some categories are particularly large even if this characteristic is taken into account. Comparison with the complete classificatory scheme of the *Thesaurus* draws attention to the fact that *sl*-words, whether obviously phonaesthetic or not, do seem to cluster in particular fields and not in others; such clustering suggests that phonaesthesia is more widespread than has been sometimes supposed hitherto, though it is a conclusion which Käsmann's work inescapably points towards. Each lexeme has been classified under the principal

41 For details of the precise meanings of these lexemes, see further Roberts and Kay, *Thesaurus*, pp. 1320–4, the ongoing Toronto *Dictionary of Old English*, and of course still J. Bosworth, T. Toller and A. Campbell, *An Anglo-Saxon Dictionary, with Supplements*, Oxford, 1898–1972.

categorisation given in the Contents list to the *Thesaurus*; for a more delicate categorisation, the *Thesaurus* should be consulted.

01.01 Surface of the earth

slæd, *(?A) slæf, *(B) slæp, *(A) slēa, *(B) slidor, *(B) slidornes, *(B) slīm, slind, slinu, *(B) slōh (n.), *(B) slōhtre

01.03 Air surrounding earth, atmosphere

*(A) slege, *(A) slieht

02.01 Existence, life

*(B) slæpan

02.02 Death

*(A) slæhtan, *(B) slæp, *(B) slæpan, *(A) slaga, *(A) (ge)slēan, *(A) slege, *(A) slegefæge, *(A) slieht, *(A, ?C) slitcwealm

02.05 Sensation, perception, feeling

*(B) (ge)slæpan, *(B) slæpbære, *(B) slæpdrenc, *(B) slæpe tōbregdan, *(B) slæpere, *(B) slæping, *(B) slæplēas, *(B) slæplēast, *(B) slæpnes, *(B) slæpor, *(B) slæpwērig, *(B) slāpian, *(A) slēan, *(B) slūma, *(B) slūmere

02.06 Animal

*(?B) slāwyrm, *(A) sleghrȳþer, *(A) slegnēat, *(A) slieht, *(A) sliehtswȳn, *(B) slincend, *(C, ?A) slite, *(A) slīþhende, *(?B) slīw

02.07 A plant

slāh, slāhþorn, slāhþornragu, slāhþornrind, slarege, slite

O2.08 Mental/spiritual health

*(B) slæpan, *(B) slæpdrenc, *(B) slāpende, *(B) sleac, *(A) (ge)slēan, *(A) slege, *(A) geslegen, *(A) slieht, *(A, ?C) geslit, *(A, ?C) slītan, *(A, ?C) slite

03.01 Properties of matter

*(B) slæpe, *(A) slica, *(B) slid, *(B) slidor, *(B) slifer, *(B) slipeg, *(B) slipor, *(B) slypa, *(B) slyppe

03.03 Measurement, determination of amount

*(?C) slota

04.01 Digestion

*(A) sleghrȳþer, *(A) slegnēat, *(A) slieht, *(A) sliehtswȳn, *(A) geslit, *(A) slītendlic, *(A) slītere

04.02 Farm

(A) slæget

04.03 Hunting, the chase

(A) slætan

04.04 Weaving

*(A) slēa, *(?B) slēfan, *(?B) geslēfed, *(B) slēfescōh, *(A) slege, *(B) slīefe, *(B) slīeflēas, *(B) slȳpan, *(B) slȳpescōh*

04.05 Building, construction

*(B) slæpern, *(A) (ge)slēan, *(B) slypræsn*

04.06 Salubrity

*(B) slipor, *(B) slipornes*

05.06 Destruction, dissolution, loss, breaking

*(A) (ge)slēan, *(A) (ge)slēan of, *(A) slege, *(A) geslit, *(A) (ge)slītan, *(A, ?C) slite, *(A) slītere, *(A) slītnes, *(A) slitung, *(A) slīþan*

05.07 Ending of existence, end of world

(B) slīdan

05.08 Strength

*(A) slīþe, *(A) slīþen*

05.09 Weakness

(B) gesleccan

05.10 Space, extent

(B) slingan

05.12 To move, be in motion

*(B) slæcnes, *(B) slāwian, *(B) slāwlīce, *(B) sleac, *(B) sleacian, *(B) sleaclīce, *(A) slēan, *(A) slecgettan, *(A) slege, *(B) slīdan, *(B) slide, *(B) slidor, *(B) slidrian, *(B) slincan, *(B) slingan, *(B) slipor, *(B) slūpan*

06.01 The head (as seat of thought)

*(B) slīdan, *(B) slide*

07.03 Evil

(?A, ?B) slīþelic

07.05 Disrespect, irreverence

*(A) geslit, *(A) slītan*

08.01 Heart, spirit, mood, disposition

*(A) (ge)slēan, *(B) slīdan, *(B) slide, *(A, ?C) slītan, *(A) geslītglīw, *(A) slīþful, *(A) slīþheard, *(?A) slīþnes*

10.04 To take

(B) geslæccan

11.06 Disinclination to act, listlessness

*(B) slacful/slæcful, *(B) slægu, *(B) slæwþ, *(B) slāpan, *(B) slāpol, *(B) slāpolnes, *(B) slāpornes, *(B) slāw, *(B) slāwa, *(B) slāwian, *(B) sleac, *(B) sleaclic, *(B) sleacmōdnes, *(B) sleacnes, *(B) sleacornes*

11.09 Peril, danger

*(B) slincan, *(B) slincende*

11.10 Safety, safeness

(B) slincan

11.11 Difficulty

(B) sleacian

11.12 Easiness

(B) sleac

12.08 Principle, character

(B) sleac

13.02 War

*(A) geslēan, *(A) slege, *(A) geslieht*

14.01 Law, body of rules

(?A) slæting

14.04 Making of terms, agreement, convention

slēan wedd

14.05 Punishment

*(A) slaga, *(A) slēan on racentan, *(A) slege*

15.01 Property

(A) slege

16.02 Religion

*(B) sliten, *(B) slīþnes*

17.02 Work, occupation, employment

*(A) (ge)slēan, *(A) slecgwyrhta, *(A) geslegen*

17.03 Implements, tools etc.

*(A) slecg, *(A) slege, *(A) slegebȳtl, *(A) slic*

17.05 Fuel, fire, lightning

(A) slēan

18.01 Stringed instrument

(A) slegel

18.02 Amusement, revelry, festivity

*(A) slēan, *(A) slege*

NOTE

I am much indebted to Ros Allen, Simon Horobin, Sue Powell, Liz Reay, Louise Sylvester, Jane Roberts and Theo van Heijnsbergen for comments, bibliographical references, suggestions and discussion. I am alone responsible for any shortcomings.

PART II

THE LINKS IN THE *CANTERBURY TALES*

NORMAN BLAKE

I

THE SCHOLARSHIP of the manuscript tradition of the *Canterbury Tales* has been dominated by the relationship between the Hengwrt [Hg] and Ellesmere [El] manuscripts, although the transcriptions and investigations of the witnesses of the poem made by the *Canterbury Tales* Project have revealed that other manuscripts may be just as significant in the early history of the text.[1] It is no longer certain that El is so central to the textual tradition as its use as base manuscript for most editions in the twentieth century would suggest. The initial analysis of the *Wife of Bath's Prologue* on CD-ROM indicated that its position in the textual tradition may well be among the second wave of manuscripts, although its scribe does appear to have had access to more than one copy-text, unless he altered his copying procedure about the middle of this Prologue.

The manuscript tradition and the implied way in which the poem developed that have been generally accepted hitherto are those put forward by Manly and Rickert and adapted more recently by scholars like Ralph Hanna.[2] The Manly and Rickert analysis of the textual tradition is so complicated that it is not easy to assimilate. Their edition has been interpreted to mean that Hg, the earliest extant manuscript, has the best text and should form the base text of a modern edition – even though it is at least one stage from Chaucer's original and Manly and Rickert never claimed that it was used as the base text for their edition. They accepted that El is closely associated with their *a*-group, which is at least one and possibly two stages removed from Chaucer's original.

---

1   See P. Robinson, 'A stemmatic analysis of the fifteenth-century witnesses to The Wife of Bath's Prologue', in *The Canterbury Tales Project Occasional Papers Volume II*, eds N. F. Blake and P. Robinson, London, 1997, pp. 69–132.

2   See J. M. Manly and E. Rickert, *The Text of the Canterbury Tales* (8 vols), Chicago, 1940, especially volume II, and Ralph Hanna III, 'The Hengwrt manuscript and the canon of *The Canterbury Tales*', *English Manuscript Studies* 1 (1989), 64–84.

However, Manly's and Rickert's view of the textual tradition involves several interlinking hypotheses. First, no extant manuscript dates from before Chaucer's lifetime so that all existing manuscripts are composites, made up by editors from the fragments they had at their disposal. When Chaucer had finished a tale, he circulated it privately among his friends and gradually these texts were copied and, during this process, became corrupted. Hence many different versions of any one tale were available to editors after Chaucer's death, for these exemplars ultimately derive from the booklet versions of the individual tales distributed in his own lifetime by Chaucer. This series of hypotheses makes it difficult to decide which manuscripts are central to the establishment of that copy of the original which they tried to recreate in their edition, for every tale has a different textual tradition.

Added to this, Manly and Rickert accepted the principle that some tales may have been revised by Chaucer so that some tales may have circulated in more than one authorial version as well as in scribally corrupt copies. Some scribes and/or editors might, therefore, have had both good and bad copies of different tales. It was difficult for the editors to make a reasoned choice among these differing versions. In their discussion emphasis was on the textual tradition of the tales; the links were largely ignored, perhaps because of their short length.

For his part, Hanna accepts that Hg is the earliest extant manuscript, though it has a faulty order and contents. Following the lead of Manly and Rickert, he suggested that individual tales existed at first in a 'stripped' form, i.e. without any link to the poem as a whole, and that in this form they were often revised by Chaucer. These versions of the tales 'were drafts prepared as pre-publication samples of the "work in progress" for the poet's immediate audience'[3] and were circulated individually without other tales. When Chaucer revised a tale, he would keep a copy of the revised, and from then the approved, version of the tale in his home.

In this hypothesis, it was only later that Chaucer joined the tales together within the poem by composing links. Hanna appears to accept that, unlike the tales, there was only a single authorial form for each link. However, some of these links, which are accepted as genuine and reflect Chaucer's preferred order, may exist in manuscripts side by side with links adapted or even composed by scribes to fit in with the order which for one reason or another they or their editors imposed on the poem. Hanna suggests that Chaucer's own version of the poem embracing his preferred order and genuine links existed only in the poet's home, and none of his friends had access to this definitive, but incomplete, text before his death. Hence the scribes of some early manuscripts like Hg cannot have had access to the incomplete version of the poem in the author's home, for otherwise they would have had access to the poem in its

---

3   Hanna, 'The Hengwrt manuscript', p. 72.

most complete and authentic form. Consequently, such versions with their non-authentic orders are based on the freely-circulating tales and on links, which may be genuine or adapted to fit in with the order superimposed by scribe or editor on the tales. On the other hand, later manuscripts like El are based on the poet's final (though incomplete because of his death) and definitive holograph copy.

However, it is not clear in Hanna's account why scribes like the Hg scribe should not have had access to the poet's own copy, which many people must have known about given the fact that Chaucer was circulating tales long before his death, or how one can determine today what is genuine in the various fragments which survive. Hanna's theory also assumes that these early scribes imposed their own order on the tales which were free-floating, although they had access to links which suggested a different order. It presupposes one of two possible scenarios: first, haste in the preparation of the early manuscripts whose scribes had access to much genuine material, but who were also prepared to adapt that material when they pleased; or secondly, the piecemeal acquisition of bits of the poem which were assembled before the editor or scribe had any precise knowledge how many tales were to be included in the final version or what their 'approved' order might be. Either hypothesis leaves many unanswered questions, though it may be admitted that, as so many strange things happened with manuscripts and texts, neither is beyond the bounds of possibility.

This general scenario, as outlined by scholars like Hanna, is primarily devised to explain why Hg, the earliest extant manuscript, has what is taken to be an order – which was not Chaucer's approved one – with adapted links and incomplete contents as compared with El, the base text preferred by most modern editors. It seems to be motivated by a desire to establish the centrality of El rather than to evaluate the manuscript evidence as such. Among the other weaknesses of this hypothesis is the question of the links, for although many of the links, like the tales, exist in more than one version, they are treated differently. Why should we assume that the tales existed in more than one authorial version (though the possibility of scribal interference at a later date is not excluded in this hypothesis), whereas the links exist in only a single authorial version as well as several scribal ones? Not only is this illogical, it is also difficult to justify. If the tales exist in several authorial versions, it is more sensible to allow for the possibility that the links also exist in several authorial versions. The rest of this paper explores that possibility.

II

A point that might need to be borne in mind in the following discussion is the dating of the manuscripts. Manly and Rickert accepted that no extant manuscript dates from Chaucer's own lifetime and that no full manuscript was produced by or for him. This theory has become part of the standard view of the manuscripts ever since, and has been strengthened by the dates proposed in many facsimiles, like that of Hg.[4]

However, the question of whether all manuscripts must be dated after Chaucer's death in 1400 has recently been reopened. Kathleen Scott's examination of El and related illuminated manuscripts led her to conclude that El might be at or just after the turn of the century.[5] She recognised that this conclusion would have significant implications for the dating of Hg and other early manuscripts, such as British Library Harley 7334 [Ha4], Corpus Christi College Oxford 198 [Cp] and British Library Lansdowne 851 [La], in so far as the standard modern dating for El puts it about ten years after Hg.

I have followed up the tentative suggestion made by Scott in my 'Geoffrey Chaucer and the manuscripts of the Canterbury Tales'.[6] In that paper I reviewed the reasons which have led us to assume that all extant manuscripts have to be dated post-1400 and to what extent these reasons are justified. The conclusion I offered there is that there are no conclusive arguments to prove that all extant manuscripts of the *Canterbury Tales* must be dated after Chaucer's death; on the contrary, there are arguments in favour of an earlier dating for some of them. Acceptance of this position would put the clock back to the views held by Skeat and others, for Skeat accepted that El was the first manuscript to be written after Chaucer's death and that others like Hg, Ha4 and Cp were all written in his lifetime and reflect his revisions of the text.[7]

III

With this in mind, let us consider some of the links. In Hg there are two links which are generally regarded as scribal adaptations, because they differ from the links found in El and thus from the versions usually printed in modern editions. These are the ones that appear in Hg as the Squire-Merchant and the Merchant-Franklin links, which correspond in modern editions to the Merchant-Squire and Squire-Franklin links [E2419–F8 and F673–708].[8] I have myself argued elsewhere that the Hg versions are the earlier ones, which were later adapted to refer to different tellers when the order of the tales was

4   A. I. Doyle and M. B. Parkes, 'A palaeographical introduction', in *The Canterbury Tales, Geoffrey Chaucer: A Facsimile of the Hengwrt Manuscript*, ed. P. G. Ruggiers, Norman, 1979, pp. xix–xlix.

5   K. Scott, 'An Hours and Psalter by two Ellesmere illuminators', in *The Ellesmere Manuscript: Essays in Interpretation*, eds M. Stevens and D. Woodward, San Marino and Tokyo, 1996, pp. 87–119.

6   *Journal of the Early Book Society* 1 (1997 [1998]), 96–122.

7   W. W. Skeat, *The Evolution of the Canterbury Tales*, Chaucer Society 2nd ser. 38, London, 1907.

8   The group letters and line numbers are those from L. Benson, *The Riverside Chaucer*, 3rd edn, Boston, 1986.

changed.[9] The standard view, on the other hand, is that found in Hanna, namely that the Hg versions are scribal adaptations of the original links, which are found in El and other manuscripts, because the scribe of Hg had to adapt them to fit the order of the tales which had come to him in a piecemeal fashion. The only link for which this might not apply is the Nun's Priest's Prologue, though that does not involve any change to or uncertainty over the order of the tales. Manly and Rickert also refer to the Merchant-Squire link as found in El and other manuscripts as 'its correct place' (II.284).[10]

The claim that the Hg versions of the links are inferior, and therefore scribal, adaptations is based on the posited unsatisfactory nature of the metre in the presumed changes found in Hg as compared with El. Benson, for example, has claimed that 'if El contains the authentic versions and Hg spurious adaptations, the links in Hg and the order they serve are derivative from some previously established order rather than the creation of the Hg director'.[11] He justifies this statement by examining only three lines in the two links; it is asserted that in each one of these three lines a syllable missing in Hg makes the line defective, whereas each line in El is a pentameter and hence must be the correct, i.e. Chaucerian, reading. Benson states that 'Fifteenth-century versifiers did not always aim at, or achieve, exact pentameters in every line, but it is beyond probability that the original composer would have missed all three times.'[12]

It is difficult, if not impossible, to substantiate claims like this. Although we are beginning to understand Chaucer's metre better than we did, and although it now seems as though Hg may reflect what we understand as Chaucer's metre more satisfactorily than most other early manuscripts, it is difficult to achieve certainty in such matters, particularly when the number of disputed lines is so small.[13] Even if it could be accepted that the metre in Hg is less satisfactory than that found in El, it would not be possible to prove that it was not a first draft which Chaucer himself improved when he revised the link (on the assumption that a revision of links was just as acceptable as the revision of tales). It, therefore, seems more sensible to consider the links as a whole to review whether revision in them could be accepted as probably Chaucerian. In

9   N. F. Blake, 'The relationship of the Hengwrt and Ellesmere manuscripts', *Essays and Studies* n.s. 32 (1979), 1–18, and *The Textual Tradition of the Canterbury Tales*, London, 1985.

10 Manly and Rickert, *Text*, vol. II, p. 284.

11 L. Benson, 'The order of The Canterbury Tales', *Studies in the Age of Chaucer* 3 (1981), 77–120; this quotation is on p. 105.

12 Benson, 'Order', p. 106.

13 For recent studies on Chaucer's metre, see E. Solopova, 'Chaucer's metre and scribal editing in the early manuscripts of *The Canterbury Tales*', in *Canterbury Tales Project Occasional Papers Volume II*, eds Blake and Robinson, pp. 143–64, and S. Barney, *Studies in Troilus: Chaucer's Text, Meter, and Diction*, East Lansing, 1993.

this process it is less prejudicial to start with links other than those which have hitherto provided the battleground between Hg and El.[14]

IV

The Man of Law's Endlink [B1.1163–90], though its status is ambiguous, is usually included in modern editions of the poem, more often than not in square brackets as in *The Riverside Chaucer*. The justification for its inclusion is that, although it is regarded as written by Chaucer, it may at some stage have been deleted by him. This is an odd reason for including it, since modern editors usually base their editions on the author's final version of his work rather than on his early drafts.

The position of this endlink in early manuscripts is as follows. In Hg there is a blank of a whole page (fol. 128v) after the Man of Law's Tale; it contains no endlink to the tale. Since in Hg there are forty lines of writing per page, this blank page would provide more than enough space to accommodate the thirty-two lines which elsewhere make up the Man of Law's Endlink and also leave enough space for a heading and a final rubric, though the explicit for the Man of Law's Tale is already found on folio 128r. This blank page in Hg (fol. 128v) was never written on or filled before the seventeenth century when various family genealogies were inserted, though the blank clearly indicates that the scribe expected and made provision for a link to be included. This could mean that a link was going to be written to fill this blank (either by the author or someone else) or that it was known a link existed, but it was not immediately at hand to be copied by the scribe. One may note that leaving a whole page blank looks suspiciously as though it was a random amount of space which was set on one side, and that the endlink and its accompanying rubrics when they came fitted comfortably into the space available.

The endlink, as it survives, has some relevance for the order of the tales since, although it is primarily designed to conclude the Man of Law's Tale, it contains a reference at line B1.1179 to the pilgrim who is going to tell the following tale. In the extant copies of the Man of Law's Endlink thirty-five manuscripts read Summoner, twenty-five read Squire and one late manuscript Shipman. A few manuscripts do follow the Man of Law's Tale with the Squire's Tale and others look as though they intended to do so. No witness follows it directly with the Summoner's Tale, although that tale is the last tale in Group D, which does follow the Man of Law's Tale in many manuscripts. The introduction of Shipman at B1.1179 is late and suggests a desperate solution, though it has provided justification for some modern editors to place Group B2 after Group B1 so that the Shipman's Tale follows the Man of Law's Tale.

14 In what follows I have been able to draw upon the work done by two former postgraduate students, Dr Simon Horobin and Mrs Linda Cross, and I am grateful to them for their help.

However, Hg does follow the Man of Law's Tale with the Squire's Tale, though it does not include this endlink. It is perfectly possible that the endlink was written with the order in Hg in mind.

Two other blanks for the possible inclusion of links are found in Hg: one extending over the whole of folio 137v except for the top three lines, which contain the end of the Squire's Tale, and the other including the bottom half of folio 152v with the top half of folio 153r. These blanks were filled in with links written by the same scribe in ink of a different colour from that used for the tales which they join together. In Hg these links are the Squire-Merchant link and the Merchant-Franklin link. The first of these links fills the blank more or less adequately, but the second is far too short for the space allowed and so the scribe was forced to leave substantial gaps. In this latter case one may assume that the scribe, when he left his blank, had no idea how long the link which was missing was going to be or alternatively the person who wrote the link had no idea how much space had been allowed for it. A fourth blank in Hg at the end of the Franklin's Tale (which occupies only the bottom half of fol. 165r) was not filled in until the sixteenth century when further genealogical entries were inserted.

On the basis of the insertions in the blanks on folios 137v and 152v–153r one may assume that there was an intention to fill the blanks on folios 128v and 165r. The failure to do so, as already suggested, may be explained either because the links were not yet written or because, although they had been written, they were not available to the scribe or were no longer considered appropriate for the position which they were intended to occupy. It is the second of these suggestions which is usually accepted by modern editors, but the first is just as, if not more, likely. In this matter the evidence of Ha4 is significant.

In Ha4 the Man of Law's Endlink is included on folios 86r–v, but in an incomplete form. The endlink starts without a gap after the end of the Man of Law's Tale with a two-line illuminated capital *O* in *Our*. But the first line of the couplet B1.1175–76 on folio 86r is not included, and a blank is left for this missing line, which appears in *The Riverside Chaucer* as *Abydeth, for Goddes digne passioun.* Folio 86r ends with line B1.1179, and this folio has, counting the blank line as one line, the thirty-eight lines which are characteristic of each page of Ha4. Folio 86v continues with the endlink, but it includes only B1.1180–85. The last five lines of the endlink, namely B1.1186–90, are missing, though no gap is left for them before the rubrics to terminate the Man of Law's Tale and to introduce the next tale. The result is an incomplete and apparently unfinished endlink, though there is no suggestion that the scribe was worried by the situation, and apart from the blank left for B1.1175, no allowance is made for any additional text. The endlink is followed directly without a gap by the single line explicit for the Man of Law's Tale *Here endith the man of lawe his tale* (and it is notable that the rubric is for his tale rather than for his endlink) and by a single line implicit for the Wife of Bath's Prologue *Here begynneth the prologue of the Wyf of Bathe.*

The normal interpretation of this situation is that Ha4 represents a scribally truncated version of the link. But there is no evidence in the manuscript that the scribe of Ha4 left a blank and subsequently filled it in with only part of the link so that it fitted the blank which had been left. The lines of the endlink appear to have been written at the same time as the surrounding text. The final lines do not seem to have been omitted through lack of space, and if space was short it was silly to leave a blank for one line (B1.1175) of a couplet; it would have been more sensible to leave out the couplet for which the one line was missing. That being the case we ought to reconsider why the final lines and one intermediate line are not there. One explanation is naturally that they had not yet been written. The endlink in Ha4 may represent a link which was almost, but not quite, completed, and this incompleteness may reflect uncertainty (authorial or scribal) at the time as to what was to follow this tale.

That the tale to follow the endlink in the order remained uncertain for some time is indicated by the change of names of the next teller at B1.1179. Ha4 in fact reads *Summoner* at B1.1179, although from its *ordinatio* it appears as if the Squire's Tale was originally destined to follow the Man of Law. In fact, the Wife of Bath's Prologue follows it in Ha4 so that the Summoner's Tale follows at the end of that Group. However, Cp has the link in its complete form as we accept it today with the reading *Squire* at B1.1179 and with the Squire's Tale before the Wife of Bath's Prologue and Tale. Cambridge University Library Dd 4.24 [Dd] has no endlink and is followed by the Wife of Bath's Prologue and Tale; this established the pattern for many later manuscripts and modern editions.

It is perfectly reasonable to suggest that Chaucer himself was undecided as to the most appropriate order for the tales following the Man of Law and that it was he who experimented with different orders and revised the appropriate link accordingly. An explanation of this variation in the manuscripts is that at first there was no Man of Law's Endlink, as in Hg, though Chaucer made allowance for one which he proposed to write or had already started to write. Its omission in Hg may be caused by the fact that the link had not been completed because it was going through several drafts. His initial version, although incomplete, is the one found in Ha4, but its composition was impeded by the continuing uncertainty as to what tale should come next – hence it was not completed in Ha4. Chaucer completed what he had started in what is now its final form of this endlink for Cp with *Squire* at B1.1179 and with the intention that the Squire's Tale should follow the Man of Law. His final solution may have been no endlink when the tale order was changed to allow the Wife of Bath's Prologue to act as the link between the Man of Law and the Wife of Bath, when her tale was reordered to follow the Man of Law. This may have been occasioned by the rewriting of the Wife of Bath's Prologue as suggested by Peter Robinson to allow for a different tale to follow and a less aggressive wife.[15] If this were the case, it is hardly

15 Robinson, 'Stemmatic Analysis', especially pp. 124–6.

surprising that, with so many authorial versions and orders, later scribes were uncertain precisely what to do: some omitted the endlink, whereas others included it and made a guess as to which pilgrim's name should be inserted at B1.1179 for none of the names that were there fitted precisely with the orders they had.

Authorial revision may also be the best explanation of the two forms of the Nun's Priest's Prologue. A shorter and a longer version exist, with the shorter missing lines B2.3961–80. The explanatory notes for *The Riverside Chaucer* refer to the later version as 'Chaucer's latest intention' with the shorter version being his first draft.[16] If so, Chaucer would have first written the short form substantially as it appears in Hg and then composed the extra lines which appear in many manuscripts and most modern editions. It is easier to accept that this is the order of composition rather than that Chaucer wrote only the longer version and that scribes for some reason deleted some of its lines when copying their manuscripts.

The Nun's Priest's Endlink, which is found in only nine manuscripts with the earliest being Dd, may have a similar, but different, explanation. If it is genuine,[17] it may be that Chaucer started to write a link, but never finished it because of uncertainty as to which tale was ultimately going to follow the Nun's Priest. At first it looked as though a link would not be needed because it was to be followed by the Manciple's Tale with its own prologue. When an alternative order arose with the (Second) Nun's Tale following the Nun's Priest, a link became necessary. But this link was never finished, partly because the decision to have a revised order was reached relatively late and partly because Chaucer or someone else then decided to adopt a different strategy in the ordering of the tales. When the Canon's Yeoman's Prologue and Tale was written, it was included before the Manciple's Tale, but as this tale had its prologue there was no need for an endlink for the Nun's Priest's Tale. It was only when the Canon's Yeoman's Tale attracted the (Second) Nun's Tale to a position after the Nun's Priest's Tale that an endlink to form a link became necessary. However, a decision to construct a prologue from within the (Second) Nun's Tale itself made an endlink for the Nun's Priest's Tale unnecessary since the new prologue could act as the linking device. Most scribes disregarded this incomplete endlink because it was unfinished and served no

---

16 Benson, *Riverside Chaucer*, p. 935. This was also the view of Manly and Rickert who wrote: 'It seems probable therefore that Miss Hammond was right in maintaining that Chaucer wrote both forms. The S[horter] F[orm] with the Host as interrupter came first and it was later – though not necessarily much later – that he fortunately thought of varying his interruption by transferring this to the Knight and enlivened the incident by adding [B2.]3961–80' (II.412).

17 Manly and Rickert claim that this endlink 'is distinctly Chaucerian', but it was cancelled by Chaucer and so is like the Man of Law's Endlink 'an atrophied residual element' of the poem (II.422).

function once the prologue to the (Second) Nun's Tale became available. It was a situation which is parallel to, but not identical with, the uncertainties surrounding the Man of Law's Endlink. The incomplete version of that endlink found in Ha4 resembles the incomplete version of the Nun's Priest's Endlink in Dd and other manuscripts. The difference lies in the fact that the Man of Law's Endlink was ultimately completed, whereas as far as we can tell the other was not.

It follows from this that the two most controversial links (what in Hg are the Squire-Merchant and the Merchant-Franklin links, which in later manuscripts became the Merchant-Squire and Squire-Franklin links) may also exist in two authorial forms. If so, it means that Chaucer experimented with the order of these tales, as suggested long ago by Skeat. Chaucer's first solution was the order in Hg which he later modified in stages until he arrived at the order found in such manuscripts as Ellesmere. It is easier to consider this to be the way things developed rather than to assume, as is often done, that the Hg scribe adapted the Chaucerian links to the order he had imposed on the free-floating tales. These links then fall into the same pattern as the other links in the poem. An initial attempt at providing an order demanded the writing of possible links to fill the gaps left by the proposed order, but some of them were incomplete because they were no more than first drafts. As the order underwent change at Chaucer's hands, because once a sequence was established he would get ideas as to how to improve it, Chaucer (and probably later some scribes or editors) altered the links to fit in with what had become the revised order.

Another example of this process is provided by the omission in British Library MS Additional 35286 [Ad3] of the first couplet of The Canon's Yeoman's Prologue, which in most manuscripts anchors his tale to the (Second) Nun's Tale.[18] In *The Riverside Chaucer* these lines read:

> Whan ended was the lyf of Seinte Cecile,
> Er we hadde riden fully fyve mile.   [G544–5]

It is possible that Ad3 reflects the original version, whether by Chaucer or another. Ad3 is a manuscript which is thought to have a good text, and for this reason it is included as one of the ten manuscripts collated as part of the Variorum Edition of the *Canterbury Tales*. In the *Canterbury Tales* Project's analysis of the textual tradition of the Wife of Bath's Prologue on CD-ROM, Ad3 is a member of the O-Group – that group of manuscripts which is closest to Hg and therefore probably to Chaucer's original. Despite its somewhat later date, its scribe must have had access to a good copy-text. If we assume that it was Chaucer who wrote the Canon's Yeoman's Tale, which most Chaucerian

18   On this manuscript, see Simon Horobin, 'Editorial assumptions and the manuscripts of *The Canterbury Tales*', in *Canterbury Tales Project Occasional Papers Volume II*, eds Blake and Robinson, pp. 15–22.

critics take for granted, it is possible to believe that at first he had not decided with which tale(s) to join it. This was after all the likely way in which he gradually built up his tales and joined them together. He may have thought, when he was composing it, of linking it with the (Second) Nun's Tale, which could account for the late insertion of that tale in Hg. The Canon's Yeoman's Tale itself, it may be proposed, was not finished in time for inclusion in Hg. When the prologue of the Canon's Yeoman (without that initial couplet G554–5) and his tale were completed, they were placed without any linking device before the Manciple's Tale, as we find in Ad3. In this and other manuscripts which have a good text, the (Second) Nun's Tale and the Canon's Yeoman's Prologue and Tale are some way apart in the tale order, for the former tale precedes the Physician's Tale. This is the position of these two tales in such early manuscripts as Ha4, Cp and La. At some stage the (Second) Nun's Tale was joined to the Canon's Yeoman's Tale and it was placed further back in the order, namely after the Nun's Priest's Tale. In other words the linking of the (Second) Nun with the Canon's Yeoman led to the former's tale being pushed further back to where the Canon's Yeoman's Tale was. It was only when this tale changed its position in the order that the couplet [G544–5] was included – presumably by Chaucer if the change took place early enough. The uncertainty about what tale would follow the Nun's Priest's Tale (whether in fact it would be the (Second) Nun's Tale or not) accounts for the hesitation and ultimately incomplete form of the Nun's Priest's Endlink, as suggested earlier.

V

It is not necessary to investigate other links in the poem to establish as a principle the concept that, if the tales exist in more than one authorial version, the same could apply to the links. Indeed, the matter of different authorial versions of the links is more important than authorial versions of the tales, for different links imply different orders and, if there are different orders, these may have been arranged by the author himself.

It may be for this reason that many scholars have been unwilling to consider different authorial versions of the links because it throws open the whole question of Chaucer's intentions for the order of the tales. Different authorial versions of the links would also make the theory of prior circulation of tales in a free-standing form in the author's lifetime unnecessary, since it would mean that Chaucer prepared certain orders himself and supervised the preparation of at least some early manuscripts.

This hypothesis makes the development of the manuscript tradition much easier to understand, though it might make it much more difficult to chart since a single stemma would no longer be possible. Although the later scribes may readily have altered what Chaucer wrote – partly because he had left so many versions – most of what appears in the early manuscripts may reflect Chaucer's own experiments and alterations.

There seems no reason why we should not accept that after a certain point in the composition of various parts of his poem, which may well have been characterised by writing tales in isolation as Hanna and others have suggested, Chaucer decided that he wanted to see how the poem was shaping up. So he assembled the various pieces already written in some kind of order. The existence of the Parson's Tale and the Retraction may indicate that Chaucer realised he might never finish his original plan and he would have to reduce the planned scope of the poem. Surely the arrangement of the parts he had completed into an order would provide that spur which would lead him to revise some of the tales and, especially, to write new or revise existing links.

Given this possible scenario, it makes it easier to understand why later scribes were led to experiment; the multiplicity of authorial versions meant that they were uncertain which was the best or final arrangement in what still remained an unfinished poem and so they experimented with various possible groupings. If Chaucer had been playing with the order up to his death, it would provide a reason for others to do the same after his death, and if he was responsible for more than one overall version of the poem, it could explain why Hg, the earliest extant manuscript, has a good text but does not contain what most modern scholars prefer as the best order.

It would also allow us to accept that the Canon's Yeoman's Prologue and Tale could be genuine Chaucerian pieces, even though not in the earliest manuscript, because prologue and tale were inserted into the poem at a late stage in Chaucer's own lifetime. Indeed, once he had arranged the poem in a first draft, as found in Hg, he might easily have decided that the pilgrimage framework needed livening up – something he could do by devising new or revising old links and by inserting a tale which introduces pilgrims who were not members of the original party. If this is so, it would also raise the question of the authenticity of the Tale of Gamelyn, with which Chaucer may have experimented before he decided not to include it in what was taking shape as a more definitive order and form for the poem. But it would still have to be thought of as written by Chaucer, if this were the case, even though he decided in the end not to include it in this poem. But these are matters which lie outside the scope of this paper. To accept different authorial versions of the links, which most scholars do for the Nun's Priest's Prologue, has considerable implications for our understanding of the textual tradition of the poem.

If it is accepted that some manuscripts date from Chaucer's lifetime, the next task will be to determine which manuscripts date from before 1400 and which were prepared for him or under his direction. It makes the study of the early manuscripts much more exciting, if potentially more complicated, and it should break that unfortunate stranglehold which Hg and El have for too long exercised over scholarly debate on the poem's textual history. It is one of the matters towards which we on the *Canterbury Tales* Project are directing our attention.

MIDDLE ENGLISH VERSE IN CHRONICLES[1]

JULIA BOFFEY and A. S. G. EDWARDS

T he interpolation of vernacular verse into prose chronicle writings has a tradition extending back to the *Anglo-Saxon Chronicle*, which includes poems ranging from *The Battle of Brunanburh* (937) to *The Rime of William* (1086). But the occurrence of Middle English verse in prose works in either the vernacular or Latin, the factors that determine its occurrence and the forms in which it appears, do not seem to have been the subject of much enquiry.[2] A full discussion of this question cannot be attempted here; but it seems appropriate to offer some account of the appearance of such verse in historical writings on the present occasion, in an essay dedicated with affection and respect to Ron Waldron, the editor of Trevisa's *Polychronicon*.

There was an intermittent tradition of verse chronicle or historical narrative in Middle English verse running from Laȝamon's *Brut* in the early thirteenth century to Laurence Minot in the late fourteenth to the more widely circulating John Hardyng in the fifteenth century, as well as a developed tradition of Middle Scots historical verse in the works of Wyntoun and Barbour.[3] But prose

---

1 The following abbreviations are used: IMEV: *The Index of Middle English Verse*, eds Carleton Brown and Rossell Hope Robbins, New York, 1943; IMEVS: *Supplement to the Index of Middle English Verse*, eds Rossell Hope Robins and J. L. Cutler, Lexington, Ky., 1965. References to individual entries within both works appear in arabic numerals within round brackets after particular works or manuscripts.

2 We are concerned with verse texts deliberately incorporated into prose chronicles, not those unrelated ones added on flyleaves or in margins of such works. For examples see J. Boffey, *Manuscripts of English Courtly Love Lyrics in the Later Middle Ages*, Cambridge, 1985, p. 98 and A. S. G. Edwards, 'A Chaucerian Reader of Trevisa', *Medium Aevum* 62 (1993), 288–9. Nor are we concerned with verse incorporated into other prose texts containing historical materials, like the *Coventry Leet Book*, which preserves some historical verse, or the *City of York House Book VI*, which includes a pageant for Henry VII.

3 For a concise enumeration of verse historical writings see E. D. Kennedy, *A Manual of the Writings in Middle English*, New Haven, Conn., 1989, 8: 2599; see also for additional relevant information Rossell Hope Robbins, 'Poems Dealing With Contemporary Conditions,' in *A Manual of the Writings in Middle English*, general ed.

remains the dominant mode for the Middle English transmission of historical narrative. It achieves its most popular manifestation in the Middle English prose *Brut* which survives in over 170 manuscripts[4] and its most extended one in Trevisa's massive translation of Higden's *Polychronicon*, which survives in fourteen complete manuscripts and a number of selections.[5]

Both these works are relevant to our present concerns. They, like a number of others which we will also briefly discuss, often include texts or passages in verse. But they are not the earliest chronicles to include Middle English verse. Among the earliest to do so are Roger of Wendover's *Flores Historiarum* which includes, in his *Life of St Godric*, a verse prayer to St Godric (IMEV 2988).[6] This is a short poem which enjoyed a quite extensive circulation in different contexts, all prose.[7] The relative brevity of this and its associated prayers may have permitted oral transmission.

Other early instances of Middle English verse in similar contexts include the famous lines in the Latin *Liber Eliensis* ascribed to King Canute, 'Merie singen the munaches binnen Ely' (IMEV 2164),[8] and a couple of brief verse fragments, seemingly quotations from songs, in Matthew Paris's *Historia Anglorum*.[9] All these instances represent the most typical function of surviving verse in chronicles: to furnish a song or other utterance linked to a specific occasion or individual.

A more extensive early use of Middle English appears in the verse chronicle of the early fourteenth-century Austin canon Peter of Langtoft. Most of this work is in Anglo-Norman but in its final section, which examines Edward I's

A. E. Hartung, New Haven, Conn., 1975, 5: 1385–1536, 1639–1725.

4   For enumeration of these manuscripts see Lister Matheson, *The Prose Brut: The Development of a Middle English Chronicle*, Medieval & Renaissance Texts & Studies 180, Tempe, Az., 1998.

5   For the most recent bibliography of Trevisa's manuscripts see David C. Fowler, *John Trevisa*, Aldershot, 1993, p. 46; for descriptions of all the major ones see R. A. Waldron, 'The Manuscripts of Trevisa's Translation of the *Polychronicon*', *Modern Language Quarterly* 51 (1990), 281–317.

6   Ed. H. O. Coxe (4 vols), Oxford, 1841, II, 348–9.

7   IMEV/S lists twelve manuscripts; to these can be added Paris, Bibl. Mazarine 1716, folio 207v: see Alexandra Barratt, 'The Lyrics of St Godric: a new manuscript', *Notes & Queries* n.s.32 (1985), 439–445, pp. 443–4. The only other verse items with which it is collocated are related to St Godric and include a brief (a single couplet) prayer to St Godric in four manuscripts (Bodleian Laud misc. 423: BL Harley 153, BL Royal 5 F.vii, and the Paris manuscript) and Godric's prayer to St Nicholas in the Royal and Paris manuscripts.

8   *Liber Eliensis*, ed. E. O. Blake, Camden Society, 3rd ser. 92, London, 1962.

9   These are IMEV 1252, 1335; see *Matthaei Parisiensis Historia Anglorum*, ed. F. Madden, Rolls Series, London, 1866–69, I, 271, 381; it should be noted that IMEV includes two further passages, 2830, 4284.8, but these are not verse. For discussion of the verse passages see A. B. Friedman, 'Medieval Popular Satire in Matthew Paris', *Modern Language Notes* 74 (1959), 673–78.

wars with the Scots, a number of passages of Middle English tail-rhyme verse are interpolated.[10] Langtoft's motives for including these verses are unclear – were they his own interpolations or was he incorporating material that may have circulated independently as patriotic responses to these anti-Scottish campaigns? The fact that they are all in the same verse form, six-line tail-rhyme stanzas, suggests the former possibility. The impact of these verses is primarily linguistic. They suggest an impulse to underscore the triumph of the English by its expression in triumphant English. They offer forms of invective against the Scots in general (IMEV 841, 3352) or against particular figures like Wallace (IMEV 313) or John Balliol (IMEV 814). But the use of English verse is not simply xenophobic. It is also used to dramatize Scottish voices in poems against Edward I (IMEV 2574, 3352). This shared language and voice provide a reminder of the cultural and linguistic distance that separates the combatants from the larger Anglo-Norman narrative. It also initiates a tradition in chronicle writing, to which we will return, whereby the Scots and/or Anglo-Scottish relations become a recurrent subject for such verse interpolations.

The impact of the Middle English verse passages in Langtoft is rather different as they are subsequently incorporated in Robert Mannyng's *Chronicle*. This is itself a free redaction of Langtoft in Middle English couplets.[11] In the earliest and seemingly most authoritative version of Mannyng's *Chronicle*, in London, Inner Temple Petyt 511.7, only one passage is preserved in tail rhyme – the others are written as long line, three short lines to a line.[12] Interestingly however, all of these are prefaced by the note 'Couwe' (that is 'rime couvé' or tail rhyme), thus drawing attention to their formal distinctiveness. Mannyng does on occasions introduce variant verses; given their nature as

10 *The Chronicle of Pierre de Langtoft*, ed. T. Wright (2 vols), Rolls Series, 1866–68. The poems appear in vol. II; they occur at pp. 234, 236 (three stanzas: IMEV 2574), 244 (one stanza: IMEV 2686), 248 (two stanzas: IMEV 3352), 252 (one stanza: IMEV 841), 258 (one stanza: IMEV 814), 264 (two stanzas IMEV 310), 364 (one stanza: IMEV 313), although there are variants and additions in various manuscripts some of which are printed in Wright's *Introduction* to vol. II, x–xii. For some account of the manuscripts and their relationships see T. M. Smallwood, 'The Text of Langtoft's Chronicle', *Medium Aevum* 46 (1977), 219–30; for the English verses see especially 220–1, 226–7.

11 For the manuscripts of Mannyng's *Chronicle* see IMEV 1995; to the manuscripts listed there can be added Merton College, Oxford C.23.b.6 (a fragment from the same manuscript as Bodleian, Rawlinson D. 913, folio 4); see N. Davis, 'Another Fragment of "Richard Coer de Lyon"', *Notes & Queries* n.s. 16 (1969), 447–52 (especially 451–2).

12 We follow the edition of Mannyng's *Chronicle* by Idele Sullens, Binghamton, NY, 1996, who reproduces the actual arrangement of the tail rhyme passages in this manuscript (p. 727). The relevant passages are on pp. 647 (lines 6424–28), 651 (lines 6599–6604), 653 (lines 6683–88), 654 (lines 6711–16, 6735–6), 655 (lines 6765–6778), 656–7 (lines 6813–52); only the first of these is actually set out in the manuscript as tail-rhyme.

popular invective, it is possible that these represent other orally circulating sources.[13]

The Middle English prose *Brut* remains the most variegated source for the incorporation of Middle English verse. The most popular single verse text it incorporates is Page's *Siege of Rouen*, a seemingly autobiographical account of Henry V's siege of the city in 1421. In ten copies of the *Brut* Page's account appears at the appropriate point, in part or in whole, in place of the prose narrative.[14] Sometimes in these manuscripts Page's narrative is actually written as prose to seek to merge it seamlessly with the dominant prose form into which it has been incorporated.[15]

There are other collocations of verse texts in *Brut* manuscripts. The most extensive is London, College of Arms, Arundel LVIII which seems to reflect a nexus of verse additions from which other manuscripts draw in varying degrees. It includes both *Richard Coeur de Lion* (IMEV 1979) and *The Battle of Halidon Hill* (IMEV 3539) as well as the couplet version of 'Verses on the Kings of England' (IMEV 444) and the continuation of Robert of Gloucester's *Chronicle*. The layout of materials in this manuscript suggests some of the scribal difficulties in accommodating verse and prose together consistently even in a large and well produced manuscript. Here the verse is generally copied in a single column, enhanced at various points with illuminated borders. But on occasions there are problems. On folio 145r, for example, a verse passage has to be crammed into the smaller than usual space on the right-hand side of a column of prose; a marginal note 'rhyme' marks its beginning. The verso of this leaf is then taken up with a single column of verse; but on folio 146r the text is set out in double column, with verse being replaced by prose partway down; the change is signalled by the marginal notation 'prose'. *Richard Coeur de Lion* and *The Battle of Halidon Hill* also appear in another *Brut*

13   Mannyng also translates into tail-rhyme passages in Anglo-Norman tail-rhyme in Langtoft. For a helpful overview of the verses in both chronicles see Thea Summerfield, 'The Political Songs in the *Chronicles* of Pierre de Langtoft and Robert Mannyng', in *The Court and Cultural Diversity*, eds Evelyn Mullally and John Thompson, Cambridge, 1997, pp. 139–48; see also her *The Matter of Kings' Lives: The Design of Past and Present in the early-fourteenth-century Verse Chronicles by Pierre de Langtoft and Robert Mannyng*, Amsterdam, 1998, pp. 31–35, 153–4, 165–6.

14   Cambridge University Library Hh.6.9; Trinity College, Cambridge O.9.1; BL Harley 753 and Harley 2256; Lambeth Palace 331; Holkham Hall 670; Huntington Library HM 131; University of Chicago 254; University of Illinois 116. For the most recent listing of manuscripts of Page's work see A. S. G. Edwards, '*The Siege of Rouen*: A Bibliographical Note', *Notes & Queries*, n.s. 43 (1996), 403–4, correcting that by Rossell Hope Robbins in the revised *Manual of the Writings in Middle English*, vol.V, New Haven, 1975, 1665 [74].

15   As, for example, in Holkham Hall 670, BL Harley 266, BL Harley 753, Lambeth Palace 331, University of Illinois 116; for discussion of these manuscripts see Matheson, *The Prose Brut*, pp. 133–56.

manuscript, BL Harley 4690, while BL Stowe 69 includes Lydgate's 'Verses on the Kings of England', and Cambridge University Library Ee.4.31 and BL Sloane 2027 contain the continuation of Robert of Gloucester's *Chronicle*.

Such collocations indicate the ways in which some copyists or redactors of the *Brut* felt sufficiently unconstrained by the main form of their work to include relevant verse texts at various points. But some verses may have been part of the textual tradition of the *Brut* in a more rooted way and invested with a deeper ethnic and political significance, particularly with reference to Anglo-Scottish relations. There is, for example, the song supposedly sung by the victorious Scots after Bannockburn in 1314, 'Maydenes of Engelande sare may ye morne' (IMEV 2039.3) which appears in many manuscripts. The attempt to offer some version of a Scottish dialect here may bespeak the authentically Scottish nature of the text.

Nationalist factors also seem to obtain elsewhere. Many manuscripts include what is described as a 'tag made by the Scots in the reign of Edward III against the effeminate English' (IMEV 1934), 'Longe berdes herteles / peyntede hoode wytles'. In these instances verse is an anti-English mode: it is England's enemies alone who are given verse formulations in English. But many *Brut* manuscripts also include versions of one of the anti-Scottish verse passages from Langtoft.[16] All these passages are usually written as prose, but often rubricated or underlined in red to establish their verse identity. Occasionally, they are sometimes given an even more distinctive emphasis. One recurrent passage is an attack on Edward I.[17] In Cambridge University Library Ll.2.14, folios 144v–162, the phrase 'Edwarde with longe shankes' is used as the running title to the account of Edward's reign. Verse is used elsewhere in particular *Brut* manuscripts to underscore other ethnic antipathies, as in the verses against Flemings (IMEV 2657, 4034) found in two *Brut* manuscripts (Lambeth Palace 84 and 6 respectively) or in the verses added in National Library of Wales 21608, folio 88v, to present views 'in commendacioun' and 'in discommendacioun' of Llywelyn ap Gruffyd.[18]

Other chronicles regularly incorporate verse on principles of varying degrees of discernibility. In Trevisa's translation of the *Polychronicon* the great majority of the verse passages, and all those that have been hitherto recorded, occur in the translation of the opening book of the *Polychronicon*, on geography.[19] To some degree Trevisa's translations here are a reflection of his

---

16   IMEV 3558.5: 'These scaterande scottes / holde I for sottes'; cf. IMEV 841

17   IMEV 3918.5: 'Wende kynge Edwarde with his longe shankes to haue goten Berwike alle oure vnthankes'.

18   These are printed by William Marx, 'Aberystwyth, National Library of Wales, MS 21608 and the Middle English Prose *Brut*', *Journal of the Early Book Society* 1 (1997), 1–16.

19   Trevisa's treatment of verse in the *Polychronicon* has been the subject of some bibliographical confusion. The original IMEV did not include any apart from a verse

fidelity to Higden's original. For example, Higden did write one chapter, On Wales (Book I, ch.38), in verse, and Trevisa follows him in this respect. This is the longest of the verse passages in the *Polychronicon* and is regularly set out as verse in the manuscripts. But a number of the other passages Trevisa translates as verse in Book I seem to reflect conscious decisions to present passages in this way when Higden does not do so. The force of such decisions is, nonetheless, often obscured by scribes who, in most manuscripts, render many of these shorter verse passages as prose. There seems a general tendency either not to recognize or to suppress verse as a distinctive form, and to reduce it to the dominant prose mode.[20]

A not dissimilar situation occurs, albeit on a smaller scale, in John Capgrave's mid-fifteenth-century *Abbreuiacion of Chronicles*[21] where there are a few brief verse passages, usually in couplets. With one exception[22] these are all translations of Latin passages in Capgrave. In only one instance in Capgrave's holograph, Cambridge University Library Gg.4.12,[23] is the verse actually set out as verse. Even though Capgrave himself was an accomplished versifier, he does not seem to have felt that verse was a sufficiently significant or distinctive mode in his chronicle to be signalled as such.

The same may perhaps be said of the late-fifteenth-century *Scotichronicon* of Walter Bower. Although primarily in Latin prose, this does include a number of passages in Latin verse, and in its later books, particularly Book XIV, incorporates a number of passages in Scots verse.[24] In Bower's autograph manuscript, Corpus Christi College, Cambridge 171, all these passages are written as prose and are not distinguished in any way from the surrounding

---

preface occurring in a single manuscript, seemingly not by Trevisa himself (3252). IMEVS incorporated nine verse passages, but does so with less than total accuracy: it notes the inclusion of these verses in one manuscript, Pierpont Morgan M 875, where they do not appear at all, since this is a manuscript of Trevisa's translation of Bartholomaeus Anglicus's *De Proprietatibus Rerum*. And several verse passages are not noted in IMEVS in later books. (The latter will be detailed in our forthcoming revision of IMEV.)

20 Matters are further complicated by the decision of the editors of the only accessible edition, in the Rolls Series, to print some passages in later books as verse, particularly in Book VI, which are not verse, and which are not presented as such in the manuscripts, but which are Trevisa's prose translations of Higden's original Latin hexameters.

21 P. J. Lucas (ed.) *John Capgrave's Abbreuiacion of Cronicles*, Early English Text Society 285 (1983), pp. 134 (a quatrain), 173 (a couplet), 228 (2 couplets), 248 (3 couplets). None of these appears in IMEV/S.

22 That on p. 248.

23 That on p. 173.

24 All references are to *Walter Bower: Scotichronicon*, general ed. D. E. R. Watt (9 vols), Aberdeen, 1987–98: Book XIV, ch.4 (Watt 7: 262), Book XIV, ch.30 (Watt 7: 344), Book XIV, ch.31 (Watt 7: 348, 350), Book XIV, ch.32 (Watt 7: 352), Book XVI, ch.1 (Watt 8: 218).

prose narrative. Their significance is particularly hard to determine; are they material incorporated from other sources, oral or written, or were they composed specifically for the work itself?[25] Their localization to particular parts of the *Scotichronicon* seems to suggest access to a range of apposite vernacular verses rather than any more deliberate impulse to versify for particular purposes.

Matters are even more complex in the case of another brief verse passage in the *Scotichronicon*. It occurs in Book XVI, ch.1, beginning 'lauch liis down our all', and comprises four macaronic lines.[26] This is a passage that appears elsewhere as part of a longer work (IMEV 2787) of which it forms lines 13–16.[27] But confusingly the IMEV entry lists under this longer work a number of witnesses to the passage's independent circulation;[28] and further witnesses still are recorded separately as IMEV 1870.[29] Not surprisingly, the appearance of these lines in Bower is rather opaquely signalled in IMEVS.[30] But the implications of the fact are not explored. It would seem quite likely that Bower is drawing here on aphoristic material of a wide circulation over a long period in both Scotland and elsewhere.

Much the same issues are posed by another Scottish chronicle, that of Andrew Wyntoun. It is written chiefly in couplets, but one or two parts, like a passage on the defence of the Scots by the Duke of Orleans (IMEV 2697), survive separately in other manuscripts as well as in an extended version in the Maitland Folio Manuscript (Magdalene College, Cambridge Pepys 2553). Are Wyntoun and Maitland independently adapting a common source or is the latter extracting material from a manuscript of Wyntoun outside the surviving manuscript corpus? Elsewhere, in a lament on the death of Alexander III, the verse changes briefly from couplets to quatrains, a move that has earned this passage the status of 'a popular lament'[31] incorporated into Wyntoun. Could this metrical shift signal the incorporation of material otherwise circulating

---

25   For discussion of this problem see R. J. Lyall, 'The Lost Literature of Medieval Scotland', in *Bryght Lanternis*, eds J. Derrick McClure and Michael R. G. Spiller, Aberdeen, 1989, pp. 33–47, especially p. 37.

26   Book XVI, ch.1 (Watt 8: 218).

27   The fullest discussion of this entry and the manuscripts versions of it is in Nancy P. Pope, 'An Unlisted Variant of *Index of Middle English Verse* No. 2787', *Notes & Queries* n.s. 28 (1981), 197–99, to which we are indebted.

28   BL Royal 17 B.xvii, folio 99; Merton College, Oxford 248, folio 166v; the latter comprises only lines 13–14.

29   Three manuscripts are recorded here: Bodleian Laud misc. 213 (SC 1045), Bodleian Tanner 407 (SC 10234), and *olim* Brome, now Beinecke 365; for discussion of these versions see C. Louis (ed.) *The Commonplace Book of Robert Reynes of Acle*, New York, 1980, p. 398, where the relationship to 2787 is also noted.

30   Under 2787 there it is noted that '[vv. 13–16 occur in Joannis de Fordun [*sic*], Scotichronicon ...]'.

31   It is so characterized at IMEV 3923.5.

separately? Or could it be simply a way of underscoring a modal shift? There is no evidence that this passage did have any separate existence, so speculation as to its 'popularity' must remain wholly speculative.

Some other chronicles employ verse for an exemplary, summarizing function. There is a late-medieval Middle English prose chronicle in London, MS British Library Lansdowne 210, folios 14v–42v *passim*, which incorporates Lydgate's 'Verses on the Kings of England'.[32] Lydgate's poem is regularly written as verse; however it is not copied continuously but interspersed throughout the chronicle with the verse on each king accommodated to the appropriate reign. The verse seems to function as some sort of encapsulization of the larger prose narrative. A similar function is served by the verses that conclude John Shirley's chronicle of the death of James I of Scotland, a translation of lines ascribed to Jean de Meun.[33] Other verses seem to be inserted into chronicles through random access to illustrative material, as in the case of 'Davies' *Chronicle*'.[34] It includes, in what is otherwise almost wholly prose,[35] 'a balat . . . sette vppon the yates of the cyte of Caunterbury' in 1460 (folios 203-4).[36] Similarly there are only scattered verse passages in the so-called 'Gregory's *Chronicle*', BL Egerton 1995, the most extensive being the 'sotelties' for the banquet for Henry VI's coronation in 1432 (IMEV 1929). Here, as with other brief verse passages, the verse is once again written as prose, but underlined in red to signify its formal distinctiveness.[37]

In other chronicles the inclusion of verse is different again. The late-fifteenth-century *Liber Pluscardensis*, a Latin prose history of Scotland, includes only two poems in Middle English. One is an 'advice to princes' poem (IMEV 2818.8), that seems rather indeterminately located in the textual tradition: it does not appear in all the manuscripts of this work, and occurs elsewhere separately (in the Maitland Folio). The other poem, a lament of the Dauphin of France for the death of his wife Margaret (IMEV 3430), a Scottish

32 On Lydgate's poem see Linne R. Mooney, 'Lydgate's "Kings of England" and another Verse Chronicle of the Kings', *Viator* 20 (1989), 255–90, especially 277–8. To the manuscripts noted there may be added: Hatfield House, Cecil Papers 281, folios 139v–141; see Sarah Horrall, 'Lydgate's Verses on the Kings of England: A New Manuscript', *Notes & Queries* n.s. 35 (1988), 440; and BL Harley 2169, folios 1, 2, 3 (we owe this to the kindness of Professor Stephen Reimer).
33 See Margaret Connolly, '*The Dethe of the Kynge of Scotis*: A New Edition', *Scottish Historical Review* 71 (1992), 46–69, especially p. 69.
34 Now Bodleian Lyell 34; it was edited by J. S. Davies, *An English Chronicle from 1377–1461*, Camden Society, 1856.
35 It does also include (folio 194), two couplets ascribed to Peacock (IMEV 4181).
36 Edited by R. H. Robbins, *Historical Poems of the XIV and XVth Centuries*, New York, 1959, pp. 207–10.
37 The other verse passages are IMEV 1147.9 and 1240.5; see *The Historical Collections of a Citizen of London in the Fifteenth Century*, ed. James Gairdner, Camden Society, 1876, pp. 169–70, 174, 215.

princess, is similarly not a fixed part of the textual tradition. It survives in only two manuscripts, and is a translation of a French anonymous verse complaint on the same subject. It clearly suggests some form of opportunistic interpolation in some manuscripts based on the availability of such a translation, not on any more purposive sense of a relationship between verse and prose.[38]

In its mode and tone the lament for Margaret adumbrates the admixture of elegy and eulogy that is found with much greater frequency in later chronicles, particularly among the verse passages in Fabyan's *Chronicle*. This *Chronicle* survives in both manuscript and contemporary print[39] and contains about twenty-five separate verse passages which vary greatly in length and verse form, from two lines in poulters measure (TM 892) to fifty-eight lines in various verse forms (TM 1890). Most of the passages are in rhyme royal, but eight-line stanzas, quatrains and couplets are also used. Rhyme royal is used invariably in the predominant mode of the verse passages, laments for notable figures, particularly kings or emperors. Kings commemorated in this way include Richard I (TM 308), Richard II (TM 1323), Edward I (TM 1672, 1934), Edward II (TM 1264) and Edward III (TM 1265), Henry III (TM 1522) and Emperors Frederick I (TM 442) and II (TM 716); such verses may in some cases preserve epitaphs and the poems on funerary 'tables' which were sometimes displayed alongside tombs and burial places. Other verses in Fabyan are linked to specific occasions: the wind and snow on 24 May, 1294 (TM 1569), the execution of Hugh Spenser in 1316 (TM 2007), the death of the Lollard John Badby in 1410 (TM 1579) or are encomiastic as in the two poems in praise of Henry V (TM 910, 1201). Several of the verse passages in Fabyan's chronicle seem to have had a long prehistory in other contexts, as with the tag 'longe beerdys hartless' sung by the Scots in 1328 and incorporated into the *Brut*.

As its title suggests the interests of *The Great Chronicle of London* are much more parochial and the verse it contains reflects this. There is very little in it before the early sixteenth century: a Latin couplet on the early fifteenth-century heretic, John Badby;[40] *sotiltes* on the coronation of Henry VI in France in 1429 (IMEV 1029) and the 'ordenaunces made … a yenst the comyng of the kyng from his coronacion oute of Fraunce' in 1432 (IMEV 3799) (both these

---

38   For discussion of this poem see Priscilla Bawcutt, 'A Medieval Scottish Elegy and its French Original', *Scottish Literary Journal* 15 (1988), 5–13.

39   There are at least three manuscripts of Fabyan: BL Cotton Nero C. xi, Holkham Hall 671, and Harvard, Houghton Library Eng.766. There are editions by Pynson (1516, STC 10659) and Rastell (1533, STC 10660) as well as by later printers. Parenthetical references to 'TM' are to William A. Ringler Jr., *Bibliography and Index of English Verse in Manuscript 1501–1558*, London, 1992.

40   *The Great Chronicle of London*, eds A. H. Thomas and I. D. Thornley, London, 1938, p. 88. All references to the text of the *Chronicle* are to this edition, cited parenthetically by page.

also occur in Fabyan and Gregory). But from the early sixteenth century its poems are more extensive in their recording of metropolitan events. At times they celebrate the identity of London itself, as in the poem on the city sometimes ascribed to Dunbar (IMEV 1933.5) or recall moments of civic triumph, as with the reception of Katherine of Aragon in November 1501 (IMEV 1322.8). Some attack those who threaten the economic well-being of Londoners, like Empson (TM 1204) or John Grimald (TM 383). Others offer more generalized moral reflections (TM 986). As with earlier chronicle verse discussed here, *The Great Chronicle* draws largely on a sense of the potentiality of verse at a particular, contemporary moment in the sequence of events being tabulated and recalled. There is no sense of any larger design in which verse and prose were seen as complementary in contributing to the effect of such writing.

Indeed, this is the general conclusion one can reach about verse in chronicles. In both Middle English and Middle Scots it seems to have been incorporated randomly with no real suggestion that it possesses any distinct identity as verse; this much is clear from the difficulties that its recovery can often pose when it is embedded without differentiation into larger prose works like the *Polychronicon* and the *Scotichronicon*. Its identification remains a challenge for the bibliographer, the historian and the textual critic given the nature of its composition, circulation and preservation. The textual history of some verse fragments still remains obscure, as for instance, the famous warning 'Jack of Norffolke be not to bolde / For Dykon thy maister is bought and solde' (IMEV 1654.5), given to the Duke of Norfolk during Richard III's reign, but only preserved in the sixteenth century by Hall and Holinshed. Much remains to be clarified in relation to verses in chronicles, and it is likely that some further portion of 'lost' Middle English verse still remains to be identified within this corpus.[41]

---

41 Our forthcoming revision of the *Index of Middle English Verse* will seek to clarify a number of the bibliographical and textual questions we raise here.

AN ENGLISH READING OF BOCCACCIO: A SELECTIVE MIDDLE ENGLISH VERSION OF BOCCACCIO'S *DE MULIERIBUS CLARIS* IN BRITISH LIBRARY MS ADDITIONAL 10304

JANET COWEN

T HE TEXT which forms the sole item in British Library MS Additional 10304 has received little attention in recent decades. The quarto volume, of mixed paper and membrane, contains an anonymous rendering of selected chapters from Boccaccio's work on famous women, *De Mulieribus Claris*, into Middle English seven-line stanzas of the 'rhyme royal' type.[1] The English verses are written in a cursive script with mixed forms.[2] There are also chapter headings and some prefatory Latin verses in red in a humanistic script. The manuscript has no distinguishable contemporary marks of ownership.[3] Extracts were published in 1892,[4] and the whole text was edited in 1924,[5] since when the work has received a number of notices and brief discussions.[6]

---

1 See *List of Additions to the Manuscripts in the British Museum in the Years 1836–1840*, London, 1843, p. 28.

2 Ian Doyle has dated the hand to c.1440–60 (private communication). Watermarks resembling Briquet nos. 8597, 8601, 8602 and 8607, though inconclusive, appear consistent with this dating.

3 An erased inscription on fol. 46v, below the end of the main text, written apparently in English in a secretary hand, is not fully legible even under ultra-violet light. A note on fol. 1r attributes to the hand of Lady Elizabeth Darcy an English verse inscription on fol. 1v in a hand of the mid to later sixteenth century. I am grateful to Rivkah Zim for an opinion on this hand.

4 Julius Zupitza, 'Über die mittelenglische Bearbeitung von Boccaccios *De claris mulieribus* in der Handschrift des Brit. Mus. Add. 10304', in *Festschrift zur Begrüssung des fünften Allgemeinen Deutschen Neuphilologentages*, ed. J. Zupitza, Berlin, 1892, pp. 93–120.

5 G. Schleich (ed.) *Die mittelenglische Umdichtung von Boccaccios De claris mulieribus*, Leipzig, 1924.

6 J. Raith, *Boccaccio in der englischen Literatur von Chaucer bis Painters Palace of*

The opening stanzas of the text include a reference to Boccaccio's work on famous men:

> Iohn Bokase, so clepyde is his name,
> That wrote the fall of pryncys stronge and bolde,
> And into Englissh translate is the same.   (16–18)[7]

That this is a reference to Lydgate's translation of Boccaccio's *De Casibus* is indicated by the lines:

> Whan Iohn Bochas determyned was in mynde
> Of noble wymen a volume to wrytyne ...   (218–19)

which echo the opening lines of *The Fall of Princes*:

> Whan Iohn Bochas considred hadde & souht
> The woful fall off myhti conquerours ...   (I. 470–71)[8]

On this indication the composition of the translation can be dated after Lydgate's *Fall of Princes*.[9] A further implication is that the translator views his English version of Boccaccio's work on famous women as an extension of Lydgate's project; this is not dissimilar to the way Boccaccio, in his own preface, had referred back to Petrarch's compilation on famous men.[10] The

Pleasure, Leipzig, 1936, pp. 73–4; C. Brown and R. H. Robbins, *The Index of Middle English Verse*, New York, 1943, item 2642; F. L. Utley, *The Crooked Rib*, Columbus, Ohio, 1944, p. 219; H. G. Wright, *Boccaccio in England*, London, 1957, pp. 28–32; R. H. Robbins and J. L. Cutler, *Supplement to the Index of Middle English Verse*, Lexington, 1965, item 2642; P. M. Gathercole, 'Boccaccio in English', *Studi sul Boccaccio* 7 (1973), 353–68; E. Reiss, 'Boccaccio in English Culture of the Fourteenth and Fifteenth Centuries', in *Il Boccaccio nella Cultura Inglese e Anglo-Americana*, ed. G. Galignani, Florence, 1974, pp. 15–26; C. M. Meale, 'Legends of Good Women in the European Middle Ages', *Archiv* 229 (1992), 55–70; F. S. Stych, *Boccaccio in English: A Bibliography of Editions, Adaptations, and Criticism*, Westport and London, 1995, p. 77, item 683; p. 104, item 989 (where Schleich is listed misleadingly under criticism rather than under editions). Certain of these notices perpetuate the mistaken supposition that there existed a former Phillipps manuscript containing a second witness to the text, a mistake based on a confusion between the Middle English verse translation and the later prose translation by Henry Parker, see J. M. Cowen, 'The Translation of Boccaccio's *De Mulieribus Claris* in British Library MS Additional 10304 and "The Forty-Six Lives" Translated from Boccaccio by Henry Parker, Lord Morley', *Notes and Queries* 243 (1998), 28–9.

7   In citations from the text Modern English punctuation and capitalisation have been adopted, and abbreviations have been expanded silently.

8   H. Bergen (ed.) *Lydgate's Fall of Princes* Early English Text Society, e.s. 121–24, London 1924–27.

9   The composition of *The Fall of Princes* is dated 1431–38; see D. Pearsall, *John Lydgate (1371–1449): a Bio-bibliography*, Victoria, BC, 1997, p. 51.

10   Cf. the opening words of Boccaccio's preface: *Scripsere iam dudum non nulli veterum sub compendio de viris illustribus libros; et nostro evo, latiori tamen volumine et*

translator's apologia includes the lines:

> The whiche boke I haue had in purpose,
> If I in Englisshe cowde it clere expresse,
> To haue translatyd, but euer I dydd suppose
> Wythout grete ayde of sum noble pryncess
> All in veyne shuld be my besyness,
> For poetys ben of litell reputacyon
> That of estatys haue no sustentacyon.
>
> Neuertheless, wyth all my dilygence,
> Thof all I make full rude interpretacycon,
> I shall intende brevely in sentence
> Of this boke to make a translacyon.   (22–32)

How far this is a glance towards a specific potential patron, or how far simply an allusion to Boccaccio's own dedicatee, Countess Andrea Acciaiuoli, is uncertain.

Boccaccio's *De Mulieribus Claris*, in its final form, contained 106 chapters.[11] The English translator deals with twenty-one of these, which fall into discernible groups, as follows. The first ten (Eve, Semiramis, Ops, Juno, Ceres, Minerva, Venus, Io (or Isis), Europa, Libya) follow the order of chapters in what is considered to be the later stages of revision of Boccaccio's text.

---

accuratiori stilo, vir insignis et poeta egregius Franciscus Petrarca, preceptor noster, scribit. (*Tutte le opere di Giovanni Boccaccio*, ed. Vittore Branca, Vol. X: *De Mulieribus Claris*, ed. Vittorio Zaccaria, 2nd edn, Milan, 1970, p. 22, Proemio, 1.) Unless otherwise specified, references to Boccaccio's Latin text are to this edition, abbreviated as: *DMC*, ed. Zaccaria.

11   See P. G. Ricci, *Studi sulla Vita e le Opere del Boccaccio*, Milan and Naples, 1985, esp. pp. 125–35; V. Zaccaria, 'Le Fasi Redazionali del De Mulieribus Claris', *Studi sul Boccaccio* 1 (1963), 253–332; *DMC*, ed. Zaccaria, pp. 458–9. Several phases of authorial editing have been distinguished, culminating in the autograph copy which Boccaccio continued to annotate perhaps until his death (it is this autograph, MS Bib. Laur. Cod. Pluteo 90 sup. 981, which forms the basis of Zaccaria's edition). There is a difference of view between Ricci and Zaccaria as to the exact number of phases of redaction: Ricci argues for seven, Zaccaria for nine, both counting the revisions and corrections to the autograph as the two final phrases. But both agree that in its early stages the collection consisted of two sequentially composed, chronologically overlapping series, one beginning with Eve, the other with Ops, which, together with later additions, Boccaccio integrated into a chronological sequence such as is found in the bulk of the extant manuscripts. (*DMC*, ed. Zaccaria has 106 numbered chapters, since double chapter numbers are assigned to the two pairs of subjects Marpesia and Lampedo (XI and XII) and Orythia and Antiope (XIX and XX). In the Modern English translation, Giovanni Boccaccio, *Concerning Famous Women*, trans. Guido A. Guarino (New Brunswick, 1963, repr. London, 1964) which is based on the printed edition of Mathias Apiarius, Berne, 1539, these two pairs are numbered as single chapters, hence the total number of chapters is 104.)

After the first two, the subjects in this group are goddesses. The translator says that up to this point he has followed Boccaccio in describing *thies goddessys notable / In lyke orderr as he in Latyne hase* (982–83); now he will select those who after them were most to be commended *by their dedys laudable* (985). What do the criteria seem to be?

A glance at the corresponding numbers of Boccaccio's chapters shows that after the first ten the Middle English translator has abandoned Boccaccio's roughly chronological ordering scheme. Instead we find broadly thematic groupings, the shape occasionally accentuated by the translator's comments.

Camilla, the first subject in this reordered sequence, is introduced as *a quene and also a virgyne* (987).[12] The emphasis in her story, following Livy and Virgil, is on her independent life in the wild, her self-taught skills of hunting and weaponry, culminating in her support of Turnus in the war against Aeneas. The next two, Erythrea and Almathea, are sibyls, separated in the order of Boccaccio's chapters,[13] but paired in the English, and prefaced by an introductory stanza composed of comments from Boccaccio's chapter on Erythrea, giving an etymology of the word 'sibyl' as 'bearers of God in the mind' (*That in their myndys beren Godd of myght*, 1106).

The next group comprises three enchantresses, Circe, Medea, and Mantho.[14] To link together Circe and Medea, skilled both in magical incantations and herbal lore, the translator makes explicit the blood-relationship between them which is implicit in Boccaccio:

> Anodir lady of Cyrces consanguynyte …
> The kyngys doughter of Colchos, Oethe,
> Brodyr to Cyrces as I aforn rehersed.   (1289–92)[15]

The third of this group, Mantho, ends her days at Mantua, where, the translator adds (1420–21), Virgil was born. This added detail makes a neat link with the next pair of subjects, Sappho and Carmenta, two poetesses.[16]

The final group contains two warrior queens, Thamyris, queen of Scythia,[17] and Arthemesia, queen of Caria. Linking the two, and treated briefly (1625–38), is Thamaris, the Athenian painter, famous for her depiction of the goddess Diana at Ephesus. Thamaris and Arthemisia are the subjects of adjacent chapters in Boccaccio's text, the only case in the latter part of the work

---

12   *DMC*, ed. Zaccaria, ch. XXXIX.

13   *DMC*, ed. Zaccaria, chaps XXI and XXVI respectively.

14   *DMC*, ed. Zaccaria, chaps XXXVIII, XVII and XXX respectively.

15   Cf. *DMC*, ed. Zaccaria, XVII. 1: *Medea … Oete, clarissimi regis Colcorum, et Perse congiugis filia fuit*, and XXXVIII. 1: *Circes … filia fuit Solis et Perse nynphe … sororque Oethe Colcorum regis.*

16   *DMC*, ed. Zaccaria, chaps XLVII and XXVII respectively. (Carmenta is alternatively named in both the Latin and the Middle English texts as Nichostrata.)

17   *DMC*, ed. Zaccaria, ch. XLIX.

where the translator returns to Boccaccio's sequence.[18] Perhaps the coincidence of names caught his attention and led him to his final pair.[19] The result, perhaps produced by serendipity, can be viewed as a triptych in which one figure representing the arts of peace stands between two who represent the arts of war.

All of these subjects come from among the first fifty-seven of Boccaccio's chapters. There can be no way of knowing for certain whether the Middle English translator's source contained the whole of Boccaccio's 106 chapters, but it is clear from the concluding remarks that he had available to him more than he has translated here. He ends by saying that as it is expedient for a person on a long journey to pause and rest, so he will do the same, waiting to see whether the hearers are pleased with what has been done, and if so, he will proceed with *the residue of ladyes notable* (1788). It seems likely that to a certain extent the translator was working in a piecemeal fashion, and at the outset may not have known exactly what his source contained. This is the implication of an aside at the end of the story of Eve, in which female readers are bidden to remember that Eve's *bewte, wytt and womanhede* (359) exceed Dido, Criseyde and Helen, though these three were famous *as ȝe shall after rede* (361). But in fact none of these three is among the following subjects in the Middle English translation, and although Dido and Helen are in Boccaccio's collection and among the first fifty-seven chapters,[20] Criseyde is not in Boccaccio's text at all.

Yet despite this indication that the translator may have been feeling his way into the work, it is possible to infer some criteria for the selection of subjects. The achievements of the women chosen for the sequence which diverges from Boccaccio's chapter order seem to fall into three broad, partly overlapping categories, which continue certain themes introduced in the opening ten chapters: (1) government and conquest; (2) the invention or practice of arts and crafts, including literature; (3) prophecy. In the first category are Semiramis, Camilla, Thamyris queen of Scythia, and Arthemisia. In the second category are several of the subjects in the opening sequence of goddesses and founding mothers, famed as the originators of arts of civilisation such as agriculture (Ceres, Isis), the manufacture of textiles, weapons and musical instruments (Minerva), the use of numbers (Minerva), the use of laws (Isis), and the invention of letters (Isis). Sappho is famed in particular for the invention of a new metre (1443), Carmenta as the inventor of the Latin alphabet for the people of Italy (1497). Carmenta is also noted for great skill in prophecy (1466), the skill which

18 *DMC*, ed. Zaccaria, chaps LVI and LVII.

19 The Middle English text uses the same form of name for both the Scythian queen and the painter, and refers to the painter as *Anodyr Thamyrys* (1625). It seems likely that an identical name form for the two subjects would have been present in the source text. Identical forms are found, for example, in BL MS Harley 4923, fols 405v–406r and fol. 410r, and in BL MS Harley 6348, fols 32v–33r and fol. 35v.

20 Chaps XLII and XXXVII respectively.

defines the two sibyls (*cunnynge in prophecy*, 1100) and which is displayed also by Mantho, who foretells the future by pyromancy (1390), haruspication (1399) and necromancy (1402). To account for the selection of Circe and Medea we must look back to the opening stanzas, based on Boccaccio's preface, which outline a design including both good and bad examples, where fame is taken to encompass notoriety:

> For his intent so streyghtly is not taken
> All to speke of vertue and goodenesse,
> Noon to call noble but thei that forsaken
> Of vycyous lyvynge the vnthriftynesse,
> Butt ferthermore this name of worthynesse,
> Through the goode pacyence of the herersse,
> To vndirstond both of better and of wersse
>
> Which he knew in the world ouerall
> Most notable for ony manere dede,
> Those to remembre in especyall.   (120–29)[21]

Medea is specified in this connection:

> And let no man thynke incongruent,
> Bochase seith, thof all wyth Penelope,
> Lucrece, Sulpyce, ladyes excellent,
> Chaste and goode, mengelyd be Mede,
> Vnchaste Flora and also Semprone,
> The which hadd wittys odir excedyng
>
> But neuerthelesse vnclene was their lyvyng.   (113–19)[22]

It is in this deliberately extended, morally neutralised sense of *noble* and *worthynesse* that Circe and Medea can appear among those selected for their *dedys laudable*. In the immediate context of the Middle English selection, placed as they are between the two sibyls and Mantho, the detail which stands out is their knowledge of herbs, the first skill to be mentioned in each case (1230, 1296), and one of a number of types of knowledge, natural or supernatural, literal or technical, which, taken together, form a web of links between the various practitioners of literary, manual and magic arts. A

---

21 Cf. *Non enim est animus michi hoc claritatis nomen adeo strictim summere, ut semper in virtutem videatur exire; quin imo in ampliorem sensum – bona cum pace legentium – trahere et illas intelligere claras quas quocunque ex facinore orbi vulgato sermone notissimas novero (DMC*, ed. Zaccaria, Proemio, 6).

22 Cf. *Nec volo legenti videatur incongruum si Penelopi, Lucretie Sulpitieve, pudicissimis matronis, immixtas Medeam, Floram Semproniamque compererint, vel conformes eisdem, quibus pregrande sed pernitiosum forte fuit ingenium (DMC*, ed. Zaccaria, Proemio, 5).

possible link between these skills of learning, literacy and invention and the skills of the three warrior heroines Camilla, Thamyris and Arthemisia may be inferred by reference to other early Renaissance writings in which learned women are frequently linked to the Amazon queens and to other female warriors of myth and history.[23]

If we assume that the Middle English translator had at least the first fifty-seven chapters of Boccaccio's text available, then we may draw a further inference from what is omitted from the initial project of translation. Not included are subjects famed solely or primarily as examples of chaste and faithful wifehood. Even Boccaccio's first fifty-seven chapters afford several of these: Hypermnestra, who refused her father's command to murder her husband (ch. XIV); Argia, who cremated the body of her husband Polynices, despite Creon's prohibition (ch. XXIX); the Wives of the Mynians, who delivered their imprisoned husbands by the trick of changing clothes with them (ch. XXXI); Lucretia (ch. XLVIII); and, notably, Dido, who, as mentioned above, is named but not treated in the Middle English translation, and who in the version of her story given by Boccaccio is renowned as the faithful wife of Sychaeus (ch. XLII).

Certainly the qualities of chastity and fidelity are important to the Middle English translator, who includes the striking story of how Arthemisia built the famous Mausoleum as a cenotaph for her husband, but thinking no other receptacle fitter for his remains than her faithful body, consumed his funeral ashes with her daily drink. But this instance of wifely devotion forms only part of the story, and the final emphasis is on Arthemisia's part in the battle of Salamis, as equal in strength to the mighty Xerxes. It is in this latter respect that she is explicitly commended to a certain group of implied readers:

> Thynke on this, bothe duke, erle and knyght,
> And make no boste ageyns quene Arthemyse,
> Lest womanskyns bere awey the pryse.   (1776–78)

With not dissimilar effect the Middle English translator slightly alters the balance of queenship and virginity in his presentation of Camilla. She is introduced, as in Boccaccio, as bcth queen and virgin, but the Middle English translator considerably abbreviates and tones down the conclusion, where Boccaccio commends her as a model for young girls in avoiding the dangers of an extravagant and luxurious life, and instead underlines her queenly status by adding an account of her death in which her people lament her as a peerless ruler:

---

23 For some examples see M. L. King, 'Book-lined Cells: Women and Humanism in the Early Italian Renaissance', in *Beyond their Sex: Learned Women of the European Past*, ed. P. L. Labalme, New York and London, 1980, pp. 66–90.

> And beryed hyr wyth many a wepynge teere,
> For neuer ʒitt was suyche on reygnynge there.   (1091–92)

It has been argued by Ricarda Müller that in *De Mulieribus Claris* as a whole the subjects of Amazons and other martial women, prophetesses, and learned and artistic women comprise a significant proportion (over a quarter) of the whole, and that taken together they show a significant emphasis on traditionally masculine activities as patterns for female conduct, alongside which models of domestic and familial virtues, though commended, are somewhat eclipsed.[24] Müller argues further that *De Mulieribus Claris* is a *Frauenbuch* in two senses: a book about women and for women, written for a female public of noblewomen or well-to-do citizens who would be instructed and encouraged by it. In this view Boccaccio was encouraging a new role for women, not based on Christian ascetic ideals or on skills of household management, but on scholarly and artistic work.[25]

It is tempting to extend this interpretation to the Middle English translation, where examples of domestic and familial virtue scarcely feature, but that would be to take a single view of Boccaccio's text, which has conversely been viewed as misogynistic or at least deeply equivocal in praising women deemed extraordinary for achievements deemed masculine.[26] It is, however notable that the Middle English translator omits Boccaccio's explicit comments on the incongruity of male qualities in female bodies, as for example where the jocular exhortation to male readers (1776–78, cited above) concluding the story of Arthemisia replaces Boccaccio's comment that it must have been an error of nature to give female sex to so strong a body.[27] Yet the effect remains double-edged since, as Blamires has recently emphasised, it was as exhortations to men, not models for women, that examples of strong women were particularly recommended in standard rhetorical tradition.[28]

The Middle English text constructs a mixed readership, and offers adaptable exempla:

> All people I beseche vnyuersally,
> Men and wymen, that heron cast their ye

---

24 *Ein Frauenbuch des Frühen Humanismus: Untersuchungen zu Boccaccios De Mulieribus Claris*, Stuttgart, 1992. See especially pp. 129, 138–9, 141, 145.

25 *Ein Frauenbuch*, p. 171.

26 See, e.g., King, 'Book-lined Cells', 76; Meale, 'Legends of Good Women', 61; J. L. Smarr, 'Boccaccio and Renaissance Women', *Studi sul Boccaccio* 20 (1991–92), 279–97; A. Blamires, *The Case for Women in Medieval Culture*, Oxford, 1997, pp. 70, 180.

27 *Sed quid, Arthemisie acta spectantes, arbitrari possumus, nisi nature laborantis errore factum ut corpori, cui Deus virilem et magnificam infuderat animam, sexus femineus datus sit?* (*DMC*, ed. Zaccaria, LVII. 21).

28 Blamires, *The Case for Women*, p. 176.

To deme the best, for I thynk not disprayse
Men, thof noble wymen I shall prayse.   (53–56)

How far a potential audience might construe the aims and effect of the work as exemplary, instructional, or entertaining seems to me to be an open question.

Some further changes of emphasis, apparently made with a potential audience in mind, can be observed when the Middle English is compared with Boccaccio's Latin, particularly in personal names incidental to the main events, and place names presumably unfamiliar. Thus the Middle English text does not, for example, specify that the husband of Semiramis conquered the Bactrians,[29] or that Lake Triton, where Minerva was first seen, was not far from the gulf of lesser Syrtis.[30] It does not record the name of Circe's mother,[31] or the various sites and dedications of ancient temples of Venus.[32] It is possible that metrical considerations were at work in some of these cases, but nevertheless there appears to be a tendency to simplify and reduce the encyclopaedic character of Boccaccio's accounts.

Another kind of simplification is the omission of many of Boccaccio's references to conflicting sources, most notably in relation to the main subjects. Thus, for example, the Middle English does not contain Boccaccio's record that there was another goddess named Ceres, revered at Eleusis for the same qualities as his main subject,[33] or that, as some assert, there were many Minervas,[34] or that some authorities distinguish the Arthemisia who fought at the battle of Salamis from the widow of Mausolus.[35] Yet the translator does not seek to avoid a learned air, in places adding material from Latin sources, apparently from independent reading, naming Virgil (526, 1067, 1182, 1481), Ovid (856, 919, 1257) and Sallust (83, 136) where Boccaccio refers to authorities only in general terms.[36] Some of this additional material could derive from

---

29   *Afterward the kyng Ninus dydd dy, / That many cuntreys by myght hadd subiugate* (376–77); cf. *Sane Nino, omni Asya et postremo Bacthris subactis, sagitte ictu mortuo* (*DMC*, ed. Zaccaria, II. 3).

30   *Beside a lake callid Tritonium she was first seyne* (602); cf. *apud lacum Tritonium, haud longe a sinu Syrtium minori, primo visam* (*DMC*, ed. Zaccaria, VI. 1).

31   *Hir modyr was a nymphe of the occean* (1226); cf. *DMC*, ed. Zaccaria, XXXVIII. 1, see above, fn. 15.

32   Cf. *Nec solum apud Paphos, vetustissimum Cypriorum oppidum, thure solo placata est ... verum et apud nationes reliquas et Romanos, qui templum ei sub titulo Veneris genetricis et Verticordie aliisque insignibus olim struxere* (*DMC*, ed. Zaccaria, VII. 6); this passage has no equivalent in the Middle English text.

33   *Fuit praeterea et Ceres altera apud Eleusim ... eisdem meritis penes suos clara* (*DMC*, ed. Zaccaria, V. 4).

34   *Sunt tamen non nulli gravissimi viri asserentes non unius Minerve, sed plurium que dicta fuisse comperta* (*DMC*, ed. Zaccaria, VI. 9).

35   *Sunt tamen qui velint non Arthemisiam hanc fuisse, sed Arthemidoram, eque Alicharnasi reginam* (*DMC*, ed. Zaccaria, LVII. 9).

36   See Schleich (ed.) *Die mittelenglische Umdichtung*, pp. 100–5.

Lydgate, but not all of it; for instance there are additions to the story of Camilla, who does not feature in Lydgate's works.

There is the question whether the translator was working directly from the Latin or from an intermediary, in particular from the French translation which on chronological grounds has to be considered as an available source. Previously attributed to Laurent de Premierfait but now regarded as anonymous, this French translation is dated to 1401 from the final colophon.[37] For the purposes of the present paper, comparison has been made with the modern edition and with BL MSS Royal 16 G V and Royal 20 C V, which have been placed among the earliest family.[38] This comparison has revealed nothing corresponding to the apparently distinctive features of the Middle English text, thus far bearing out the translator's claims to Latinity made both in the reference to the main source (*I haue described thies goddessys notable / In lyke orderr as he in Latyne hase*, 982–83) and in the allusions to Latin authors cited above.

One small but specific indication that the Middle English depends on a Latin rather than a French text is found in the stratagem employed by Semiramis to prevent the women of her court from seducing her son, namely by compelling them to wear lockable protective garments termed by Boccaccio *femoralia*.[39] The Middle English translator leaves out this passage, but uses this distinctive word in an earlier passage relating how Semiramis disguised herself as her son to keep control of her army:

> Femorals also of new inuencyon
> She vsyde, that noon shulde vndirstonde
> Hyr sex naturall ...   (393–95)

where Boccaccio says simply that she wore trousers.[40] The French translation does not have the word *femoralia* at either point, reading in the first case *couvry aussi ses bras et ses cuisses en certaine maniere* and in the second case *pourpensa l'usage des braiers*.[41]

There is however a notable error in the Middle English text which at first sight appears to cast doubt either on the translator's Latinity or on the quality of his source, and which has gone curiously unremarked. Boccaccio relates how Arthemisia took part in Xerxes' campaign against the Greeks, leading her

---

37   See Carla Bozzolo, *Manuscrits des traductions françaises d' œuvres de Boccace, XVe siècle, Medioevo e Umanesimo*, 15, Padua, 1973.

38   Jeanne Baroin and Josiane Haffen (eds) *Boccace 'Des Cleres et Nobles Femmes'* (2 vols), Paris, 1993–95, based on Bib. Nat. MS 12420. See vol. I, pp. x–xiii for an account of the manuscript relations.

39   *prima usum femoralium excogitavit, eis omnes aulicas cinxit sub conclavi* (*DMC*, ed. Zaccaria, II. 15).

40   *brachiis cruribusque velamentis* (*DMC*, ed. Zaccaria, II. 5).

41   Baroin and Haffen (eds) *Boccace 'Des Cleres et Nobles Femmes'*, vol. I, pp. 20, 39–40; pp. 23, 152–3; cf. BL MSS Roy. 16 G V, fols 6v, 7v; Roy. 20 C V, fols 9r, 10v.

armed ships into the battle, fighting keenly on Xerxes' side, as though she had changed sex with him, so that if Xerxes' spirit had been as bold and daring as hers, his fleet would not so easily have turned in flight.[42] The Middle English, however, reads:

> She cessyd not, but also on the ses
> Faught wyth 3erses and put hym vnto flyght.   (1772–73)

– thus placing her squarely on the wrong side in the battle of Salamis. It is easy to see how such a misunderstanding could arise from a reading of Boccaccio's account, which is very condensed at this point, relating that when Xerxes had attacked Greece, Arthemisia was sent for.[43] The agent of the summons is not specified, and without prior knowledge of the story it is possible to read Boccaccio's account back-to-front from this point on. The potential for confusion is illustrated in a textual variant found in one Latin manuscript witness at another point in the account. Where the autograph reads *in navale prelium Xerxis classis et Atheniensium ... convenissent*,[44] BL MS Harley 6348 fol. 36r reads *Arthimieñ* (or perhaps *Arthinnieñ*), a reading which may have already resulted from, and could have given rise to a confusion of names and a substitution of the name of Arthemisia at this point – a substitution which is in fact found in some early printed editions of the Latin text.[45] The misunderstanding explicit in the Middle English may have been triggered by a confusion already present in the textual tradition of the source.

Such a confusion may have also affected the French translation, as evidenced by the following reading: *Xerces, le roy des Persans qui estoit trespuissant, fust venus contre les Lacedemones, et ja oultre par devers eulx eust remply toute leur terre de gens de pié, sans nombre, et tout le rivage fust plain et occupé, de ses nefs et de ses barges, et par son jugement il cuidast non pas tant seulement prendre Grece et mettre en subjection, maiz destruire tout entierement, lors la royne Arthemese requise et mandee sy vint les secourir.*[46] The referent of *les secourir* is ambiguous, but it seems that Arthemisia is here envisaged as helping the Greeks, for the text continues with a reference to

---

42   *acriter pugnans, quasi cum Xerxe sexum mutasset, visa est adeo ut, si tam audax robustusque Xerxi fuisset animus, non facili classis eius proras vertisset in fugam* (*DMC*, ed. Zaccaria, LVII. 18).

43   *Xerxes, Persarum rex potentissimus, terras pedestribus exercitibus complesset, et litus omne occupasset classibus, omnem suo iudicio non capturus sed absorturus Greciam, requisita Arthemisia, cum armatis navibus venit in bellum* (*DMC*, ed. Zaccaria, LVII. 18).

44   *DMC*, ed. Zaccaria, LVII. 18.

45   I. Czeiner, Vlme, 1473, fol. lxᵛ; M. Apiarius, Bernae, 1539, fol. xlr.

46   Baroin and Haffen (eds) *Boccace 'Des Cleres et Nobles Femmes'*, vol. II, pp. 19–20. BL MSS Roy. 16 G V, fol. 71rv and Roy. 20 C V, fol. 93r have substantively the same reading.

battle *dedens les nefs du nauire de Xerce le roi et des Arthemesiens*, a reading which could have arisen from the substitution of *Arthemisia* for *Athenians* in an exemplar. But even if the French translation contains the same misunderstanding as the Middle English, albeit more opaquely expressed, this does not seem sufficient ground for proposing dependence of the Middle English on the French rather than the Latin, given the potential for coincident misreading embedded in the compact Latin narrative, and the indications that such misreading may have arisen early in the textual tradition.

Further evidence of the translator's Latinity is found in the two sets of Latin verses, in elegiac couplets, found respectively on folio 2r, before the beginning of the English text, and on folios 7v–8r, between the Prologue and the story of Eve. The first set, which deploys some of the topics from Boccaccio's own proem, opens:

> Anglica femineas resonancia carmina laudes
> Ordine septeno dicere Musa iubet.[47]

The references to English, and to an arrangement in sevens, allude presumably to the following translation in seven-line stanzas, and the reference to the commanding Muse implies that these Latin verses are by the translator himself.

This paper has presented indications that the Middle English translation is made from the Latin rather than the French, that the selection in the Middle English text is the translator's own, and that the selection of at least the last eleven subjects is guided by a thematic interest (albeit one which might have developed while the work proceeded). Furthermore the translator seems to have had some acquaintance with, and some reason to emulate Lydgate's verse. Not enough is yet known about the language and likely provenance of the manuscript to enable inferences to be drawn about the potential addressees or about the absence of the promised continuation, but attention to this text enhances our picture of Boccaccio's reception in the fifteenth century.[48] The Middle English version shows an appreciation of Boccaccio as a Latin writer by an English translator working in partial imitation of Lydgate.

---

47 'The Muse commands songs in English, arranged in sevens, sounding the praise of women.'

48 On the fifteenth-century English perception of Boccaccio as a Latin rather than an Italian writer see Reiss, 'Boccaccio in English Culture', pp. 23–5.

ABBREVIATIONS, OTIOSE STROKES AND EDITORIAL PRACTICE: THE CASE OF SOUTHWELL MINSTER MS 7[1]

ROGER DAHOOD

I

'**B**EFORE the advent of printing', Malcolm Parkes has observed, 'a text left its author and fell among scribes.'[2] Scribes, however, are not invariably malefactors, and knowledge of their writing habits has proven a powerful tool for deepening our understanding of manuscript texts. Copyists behave more or less consistently, and in cases of sustained copying, characteristic patterns emerge even from the work of scribes least concerned to reproduce their originals exactly.

Editors, paleographers, dialectologists, and other students of ancient language have long recognized the importance of such scribal patterns. Patterns of miscopying common to many scribes enable editors to distinguish general classes of scribal error, such as omission of lines through eye-skip or misreading of similar letter forms. Patterns within a single manuscript enable editors to identify the *modus scribendi* of a particular copyist and to distinguish with greater assurance than would otherwise be possible scribal from authorial features of a text. Patterns also form the basis of the 'linguistic profiles' in the *Linguistic Atlas of Late Mediaeval English*, from which scholars make inferences about the geographic distribution of written language features and of spoken

---

1   I am grateful to the Cathedral and Parish Church of the Blessed Virgin Mary, Southwell Minster, and the late Harold Brooke, Cathedral Librarian, for supplying a microfilm of MS 7, and to the Cathedral Council and the current Cathedral Librarian, Laurence Craik, for photographs of fols 3r and 181r and permission to publish them. I am grateful also to the Bodleian Library, Oxford, and in particular to Tricia Buckingham for supplying a microfilm of MS Gough Eccl. Top.4. The essay has benefited from T. F. Hoad's penetrating reading of an early draft.

2   M. B. Parkes, *Pause and Effect: An Introduction to the History of Punctuation in the West*, Berkeley and Los Angeles, 1993, p. 70.

features no longer directly accessible.[3] Especially important for the subject of the present essay, knowledge of scribal habits can also be a safeguard against exclusion of linguistically significant data from edited texts. The present essay focuses on one MS, but the discussion has implications for the study of other late Middle English manuscripts and the history of written English.

II

Parkes reserves the label 'otiose' for 'a superfluous stroke – one which does not form part of a letter, and which does not indicate an abbreviation'.[4] 'Otiose', it may be added, does not apply to such extra-literal strokes as punctuation marks, carryover marks that do the job of modern line-end hyphens, insertion and deletion marks, and marks indicating beginnings or ends of various kinds of formal unit, such as paragraph and section markers. The point of the label 'otiose' is to characterize extra-literal pen strokes, purely decorative in function, that might be mistaken for abbreviation marks.

Southwell Minster, Nottinghamshire, MS 7, a portion of which Saara Nevanlinna and Irma Taavitsainen have usefully edited, is a paper codex from about 1500, containing a copy of Mirk's *Festial* and eight saints' lives. The manuscript is written in Shropshire dialect in a Secretary hand with a small number of Anglicana forms.[5] My particular topic is the loop on final <r>[6] in MS Southwell. As editors have long recognized, such loops, which in Latin texts regularly stand for final <e>, may in Middle English texts be otiose.[7] Figure 3 shows a portion of the *Festial*.[8] At the beginning of line 20, in Latin quoted from Matthew 25:34–35, appears the word <manducare> with looped <r> (hereafter <r'>). From Latin grammar, morphology, and spelling we infer the loop to be an abbreviation of <e>. The inference is secure because Latin morphology and spelling are highly consistent, and final <e> is grammatically

---

3   A. McIntosh, M. L. Samuels and M. Benskin (eds), *Linguistic Atlas of Late Mediaeval English* (4 vols), Aberdeen, 1986.

4   M. B. Parkes, *English Cursive Book Hands: 1250–1500*, 1969; repr. London, 1979, p. xxvi, hereafter cited as *ECBH*.

5   M. Wakelin, 'The Manuscripts of John Mirk's *Festial*', *Leeds Studies in English* n.s. 1 (1967), 93–118, dates the manuscript to 'just after 1500' (110), citing information from N. R. Ker. N. R. Ker and A. J. Piper, *Medieval Manuscripts in British Libraries* (4 vols), Oxford, 1969–92, assign MS Southwell to the end of the fifteenth century (IV, p. 351). On the dialect and handwriting, see also S. Nevanlinna and I. Taavitsainen (eds) *St Katherine of Alexandria: The Late Middle English Prose Legend in Southwell Minster MS 7*, Cambridge and Helsinki, 1993, pp. 35, 55.

6   Throughout the present essay angle brackets designate spellings and graphemes without regard to phonemic content.

7   An explicit statement and discussion may be found in Parkes, *ECBH*, p. xxix.

8   It has been practical to include photographs only of folios 3r (Figure 3) and 181r (Figure 4).

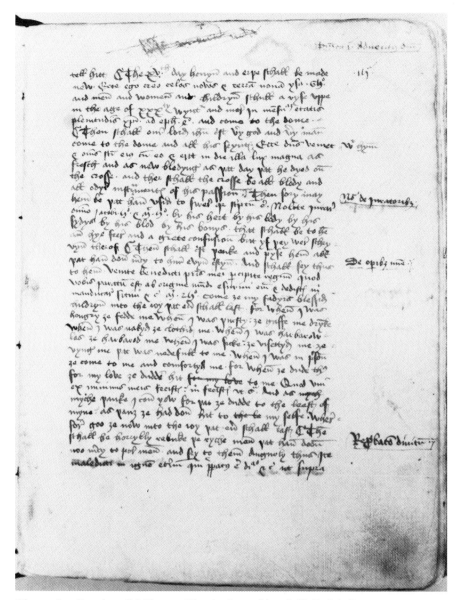

Figure 3   Southwell Minster, Nottinghamshire, MS 7, fol. 3r.

and morphologically necessary.[9] What to make of the loop in English <feer'>, the noun 'fear' (line 15), is not so clear. It could indicate final <e> or it could be

9   Parkes, *ECBH*, p. xxix.

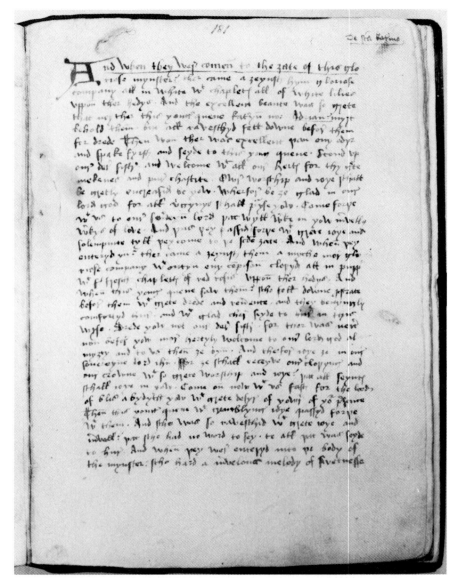

Figure 4   Southwell Minster, Nottinghamshire, MS 7, fol. 181r.

otiose, for in late Middle English a spelling with or without final <e> is conceivable.

The *modus scribendi* of MS Southwell offers little guidance, for in the case of most words ending in <r>, <r'>, and <re>, the different spellings occur in no discernible pattern. The adverb 'there' and the pronoun 'their', for example, appear indifferently as <ther> and <ther'>.[10] The adverb 'here' most frequently appears as <her'>, but in headings and explicits it appears as <here> (for example, fol. 175r, line 2).[11] Also, in the compound adverb 'hereafter', the first element appears both as <her-> (fol. 175v, line 25) and <here-> (fol. 175r, line 6).

As Figure 3 illustrates, the Southwell scribe had in his repertoire three types of <r>: the 2-shaped <r> as in <erþe> (line 1), the forked, long <r> as in Latin <erit> (line 8) and with a loop in <feer'> (line 15), and the short or right-shouldered <r> as in <harbarow-> (line 23). The 2-shaped and long <r> appear medially and finally. Examples of medial 2-shaped <r> are frequent after <o>, as on folio 181r (Fig. 4) in <gloriose> (line 2) but occur also after other letters, as in <drede> (line 7). Examples of medial long <r> appear also on Figure 4, as in <encreasid> (line 11). Examples of final 2-shaped <r>, as in <ther> (Fig. 4, line 18), and of final long <r'>, as in <mor'> (Fig. 4, line 16), are frequent. Instances of unlooped, word-final long <r> are rare (for example, fol. 1v, line 14 <ther>). The short <r> appears initially, medially, and finally. Examples of initial short <r> occur in Figure 4, lines 6 and 30 in <ravesch(y)(i)d>, and of word-final short <r> on folios 1v, line 10 <aftyr> and 5v, line 2 <Syr>. In the portions of the microfilm that I have examined, thirty-five out of 202 folios, I have found no examples of 2-shaped <r'> or short <r'>.

Final <r'> is frequent in suffixes, variously spelled and of various origin, that correspond to Modern English <-er>. Thus, <r'> appears where final <e> would be historical, for example, in 'never' and 'ever' from OE *(n)æfre*, where the modern unstressed vowel is parasitic, and in words where final <e> would be unhistorical, as in 'after', 'hither', and 'sister', from OE *æfter*, *hider*, and *sweostor*, *-er*, respectively. Final <r'> also occurs in words that ended in vowels other than <e> in earlier stages of English, for example, in 'more' from OE *mara*. It is also frequent in derivatives of Old English words that ended in <r>, such as *hwær* 'where' and *ðær* 'there'. In some words the scribe loops the second <r> of a double <r> spelling. On folio 2v, line 2 <harr'> is a comparative adjective 'higher', and a final <e> would be historical, but final <e> would not be historical in the adverb <ferr'> 'far' from OE *feor(r)* on folio 4r, line 28. On folio 178r, line 14 'far' occurs also in the historically accurate spelling <fer>. The <r'> is frequent in Old French borrowings in <- o)(u)r>, such as 'labor' and 'honor'.

For completeness I note in folio 8v, line 25 a loop that must signify final <e> in the French loan <contre> 'country'. The loop seems to my eye to be formed

10 The adverb also frequently occurs with initial <þ> instead of <th>. In such cases the standard abbreviation for <er> without final <e> is usual.

11 References to fols 175r through 189r can be checked against the printed text in Nevanlinna and Taavitsainen, *St Katherine*, pp. 67–95. The printed edition preserves manuscript lineation.

by a broad downstroke followed by a curving hairline connecting the top of the broad stroke to the right fork of the long <r>. The constituent strokes are more contrastive than are those of the other loops under consideration. The scribe conceivably differentiated two kinds of loop, corresponding, on the one hand, to stressed /e:/ and, on the other, to schwa or, if the ordinary style of loop is otiose, nothing at all, but such a distinction would be unusual, for abbreviations normally represent letters, without regard to sound. The distinctive form of the loop in <contre> seems unlikely to have significance for the present discussion.

Although the Southwell scribe's apparently indiscriminate use of his long <r'> encourages the view that the loop is otiose, Nevanlinna and Taavitsainen exhibit ambivalence about its status. In most cases they suppress the loop as otiose, but when a final <r'> would be syllabic, they expand to <re> (for example, <sistr'>, Fig. 4, line 22).[12] On folio 7v, line 26 the direct object <fadre>, corresponding to OE accusative sg. *fæder*, occurs, with unhistorical final <e> spelled out. The spelling suggests that the principle of expanding Southwell final <r'> where unexpanded <r'> would be syllabic is defensible, but the principle offers no guidance where final <r'> is not syllabic. The presence in MS Southwell of a few other final <e> spellings, however, as on folio 179v, line 26 <where> and folio 186r, line 27 <nature> (vs. fol. 186v, line 4 <natur'>), suggests that expansion of all instances of <r'> to <re> would be compatible with the manuscript orthography.

There is also positive evidence that the loop is an abbreviation for <e>. In examining the microfilm I have been able to discern a distinctive pattern of variation between <r> and <r'>. The pattern as far as I can determine is restricted to the collocations <or> and <or'>. In this part of the discussion I will rely heavily on the text of *St Katherine*, because the word index in the Nevanlinna and Taavitsainen edition greatly facilitates location of relevant forms. On folio 181r, as throughout *St Katherine*, the second element in the compounds 'before', 'therefore', and 'wherefore' invariably ends with long <r'>, whereas the free-standing preposition and conjunction 'for' appears invariably with an unlooped, 2-shaped final <r> (Fig. 4, lines 6, 7, 9, 11, 12, 20, 22, 23, 24, 25, and 27). In *St Katherine*, 'before' and 'wherefore' occur twenty-five times each, 'therefore' ten times, and free-standing 'for' 122 or 123 times.[13] Outside of *St Katherine* I have checked the microfilm of the first twenty-one folios of the *Festial* and found one instance, on folio 12v, line 32,

---

12 Nevanlinna and Taavitsainen, *St Katherine*, p. 56 and n.76.
13 Nevanlinna's and Taavitsainen's Index of Words and Forms reports 124 occurrences (*St Katherine*, p. 137), but one is an emendation in which the editors supply the missing <r>. Another has eluded me. At two places there are possible extra strokes in the vicinity of the 2-shaped <r> (fol. 184v, line 11 below the <r> and 185v, line 30 above the <r>), but it is not clear whether they are penstrokes, stray marks, or flaws in the film.

of conjunction 'for' not with 2-shaped but with long <r>. Remarkably it, too, is unlooped. The scribe could have availed himself of either the spelling <fore> or the spelling <for'> for the preposition and conjunction, or he could have written 'before', 'therefore', and 'wherefore' with <-for>, but he did not.[14] The consistency with which the scribe chooses between <-r> and <-r'> in the '-)for(e' words suggests a deliberate distinction. It is difficult to conceive of a purely calligraphic rule that would prohibit final <r'> in free-standing 'for' but would allow it when 'for' is the final element of a compound.[15] A spelling distinction seems far more likely, and a spelling distinction would imply that the loop stands for <e>.

The hypothesis of a spelling distinction is compatible with the occurrence on folio 15v, line 28 of <therfore>, showing that the scribe used the spelling with final <e>, and with his writings of the adverb 'more' and the compound 'moreover.' All nine occurrences in St Katherine of free-standing 'more' are written with long <r'>. In the compound, which occurs twice in St Katherine, on folio 175r, line 27 the first element is written with long <r'> as <mor'> and on folio 175v, line 10 with 2-shaped <r> as <more>. The treatment of 'therefore', 'more', and 'moreover' suggests that in the Southwell hand after <o> the graphs long <r'> and <re> are orthographically interchangeable, whereas the treatment of free-standing 'for' and the second element of compounds 'before', 'therefore', and 'wherefore' suggests that after <o> the graphs <r> and <r'> are orthographically distinct. That is, the loop stands for final <e>.

If I am correct that in the scribe's spelling system final <r'> is orthographically distinct from final <r> and corresponds to <re>, the alternation between <r'> and <r> is an example of 'orderly variation', to use James Milroy's phrase.[16] The variation is not based strictly on etymology, for if it were, free-standing 'for' and the second element of 'wherefore' and 'therefore', which are historically identical (from OE *for*), would be treated the same. On the other hand, etymology can explain <befor'> as reduced from OE *beforan*. The <-fore> and <-for'> spellings of 'wherefore' and 'therefore' in MS Southwell may result from analogy with spellings of 'before' or from an orthographic rule the motivation for which is lost.

Since we know, however, that by early Modern English <e> serves to indicate length in a preceding stressed vowel, it is worth considering whether <e>

---

14 The ratio of preposition to conjunction in St Katherine is about 3:4. From as early as the thirteenth century, the spelling <-e> for the preposition is attested in a range of authors and works, including Laȝamon, *Sawles Warde*, *Pearl*, Gower, and Lydgate. The spelling <-e> for the conjunction is rare.

15 The scribe also writes the conjunctions 'nor' and 'or', which occur seventeen and fifteen times, respectively, in St Katherine, like free-standing 'for' only with unlooped <r> and never with final <e>.

16 J. Milroy, 'Middle English Dialectology', in *The Cambridge History of the English Language*, ed. N. F. Blake, vol. II, Cambridge, 1992, pp. 194–6.

in MS Southwell is a diacritic. A check of the word index to *St Katherine* reveals that <e> is often superfluous, occurring after short stem vowels (for example, <gladde> beside <glad> 'glad', <hedde> beside <hed> 'head'). More often, however, the scribe appends it to words with historically long vowels (for example, <arose>, <awoke>, <feete> 'feet'). It is thus tempting to conjecture that in MS Southwell the development of <e> as diacritic, written out or abbreviated in <r'>, may be happening in an embryonic way, especially after <o>.[17] Diacritic <e> would be inappropriate after unstressed short *o* in 'for', 'nor', 'or', 'forgete', and 'forgrowe', and even after a stressed but short *o*, as in 'forrest.' From all of the preceding <e> and <r'> are consistently absent. The diacritic would, however, be appropriate in 'wherefore' and 'therefore', if as in Modern English these words in Middle English have length and perceptible stress in the second syllable.

In the frequent instances of <r'> after short suffix vowels, namely the equivalents of modern <er> spellings, a diacritic <e> is unlikely, although variant spellings <a>, <y>, and <u>, in, for example, <pledar'>, <accusars>, <undyr'>, and <bettur> (fols 3v, lines 9, 12, 22, and fol. 21r line 10), suggest distinctions in suffix vowel quality and a degree of stress. After short stem vowels a diacritic function for <r'> is almost certainly out of the question.

Still, after short suffix and short stem vowels <r'> may be susceptible of explanation. Fifteenth-century spellings of <e> after historically short suffix and stem vowels are documented and indeed occur in at least one other manuscript of the *Festial*, Oxford, Bodleian Library, MS Gough, Eccl. Top.4 (for example, fol. 24r, line 31 <afture> 'after').[18] It happens also that the Southwell scribe writes 'far' as both <ferr'> and <ferre> (for example, fol. 181v, line 29), and that <ferr'> appears in MS Southwell (fol. 4r, line 28) where in the corresponding narrative MS Gough has <ferre> (fol. 3v, line 7).[19] Although I have no sure explanation for unhistorical, non-diacritic final <e>, there can be no doubt that such Middle English spellings exist or that they are part of the Southwell scribe's repertoire. He may have used the loop in place of his exemplar's final <e>.

---

17 Final <e> as a diacritic, the culmination of pronunciational and grammatical changes that began in Early Middle English, became sufficiently established by 1582 that Richard Mulcaster recognized it as a marker of vowel quantity and quality, terming it 'qualifying e'; E. T. Campagnac (ed.) *Mulcaster's Elementarie*, repr. Ann Arbor and London, 1980, p. 123 and *passim*. The practice of using <e> as a diacritic became regular during the seventeenth century; D. G. Scragg, *A History of English Spelling*, Manchester and New York, 1974, pp. 79–80.

18 The text is printed in T. Erbe (ed.) *Mirk's Festial: A Collection of Homiles by Johannes Mirkus, Edited from Bodl. MS. Gough Eccl. Top.4, with Variant Readings from Other MSS*, Early English Text Society, e.s. 96, 1905, p. 40, line 20.

19 Erbe (ed.) *Mirk's Festial*, p. 5, line 29.

III

For its potential to contribute to a more precise history of final <e> in English spelling, the Southwell scribe's rigorous observance of the <-or>/<-ore> distinction is of special interest. If the distinction is purely orthographic, MS Southwell provides a glimpse of an early stage in the development of the modern spelling distinction between <-or> and <-ore> words. If the diacritic hypothesis has merit, MS Southwell may be taken to illustrate an early manifestation of diacritic <e> in a spelling system in which long, stressed *o* was already regularly marked but long, stressed *e* in adverbs 'where' and 'there' was not. By 1582, however, Richard Mulcaster would acknowledge final <e> in 'there' and 'where' as established by custom.[20]

The implications of MS Southwell also for editions of late Middle English manuscripts are potentially far-reaching. Expansion of <r'> in MS Southwell and possibly other late manuscripts can preserve valuable orthographic and perhaps phonological information. If orderly variation can be identified in the case of other extra-literal strokes, editors may have reason to expand those graphs as well.

Finally, the present study may have implications for the textual history of Mirk's *Festial*, now thought to be contemporary with writings of Langland.[21] The Southwell copy falls into Wakelin's Group A, manuscripts that by contents and localization are probably closest to Mirk's original.[22] Examination of final <r(e>/<r'> spellings in other Group A manuscripts, though beyond the scope of the present investigation, might prove fruitful for determining whether the pattern in MS Southwell is a feature of Mirk's own language. Even if the pattern of final <r(e>/<r'> in MS Southwell should prove uncharacteristic of *Festial* manuscripts, it may yet prove a constant in other manuscripts and perhaps an indicator for localizing such manuscripts to the region near Lilleshall.

20 Campagnac (ed.) *Mulcaster's Elementarie*, p. 138.
21 S. Powell, 'A New Dating of John Mirk's Festial', *Notes and Queries* 227 (1982), 487–9, dates *The Festial* to between 1350 and 1390. More recently, Alan Fletcher (*Medium Aevum* 56 (1987), 217–24) has argued for a date 'between 1382 and 1390, probably at the latter end of those years, on the grounds that Mirk knew something of the activities of the Lollards' (p. 218). I am grateful to Sue Powell for calling the Fletcher essay to my attention.
22 Wakelin, 'The Manuscripts', p. 113.

TEMPORAL AND SPIRITUAL INDEBTEDNESS IN THE *CANTERBURY TALES*

ELTON D. HIGGS

I

IF WE WERE to play a game of Chaucer trivia that asked about references to indebtedness in the *Canterbury Tales*, we might think immediately of the Merchant, of whom *Ther wiste no wight that he was in dette* (GP, line 280);[1] or of the Wife of Bath, who brags of having successfully manipulated the 'marriage debt' of conjugal obligation to her own advantage; or perhaps of the Shipman's Tale, in which the sly monk Daun John and the merchant's wife engage in a commercialization of the marriage debt which the Wife of Bath herself could hardly have outdone. There are, in fact, seventeen occurrences of forms of the word 'debt' in the *Canterbury Tales*,[2] ten of them explicitly referring to the conjugal debt in marriage, two (in the Parson's Tale) involving indebtedness to God, one referring to keeping a promise, and the other four having to do with financial debt.

But in addition to the verbal references to debt, there are a number of circumstances in the *Tales* in which the concept of indebtedness – an obligation to fulfil societal expectations or the terms of an agreement – form a vital part of the tale-teller's comments and the action of the story. I wish to demonstrate the extent to which the concepts of material, social, and spiritual indebtedness are outlined in the General Prologue and developed in several of Chaucer's *Tales*,

---

1 References to the *Canterbury Tales* will be from *The Riverside Chaucer*, ed. Larry D. Benson, 3rd edn, Boston, 1988. In order to facilitate reference to other editions, I will use the following abbreviations for the General Prologue and the Tales: GP – General Prologue; WBT – Wife of Bath's Prologue and Tale; PardT – Pardoner's Prologue and Tale; ShT – Shipman's Tale; FrankT – Franklin's Tale; ParsT – Parson's Tale; MLT – Man of Law's Tale; MerT – Merchant's Tale; FriT – Friar's Tale.

2 Conjugal debt: MerT 1452, 2048; WBT 130, 153, 155; ShT 397, 413; ParsT 375, 938, 941; to God: ParsT 251, 370; keeping a promise: MLT 41; financial debt: GProl 280, 582; FriT 1615; FrankT 1578.

and to argue that these various concepts of indebtedness constitute a central focus in the *Canterbury Tales*, which serves to illustrate how often in human affairs the attempt to manipulate obligations to one's own advantage ironically results in only superficial or ambivalent success.

The groundwork is laid implicitly in the General Prologue for the complex treatment of ideas of indebtedness in the *Tales*. Although the mention of the Merchant's possible concealed debt is the only explicit reference to indebtedness in the General Prologue, it is striking to notice how consistently the characters presented there are evaluated according to whether they manifest any sense of responsibility toward God or toward others – that is, whether they have any sense of indebtedness, temporal or spiritual.[3] As I have argued elsewhere,[4] the positive models of moral responsibility in the General Prologue are the Knight, the Clerk, and the Parson/Plowman pair, and each of these represents a particular kind of fulfilment of obligations and standards of behaviour.[5] The Knight, in his worthiness (GP 43, 47, 50, 68), loves *chivalrie, / Trouthe and honour, fredom and curteisie* (GP 45–46) and is summed up as *a verray, parfit, gentil knyght* (GP 72); the Clerk's sense of obligation is focused on both learning and teaching *gladly* (GP 308), as well as on praying for the souls of the friends who support him (GP 299–302); and the brotherly pair of Parson and Plowman between them fulfil the obligations to supply spiritual and physical food to society, the former by shepherding his parishioners with holy devotion and the latter by fulfilling the two highest divine commands of love (with the attendant acts of service) toward God and toward neighbour. None of the other pilgrims shows any serious sense of moral obligation, tending rather to maintain an image than to cultivate character; and most of them are characterized by the degree to which they ignore or reject expected standards of behaviour and embrace inferior, substitute objectives. The set of pilgrims presented between

---

3   P. Eberle notes that 'all the pilgrims are described in terms of how they go about getting a living or how they go about spending it' ('Commercial Language and the Commercial Outlook in the General Prologue', *Chaucer Review* 18 (1983), 162). See also R. Nevo's classic article, 'Chaucer: Motive and Mask in the General Prologue', *Modern Language Review* 58 (1963), 1–9. My treatment of the Prologue, however, puts more emphasis on the figurative and spiritual implications of indebtedness than does either of these two articles.

4   E. D. Higgs, 'The Old Order and the "Newe World" in the General Prologue of the *Canterbury Tales*', *Huntington Library Quarterly* 45 (Spring, 1982), 155–73.

5   P. Strohm, *Social Chaucer*, Cambridge, MA, 1989, pp. 85ff, identifies the Knight, the Parson, and the Plowman as the 'three most traditional characters of the Canterbury pilgrimage', representing 'the three recognized orders of feudal society' (85) and each serving as 'an exemplar of certain transcendent values' (85). Obviously my focus on the Clerk instead of the Plowman as the third ideal pilgrim places more emphasis on where the three fall in the structure of the General Prologue than on their being representative of a social class, though in the cases of the Knight and the Parson that is certainly relevant.

the Knight and the Clerk (from the Squire through the Merchant) are more concerned with creating the appearance of nobility or high social standing than with the substance of these qualities; the group coming between the Clerk and the Parson are, in contrast to the Clerk, committed to satisfying or aggrandizing themselves by irresponsibly using practical or theoretical knowledge; and the last set of pilgrims (following the Parson/Plowman pair, from the Miller through the Pardoner) includes several of the most blatantly self-serving scoundrels of the whole group, people who thumb their noses at the kind of social responsibility modelled by the Parson and the Plowman.

Chaucer extends this focus on the fulfilment or non-fulfilment of social and spiritual indebtedness from the General Prologue into the *Tales*, most obviously in those that hinge on some kind of pact or agreement set up between the characters in the stories to create indebtedness. The most salient of these (with their respective Prologues) are, I would argue, the Wife of Bath's Tale, the Friar's Tale, the Summoner's Tale, the Clerk's Tale, the Franklin's Tale, the Pardoner's Tale, and the Shipman's Tale (given in their Ellesmere MS order). These seven all show a contract purposely entered into by two or more characters, attended by the unexpected complications attached to attempts to pay, or require payment of, the contracted indebtedness. I would like to concentrate, however, on only four of this septet of tales: those by the Wife of Bath, the Pardoner, the Shipman, and the Franklin.

I justify this narrowing of focus by the following observations. (1) The Wife of Bath and the Pardoner, in their confessional Prologues, are the most forthright of all the pilgrims in their rejection of the conventional formulations of their indebtedness to moral or societal norms, and therefore an examination of their performance as pilgrims gives us special insight into Chaucer's evaluation of those strong personalities who found themselves to be at cross-currents with society but were radically motivated to justify or even glorify their wilful refusal to 'pay what they owe' (to use the words of *Piers Plowman*) to man and/or to God. Moreover, the pacts entered into in their tales show precisely the dangers of creating and committing oneself to an obligation that is inferior to the divine imperative and only personally and situationally defined. (2) Two others of the seven tales (the Franklin's Tale and the Shipman's Tale) share with the Wife of Bath's Tale the joint themes of marriage and the conjugal debt, which is the kind of debt most often mentioned explicitly in the *Canterbury Tales*.

What the four tales I have chosen to discuss have in common is that they manifest a complex interweaving of temporal and spiritual indebtedness, especially in presenting various kinds of contractual arrangements that make problematical the paying of debts or the fulfilment of obligations. Two of the four (the Wife of Bath's Tale and the Shipman's Tale) involve parodies or misapplications of conjugal debt, and the Pardoner's Tale turns on another kind of sacramental indebtedness sacrilegiously pursued; all three of these tales show the tellers and the characters in their tales choosing to make light of both divinely and socially mandated obligations. The Franklin, though serious enough about the need for honouring social debts, nevertheless proposes superficial resolutions to the conflicting obligations presented in his tale. All four of these tale-tellers underestimate or ignore humanity's ultimate indebtedness incurred through sin and the Fall.[6]

II

The Wife of Bath begins her Prologue with a long defence of her not living up to the commonly accepted religious and societal principles which would be expected to govern her life as a wife and a woman. In response to the implied reproach that she has not fulfilled her debt to the ideals of purity and abstinence, she argues rather for her indebtedness to nature and to the obligations of marriage. She does not accept the conventional doctrine outlined by the Parson in his sermon (ParsT 858–60), which warns that taking pleasure in sexual activities is spiritually dangerous, even in marriage; and she takes Paul's command to marriage partners to pay their sexual debts to each other (I Cor. 7:1–3) as an encouragement for them also to take mutual pleasure in paying that debt.[7] If this means that she is only *barly-breed* instead of *breed*

---

6   Gail M. Gibson ('Resurrection as a Dramatic Icon in the Shipman's Tale', in *Signs and Symbols in Chaucer's Poetry*, eds J. P. Hermann and J. J. Burke, University, AL, 1981, pp. 102–12), speaks of the tale's 'preoccupation with pay' even while its characters are oblivious to a 'much larger and nontemporal reckoning' (p. 104). And J. P. Hermann ('Dismemberment, Dissemination, Discourse: Sign and Symbol in the Shipman's Tale', *Chaucer Review* 19 (1985), 302–37) points out how 'each character fails to understand that there is a final reckoning of accounts … within a larger spiritual economy' (p. 327). As will be seen below in the discussion of the Pardoner's Tale, R. Adams emphasizes 'debt' understood as 'that which is owed to God', the 'debt' of sin' ('The Concept of Debt in The Shipman's Tale', *Studies in the Age of Chaucer* 6 (1984), 90).

7   Feminist literary and social critics have pointed out the ambivalent effects of medieval discussion and interpretation of the mutual conjugal indebtedness outlined and advised by Paul in this passage ('The husband should give to his wife her conjugal rights, and likewise the wife to her husband. For the wife does not rule over her own body, but the husband does; likewise the husband does not rule over his own body, but the wife does. Do not refuse one another except perhaps by agreement for a season, that you many devote yourselves to prayer; but then come together again, lest Satan tempt you through lack of self-control' (I Cor. 7:3–5, RSV)). On the one hand, a strict construction of Paul's words would have to recognize that 'Paul's purpose for marital union was not specifically procreative. He emphasized instead a conjugal obligation, binding both husband and wife, for the maintenance of conjugal chastity' (E. Makowski, 'The Conjugal Debt and Medieval Canon Law', in *Equally in God's Image: Women in the Middle Ages*, eds J. Holloway, C. Wright and J. Bechtold, New York, 1990, p. 130). On the other hand, Augustine, reinforced by Gratian and later scholars of canon law, while accepting legalistically the force of the Apostle's dictum, nevertheless so stressed the dangers of lust even in conjugal relations that 'they all but

of pured whete seed (WBT, 143–44), so be it.

> In swich estaat as God hath cleped us
> I wol persevere; I nam nat precius.
> In wifhode I wol use myn instrument
> As frely as my Makere hath it sent.
> If I be dangerous, God yeve me sorwe.
> Myn housbonde shal it have both eve and morwe,
> Whan that hym list com forth and paye his dette.
> An housbonde I wol have, I nyl nat lette,
> Which shal be bothe my dettour and my thral,
> And have his tribulacioun withal
> Upon his flessh whil that I am his wyf.
> I have the power durynge al my lyf
> Upon his propre body, and noght he.
> Right thus the Apostel tolde it unto me,
> And bad oure housbondes for to love us weel.
> Al this sentence me liketh every deel –   (WBT, 147–62)

But we see that she has given the command of Paul a twist of her own; she sees the marriage debt as a way to gain power over her husbands, at least over the first three, through whom she became rich.[8] They were *goode, and riche* (WBT, 197), and so *olde* that

> Unnethe myghte they the statut holde
> In which that they were bounden unto me.
> Ye woot wel what I meene of this, pardee.
> As help me God, I laughe whan I thynke
> How pitously a-nyght I made hem swynke!
> And, by my fey, I tolde of it no stoor;
> They had me yeven hir lond and hir tresoor.

---

stripped it [the Pauline teaching] of its positive intent' (Makowski, 'Conjugal Debt', p. 139). Dyan Elliott ('Bernardino of Siena versus the Marriage Debt', in *Desire and Discipline: Sex and Sexuality in the Premodern West*, J. Murray and K. Eisenbichler eds, Toronto, 1996, pp. 168–84) points out, moreover, that concurrent with a legalistic emphasis on the importance and inescapability of the conjugal debt was an 'apparently contradictory insistence on female subordination' (170). As to the Wife of Bath's own application of the Pauline-defined conjugal debt, Warren B. Smith ('The Wife of Bath Debates Jerome', *Chaucer Review* 32 (1997), 129–45) argues that she 'arrives at ... [an] Augustinian view of celibacy and marriage which triumphantly defends a literalist interpretation of the Bible [i.e., I Cor. 7], against the mischief of its male glossators' (130).

8   J. F. Cotter ('The Wife of Bath and the Conjugal Debt', *English Language Notes* 6 (1969), 169) observes that for the Wife of Bath, 'the *debitum* binds only one party, the husband, and it is the basis of the wife's *maistrye* over him'.

Me neded nat do lenger diligence
To wynne hir love, or doon hem reverence.

       *   *   *

And sith they hadde me yeven al hir lond,
What sholde I taken heede hem for to plese
But it were for my profit and myn ese?
I sette hem so a-werke, by my fey,
That many a nyght they songen 'weilawey'.

                        (WBT, 198–206; 211–16)

Although she invokes the authority of 'the Apostle' for the marriage debt, she puts aside the mutuality of the obligation and uses it as a weapon. We can only infer Dame Alice's justification for such cruelty as she practises toward her old husbands: that because they have used their money to gain her consent to marriage, she is free to use her sexual powers to gain control of them and thereby enrich herself with their money.[9] Indeed, she boasts that she has freed herself of any 'indebtedness' toward these three, because their relationship has become a 'free market' transaction in her eyes:

I wolde no lenger in the bed abyde
If that I felte his arm over my syde
Til he had maad his raunsoun unto me;
Thanne wolde I suffre hym do his nycetee.
And therfore every man this tale I telle,
Wynne whoso may, for al is for to selle;
With empty hand men may none haukes lure.
For wynnyng wold I al his lust endure
And make me a feyned appetit –
And yet in bacon hadde I nevere delit.
That made me that evere I wolde hem chide;
For thogh the pope hadde seten hem biside,
I wolde nat spare hem at hir owene bord,
For, by my trouthe, I quitte hem word for word.
As helpe me verray God omnipotent,
Though I right now sholde make my testament,
I ne owe hem nat a word that it is nys quit.   (WBT, 409–25)

In this passage, we see a subtle change that has developed in Dame Alice's account of the control she has exerted over her husbands. Whereas up to this

---

9   A. B. Murphy, 'The Process of Personality in Chaucer's Wife of Bath's Tale', *Centennial Review* 28 (1981), 211, says that the Wife of Bath 'claims to be talking about marital power, in terms of sexuality and misogyny, but her language is more concerned with financial power, in terms of money and land'.

point she has dealt with conjugal debt as a universal obligation (albeit one in which she takes psychological and financial advantage of her impotent old husbands), she now speaks of *quiting*, or paying back, in a specific, personal, and vengeful sense; she has slid easily from the marriage debt as a divinely sanctioned concept, however insincerely she uses it, to making sure that she triumphs in the quarrelsome verbal battles with her husbands.[10] As she alludes to making her *testament*, or will, she brings up the image of people arranging in such documents the use of their estate to pay off any debts that have been left at their death. But in her concentration on *quiting*, rather than even the appearance of the positive mutuality expected in the conjugal debt, Alice has abandoned arguing universal principles in favour of asserting her superiority in the rather tawdry exercise of marital bickering.

It is not surprising, then, that there are complications when the Wife launches out to marry for love, rather than for money. Her fourth husband was *a revelour* and led her a merry chase with his *paramour*; but she felt herself equal to the situation and once again *he was quit*, for she *made hym of the same wode a croce* (WBT, 453, 454, 483, 484). It was not until the fifth husband, however, that she was willing to relinquish control of *al the lond and fee / That evere was me yeven therbifoore* (WBT, 630–31), and that turned out to be a big mistake from her point of view. Although she endured his beatings because *in oure bed he was so fresshe and gay* (WBT, 508), when he tried to subdue her psychologically with his stories of wicked wives (as he no doubt thought it his duty to do), she reasserted herself and, evidently concluding that she could not afford to be under obligation to anyone, she regained *the governance of hous and lond, / And of his tonge, and of his hond also, so that / After that day we hadden never debaat* (WBT, 814–15; 822). She might have been satisfied with the mutual payment of the marriage debt without the security of her own financial base, but she will not tolerate a one-sided indebtedness unless she is the creditor; and it seems that having firmly established the tie between financial and sexual control, she cannot function without both.

The Wife of Bath's fable illustrates several aspects of the concept of debt: the knight is temporarily absolved of his debt of death for his crime and is obligated in recompense to perform the quest assigned him by the court ladies; he becomes indebted to the hag for the answer to the riddle and keeps his word by complying with her demand that he marry her; but he will not pay the sexual marriage debt on their wedding night, and his wife, like Dame Alice, turns his

---

10 R. A. Shoaf, *Dante, Chaucer, and the Currency of the Word*, Norman, OK, 1983, observes that the practice of perverse *quiting* in the *Canterbury Tales* reflects a pattern of human failure to practise 'mutual and just exchange', and he sees this kind of unjust exchange as manifested equally in the commercial marketplace and in the 'category of ethics from the perspective of positive justice' (167–68). In his book as a whole he explicates the historical and social context for the kind of manipulation or creation of both material and spiritual obligations for personal profit seen here in the Wife of Bath.

unpaid debt into a weapon to subdue him to her will. The hag's lecture deals with the true source of *gentilesse* (and the implied indebtedness of *noblesse oblige*), which is not based on high heritage and possessions, but on *gentil dedis*; poverty, moreover, is presented as the producer of great virtues. I submit that the lecture on *gentilesse* is of the same cloth as Dame Alice's attempt to turn over her goods to her fifth husband; both show that the Wife of Bath's desire for money is not for its own sake, but to create a context in which she can afford to chart her own course, which includes looking for the kind of mutual sexual relationship ideally assumed in the biblical doctrine of conjugal debt. But for her, paradoxically, the prerequisite for paying her marriage debt with pleasure is being free from the constraint of owing anyone anything. She soon finds, however, that such a state cannot be maintained indefinitely. As moderns steeped in secular assumptions, we are likely to miss the pathos,[11] from a medieval point of view, of her fleeting admission that her means of control – a sexual magnetism which enables her to be indebted only on her own terms – is temporal and is limited by the spirit of commercial transaction in which she has pursued it.

> But age, allas, that al wole envenyme,
> Hath me biraft my beautee and my pith.
> Lat go, farewel, the devel go therwith!
> The flour is goon, ther is namoore to telle;
> The bren, as I best kan, now moste I selle;
> Yet to be right myrie wol I fonde.   (WBT, 474–79)

We see in the offing, even if Dame Alice chooses to gloss over it, her mortality and the spectre of death, which is the final, unavoidable debt of mankind.

III

A refusal to face his debt of death also characterizes the Pardoner. Like the Wife of Bath, he must be in control of things, and he recognizes no absolute authority; but unlike her, he holds a bitter view of the world, and that makes

---

11   Several studies of the last fifteen years have noted the ambiguity of the Wife's triumphs. See R. J. Meyer, 'Chaucer's Tandem Romances: A Generic Approach to the Wife of Bath's Tale as Palinode', *Chaucer Review* 18 (1984), 221–338; Barbara Gottfried, 'Conflict and Relationship, Sovereignty and Survival: Parables of Power in the Wife of Bath's Prologue', *Chaucer Review* 19 (1985), 202–24; Peggy A. Knapp, 'Alisoun of Bathe and the Reappropriation of Tradition', *Chaucer Review* 24 (1989), 45–52; and Kathryn L. McKinley, 'The Silenced Knight: Questions of Power and Reciprocity in the Wife of Bath's Tale', *Chaucer Review* 30 (1996), 359–78. McKinley's article asserts that although the Tale presents at the end 'a state of ideal married love and reciprocity' (376), the Wife of Bath does not comprehend the deeper point of her own tale ('seems to have little residual knowledge of the *gentilesse* so carefully articulated by the hag' [375]).

him, in his own words, *a ful vicious man* (PardT, 460).[12] There is something frightening about his willingness to be openly blasphemous in his dallying with sin and forgiveness and, in his tale, with death. He sells his *relics* and chants the theme *Radix malorum est cupiditas* with astounding financial results: *By this gaude have I wonne, yeer by yeer, / An hundred mark sith I was pardoner* (PardT, 389–90). But he makes it a point to deny any actual concern for the spiritual welfare of those whom he exploits:

> Of avarice and of swich cursednesse
> Is al my prechyng, for to make hem free
> To yeven hir pens, and namely unto me,
> For myn entente is nat but for to wynne,
> And nothyng for correccioun of synne.
> I rekke nevere, whan that they been beryed,
> Though that hir soules goon a-blakeberyed!   (PardT, 400–06)

The furthest thing from his mind is to live in poverty or to do honest work (PardT, 439–51), whatever the consequences for those poor people whom he persuades to give him money. The only debt he acknowledges in Chaucer's presentation of him is to tell a tale according to the rules of Harry Bailly's game and to make it a moral tale in response to the outcry of the *gentils* (PardT, 323–28) among the pilgrims; and even that is merely to prove he can do it.

In the 'sermon' prelude to his narrative, the Pardoner deals with the tavern sins of drunkenness, gambling, and swearing, each one more sacrilegious and spiritually perilous than the one before it. In this homily there are repeated

---

12   Several critics have set forth the opinion that the Pardoner is not as bad as he makes himself out to be. See E. Reiss, 'The Final Irony of the Pardoner's Tale', *College English* 25 (1963), 260–6; J. L. Calderwood, 'Parody in the Pardoner's Tale', *English Studies* 5 (1964), 302–9; J. Halverson, 'Chaucer's Pardoner and the Progress of Criticism', *Chaucer Review* 4 (1970), 184–202; M. McAlpine, 'The Pardoner's Homosexuality and How It Matters', *Publications of the Modern Language Association of America* [hereafter *PMLA*] 95 (1980), 8–22; and J. F. Rhodes, 'Motivation in Chaucer's Pardoner's Tale: Winner Take Nothing', *Chaucer Review* 17 (1982), 40–61. I agree more with the assessment of the Pardoner's character by A. C. Spearing in the introduction to his edition of *The Pardoner's Prologue and Tale* (Cambridge, 1965), where he stresses the fascinating horror of the Pardoner's brazen, but seductive, blasphemy. E. Stockton, 'The Deadliest Sin in The Pardoner's Tale', *Tennessee Studies in Literature* 6 (1961), 47–59, says that evil and sacrilege permeate the Tale, even though the Pardoner doesn't realize the extent to which he is identified with them; and M. Storm, 'The Pardoner's Invitation: Quaester's Bag or Becket's Shrine?', *PMLA* 97 (1982), 810–18, emphasizes the Pardoner's 'function as fraudulent substitute' (p. 812) as he tries to divert the pilgrims' attention from their sanctified destination. See also M. Stevens and K. Falvey, 'Substance, Accident, and Transformations: A Reading of the Pardoner's Tale', *Chaucer Review* 17 (1982), 142–58, where the authors stress the absorption of the Pardoner into the metamorphosis of life into death and decay depicted in his tale.

references to death as the penalty of sin, and to contempt for Christ's deliverance from that death, which prepare for the haunting tale of death that follows.

> O original of oure dampnacioun,
> Til Crist hadde boght us with his blood agayn!   (PardT, 500–01)

> 'They been enemys of cristes croys,
> Of whiche the ende is deeth; wombe is hir god!'   (532–33)

> But certes, he that haunteth swiche delices
> Is deed whil that he lyveth in tho vices.   (547–48)

> 'By goddes armes, if thou falsly pleye
> This daggere shal thurghout thyn herte go,'
> This fruyt cometh of the bicched bones two –
> Forsweryng, ire, falsnesse, homycide.
> Now for the love of crist, that for us dyde,
> Lete youre othes bothe grete and smale.   (654–59)

All of the sins described by the Pardoner are exemplified by the Rioters in his story, and the connection between false swearing, greed, and death is intensified in the tale.

As has been pointed out by several critics,[13] the response of the three Rioters to the ravages of Death is a capstone of blasphemy, for the pact to slay death echoes the New Testament identification of that task solely with Christ Himself: 'For he must reign until he has put all his enemies under his feet. The last enemy to be destroyed is death' (I Cor. 15:25–26, RSV). That way of conquering death is closed to the Rioters, however, as they blaspheme the death of Christ and launch out on their own perverse and presumptuous mission:

> And many a grisly ooth thanne han they sworn,
> And Cristes blessed body they torente –
> Deeth shal be deed, if that they may hym hente!   (PardT, 708–10)

Thereby they deny their spiritual indebtedness ('The wages of sin is death': Rom. 6:23) and nullify the only source of payment for it; and in depicting their

---

13   The most incisive commentary on the theme of death in the Pardoner's Tale is, in my opinion, D. Pearsall, 'Chaucer's Pardoner: The Death of a Salesman', *Chaucer Review* 17 (1983), 358–65. He says that 'the death that the rioters find is no more than the physical correlative, an allegorical enactment, of the death that they have already undergone' and cites Romans 8:13. See also W. B. Toole, 'Chaucer's Christian Irony: The Relationship of Character and Action in the Pardoner's Tale', *Chaucer Review* 3 (1968), 37–43; and M. Pittock, 'The Pardoner's Tale and the Quest for Death', *Essays in Criticism* 24 (1974), 107–23. Both Toole and Pittock note the 'blasphemous parody' (Pittock, 'Quest', p. 113) entailed in the Rioters' actions against Death and each other. I. Bishop, 'The Narrative Art of The Pardoner's Tale', *Medium Aevum* 36 (1967), 15–24, notes the negative echoes of I Cor. 15:54 and Rom. 6:23 in their actions.

action the Pardoner unwittingly reflects the state of his own soul.[14]

When the Rioters meet the Old Man, we are presented with a contrast between rebellious seekers of death and a submissive seeker for death. Much conjecture has been set forth concerning the significance of the Old Man,[15] but I have not seen any recognition of the similarity of his ambivalent desire for death (which includes a willingness to abide alive *As longe tyme as it is Goddes wille* [PardT, 726]) to Paul's statement in Phil. 1:23–24 (RSV): 'I am hard pressed between the two. My desire is to depart and be with Christ, for that is far better. But to remain in the flesh is more necessary on your account.' Only with such submission can death be encountered without one's being destroyed by it. The three Rioters rush headlong to an accounting in which the

---

14   See Pittock, 'Quest', pp. 118–23; Pearsall, 'Chaucer's Pardoner', pp. 363–4. The reflection of death in the Pardoner himself is also noted by Shoaf (*Dante, Chaucer, and the Currency of the Word*), who says that the 'mixture of truth and lies [promulgated by the Pardoner] resembles the mixture of life and death in the Pardoner', associates him with the devil as the source of death and the Father of lies, and makes him a 'living death' (p. 212). M. Higuchi ('On the Integration of the Pardoner's Tale', *Chaucer Review* 22 (1987), 161–9), through a linguistic analysis of the frequency and pattern of *deeth* and related words in the Pardoner's Tale, concludes that 'the Pardoner associates himself with "death" both through his lack of productivity [sterility] and through his sins' (165), and that the word *deeth* is 'the integrating factor in the Pardoner's Tale' (167).

15   Nearly everyone who comments on the Pardoner's Tale has an opinion on the Old Man. In the past, the debate about his significance has centered on the extent to which he is to be interpreted symbolically or allegorically. C. Dean, 'Salvation, Damnation, and the Role of the Old Man in the Pardoner's Tale', *Chaucer Review* 3 (1968), 44–9, summarizes the major arguments in the debate up to that point and attempts a synthesis of them. The most elaborate allegorical interpretation is that of R. P. Miller, 'Chaucer's Pardoner, the Scriptural Eunuch, and the Pardoner's Tale', *Speculum* 30 (1955), 180–99, in which he identifies the Old Man with the *vetus homo* of sinfulness (cf. Rom. 6–8). One of the most recent articles in the same vein is L. O. Purdon, 'The Pardoner's Old Man and the Second Death', *Studies in Philology* 89 (1992), 334–49. In contrast to this allegorical approach, W. J. B. Owen, 'The Old Man in The Pardoner's Tale', *Review of English Studies* n.s. 2 (1951), 49–55, minimizes any symbolic significance of the Old Man. Pittock, 'Quest', pp. 115–16; Pearsall, 'Chaucer's Pardoner', p. 363; Halverson, 'Chaucer's Pardoner', p. 202; and Takami Matsuda, 'Death, Prudence, and Chaucer's Pardoner's Tale', *Journal of English and Germanic Philology* 91 (1992), 316, note, as I do, that the Old Man's sensitivity and humility in the face of death contrast with the Rioters' gross irreverence and lack of understanding. More recently, F. Hoerner ('Church Office, Routine, and Self-Exile in Chaucer's Pardoner', *Studies in the Age of Chaucer* 16 (1994), 69–98) pulls together the views of several post-modern critics (e.g. Patterson and Dinshaw) on the Old Man by saying (pp. 89–95) that the Pardoner, in his commitment to the image and the supporting routine he has created for himself, refuses to embrace the body-shattering image of the Old Man, when by doing so he might experience 'contrition's power' (92) that would bring him what he longs for but is powerless to effect (in the same way that the Old Man seeks death and can direct others to it but cannot experience it himself).

illusion of great wealth is turned into the absolute deprivation wrought by physical and spiritual death.

As he concludes his tale, does the Pardoner see the point of it in spite of his hard heart and finally try awkwardly to step aside from the callousness of his blasphemous exploitation (*And Jhesu Crist, that is oure soules leche, / So graunte yow his pardoun to receyve, / For that is best; I wol yow nat deceyve* [PardT 916–18])? Or does he merely compound his reprobate condition by seeing how far he can carry his overweening joke?[16] I'm not sure, but it seems obvious to me that after Harry Bailly's painfully pointed repartee (PardT, 946–55), by which the Pardoner is reduced to shattered silence, the man who has defied spiritual death in order to manipulate others and gain wealth has been brought face to face with a debt of death which even his rhetorical tour de force has not been able to hide completely.

IV

Robert Adams, in a seminal article, 'The Concept of Debt in The Shipman's Tale',[17] sees in the background of the Shipman's Tale the same 'biblical concept of sin as "debt"' (p. 88) which I have been pointing out in the Pardoner's Tale. While the principal characters are playing a game of monetary and sexual transactions, they (and the Shipman who relates the tale) are oblivious to the fact that no matter how clever they are with each other, 'their successfully concealed violations of accepted moral principles in trade and marriage have rendered them insolvent in the only "taillyinge" that finally matters, the "Taillynge ... unto our lyves ende"' (B2.1624) (p. 98). All three of the principals – the merchant, his wife, and the monk – are preoccupied with matters which distract them from their proper temporal and eternal obligations, that is, paying their real debts.[18] The merchant is completely taken up with his money and his business, even to the extent of not paying his 'marriage debt' to his wife; his wife is mainly concerned with her secret purchase of clothes and how to pay for them, and she thus falls prey to pride; the monk, like the one in the General Prologue, is out of his proper setting and is pulled away from his spiritual vocation by tending to the monastery's possessions – to say nothing of the sexual designs he is pursuing at the home of the merchant. In telling the story, the Shipman obviously plays with the

---

16   These two basic points of view on the mind of the Pardoner have been most ably articulated by G. L. Kittredge, 'Chaucer's Pardoner', *Atlantic Monthly* 72 (1893), 829–33 (repr. *Chaucer: Modern Essays in Criticism*, ed. E. Wagenknecht [New York, 1959], pp. 117–25); and G. G. Sedgewick, 'The Progress of Chaucer's Pardoner, 1880–1940', *Modern Language Quarterly* (1940), 431–58 (also repr. in *Chaucer: Modern Essays in Criticism*, pp. 136–54).

17   *Studies in the Age of Chaucer* 6 (1984), 85–102.

18   See Gibson, 'Resurrection', and Hermann, 'Dismemberment', cited in note 6 above.

concept of the marriage debt; that is, he uses the idea but he trivializes it. Like the Wife of Bath, he presents it as a means of a woman's gaining power over her husband, and like the Pardoner, he commercializes that which is holy.

In this atmosphere of perverted values, it appears that everyone is a winner, and that whatever debts remain can be paid off with pleasure. It would appear at the end that the wife is merely satisfying her marriage debt to her husband, but the wealth of double entendre in the last conversation between her and her husband shows that she speaks of the biblical marriage debt only on the surface; what she actually refers to is as much business as her husband's enterprises.[19]

> Ye han mo slakkere dettours than am I!
> For I wol paye yow wel and redily
> Fro day to day, and if so be I faille,
> I am youre wyf; score it upon my taille
> And I shal paye as soone as ever I may.
>
> *   *   *
>
> Ye shal my joly body have to wedde.
> By God, I wol nat paye yow but a-bedde!   (ShipT, 413–16; 423–24)

Her husband's part of the conversation ironically shows his ignorance of his complicity in his own cuckolding: be sure to let me know, he says, *If any dettour hath in myn absence / Ypayed thee* (397–98). We laugh at this ignorance, but the bliss of it is short-lived. Surely the Shipman's request that *God us sende / Taillynge ynough unto oure lyves ende* (433–34) has an especially hollow ring, coming as it does at the end of a tale where no one is in the slightest chastened by his or her foolish illusions about where true indebtedness lies.

V

Like the Wife of Bath and the Shipman, the Franklin addresses the debt incurred by marriage, but he is sanguine rather than cynical about the possibility of conflicting interests being worked out. He begins the tale with just such an accommodation of seemingly incompatible requirements between the knight and his lady:

19   The 'commercialization of the marriage relationship' in the following passage was thoroughly noted a good many years ago by A. H. Silverman, 'Sex and Money in the Shipman's Tale', *Philological Quarterly* 32 (1953), 329–36. A more recent article along the same lines is W. F. Woods, 'A Professional Thyng: The Wife as Merchant's Apprentice in the Shipman's Tale', *Chaucer Review* 24 (1989), 139–49, which he concludes with the comment that when the merchant's wife's 'debt to the monk makes her a *dettour* ... to her husband, she converts the loan by paying her marriage debt, the sexual solace married partners owe each other' (148).

... pryvely she fil of his accord
To take hym for hir housbonde and hir lord,
Of swich lordshipe as men han over hir wyves.
And for to lede the moore in blisse hir lyves,
Of his free wyl he swoor hire as a knyght
That nevere in al his lyf he day ne nyght
Ne sholde upon hym take no maistrie
Agayn hir wyl, ne kithe hir jalousie,
But hire obeye and folwe hir wyl in al,
As any lovere to his lady shal,
Save that the name of soveraynetee,
That wolde he have for shame of his degree.   (FrankT, 741–52)

But they have unwittingly laid the foundation of all their troubles. The assumption underlying this *accord* between husband and wife is that a private agreement can resolve such tensions as that between the standards of courtly love and the bonds of marriage; that so long as appearances are saved,[20] the most contradictory paths can be pursued simultaneously. Arveragus and Dorigen thus begin their married life with what seems to be an admirable sense of mutual indebtedness, each accepting the lordship of the other. But the bases of the two lordships are different and at cross purposes, and the later complications of the story spring from the tension between the two. Arveragus pursues the obligations of chivalry, but in a somewhat arbitrary absence of two years, he defaults on his marriage debt and leaves Dorigen vulnerable to the advances of Aurelius. Weakened by her grief over her husband's absence, Dorigen falls prey to questions about the sovereignty of God in her monologue about the *grisly, feendly rokkes blake* on the coast (857–94), which seem to her a symbol of the flaw of evil in the universe.[21] The combination of these two strains on her spirit, added to her tacit acceptance of the tenets of courtly love in her marriage agreement, lead to her 'playful' response to Aurelius's

20 R. A. Peck, 'Sovereignty and the Two Worlds of the Franklin's Tale', *Chaucer Review* 1 (1967), 253–71, says that the central theme of the tale is 'the difficulty of perceiving truth in a world of illusions' (p. 254), and that both the Franklin and his character, Arveragus, are more concerned with preserving appearances than with reality. D. S. Brewer, 'Honour in Chaucer', *Essays and Studies* 26 (1973), 1–19, points out that maintaining honour according to the standards of the Middle Ages was often a matter of external appearances, whereas personal fidelity (*trouthe*) was less public and therefore often in conflict with honour. He says that 'The Franklin's Tale is explicitly about *trouthe*'s superiority to honour' (p. 16).

21 See Peck, 'Sovereignty', esp. pp. 261, 268. See also E. B. Benjamin, 'The Concept of Order in the Franklin's Tale', *Philological Quarterly* 38 (1959), 119–24. Both critics see Dorigen's challenge to divine order, along with her failure to submit to the sovereignty of her husband, as major sources of the difficulties in which she finds herself.

proposition. Her sense of obligation to honour her promise, even one so lightly given, completes the web of contradictory desires and debts in which she finds herself caught.[22] Although it is clear that her first allegiance is to her husband (who *hath hir body whan so that hym liketh* [FrankT, 1005], in accordance with the marriage debt), she sets herself up to be trapped by the mere illusion that her conditions for giving herself to Aurelius have been met.

Aurelius, for his part, incurs a large debt of money with hardly a thought about it, so intent is he on fulfilling the terms of his 'agreement' with Dorigen and collecting the 'payment' for doing so. Nor does he question either the illusory nature of the removal of the rocks or the illicitness of collecting the 'debt' owed him by Dorigen as a result of the magician's work. Aurelius thus reflects the Franklin's own refusal to be worried by any awkward conflicts between desire and barriers to their fulfilment, and his incurring the money debt completes the migration of indebtedness from the idealistically conceived mutual marriage debt, to the adulterous 'courtly love' intentions of Aurelius, to the indirect payment for sexual favours.

The Franklin rather ingenuously enjoys the dilemma he has set up, because he seems constitutionally unable to encompass a sordid or tragic view of life. The other three pilgrims whose tales we have examined were vividly aware of the complexity of life in attempting to satisfy human wishes, and they were quite prepared to manipulate that complexity to bring about their own gratification. The Franklin's optimism lies in his belief that any commitment made (that is, any debt incurred) in honour and free will can transcend human limitations and be the catalyst for a kind of harmony between men and women that goes beyond possessions and social standing.[23] He, too, however, overlooks the debt incurred by mankind because of sin, preferring to concentrate on the

22 M. Golding, 'The Importance of Keeping *Trouthe* in The Franklin's Tale', *Medium Aevum* 39 (1970), 306–12, p. 309, says that when the illusion of the removal of the rocks was complete, Dorigen confronted 'a moral chaos that threatened ... the very values she had thought to preserve'.

23 A. T. Gaylord, 'The Promises in The Franklin's Tale', *English Literary History* 31 (1964), 331–65, sees the Franklin's Tale as a satirical undercutting of any idealism that might attach to the Franklin or his characters. Obviously more compatible with my interpretation of the Franklin is the view of Golding, 'Importance', who says that the Franklin is aware of the vulnerability of his idealistic fictional characters to a real world of harsh consequences, but nevertheless imposes his optimism to bring about a happy ending to his story. Recent feminist criticism is represented by S. J. McEntire, 'Illusions and Interpretation in the Franklin's Tale', *Chaucer Review* 31 (1996), 145–63, who sees the competition for most honourable person at the end of the tale to be merely 'male-bonded one-upmanship' that results in a reaffirmation that women, 'like money, can be exchanged, bartered, commodified' (155). K. Jacobs, however, argues that 'the marriage of Arveragus and Dorigen, in practice as well as promise, comes very close to achieving an ideal for the audience to emulate' ('The Marriage Contract of the Franklin's Tale: The Remaking of Society', *Chaucer Review* 20 (1985), 134).

technical definition of honour rather than on honour before God; but he does so because he thinks better of mankind than do the other three pilgrims who have ignored the need to acknowledge the debt of sin. Even though he looks more to character than to chicanery to make everything come out right, in his world of fiction he is willing to allow the *grisly, feendly rokkes blake* of life to be neutralized by a magician's trick.

VI

Thus Chaucer presents us with a wide range of responses to the various obligations that frame our existence and define our choices. He was fascinated by the complex web of voluntary and involuntary indebtedness that we must deal with, and he focused repeatedly on the tendency of human beings to manipulate or reinterpret the terms of indebtedness, whether material or spiritual, to their own advantage. But just as a lie can be effective only in a world in which truth is expected, so the manipulation of a concept of indebtedness can be advantageous only to the extent that the legitimacy of debts is the accepted norm. That lying and a lack of integrity in honouring debts are considered dangers to spiritual and social order testifies to the validity of the values they endanger, and thus every attempt to use legitimate indebtedness perversely turns in upon the very norms that make it possible for such perversity to be temporarily successful. So it is in the four tales we have examined. The Wife of Bath trades on (but bends) the legitimacy of conjugal debt to exercise her power in marriage; the characters in the Shipman's Tale wilfully confuse and conflate conjugal and monetary debt, transferring arbitrarily between sets of expectations and definitions of gain; the Pardoner's Tale shows a narrator and story teller who creates a profound verbal embodiment of spiritual bankruptcy that he simultaneously presents powerfully and rejects for himself; and the Franklin's Tale illustrates that even comparatively benevolent intentions are in dangerous territory when they depend exclusively on a social definition of honour that sets aside a higher moral obligation.

A worldly wise Chaucer realized that there are few among mortals who can resist the seduction of trying to define themselves as creditors rather than debtors, and in his society holding that perspective meant acknowledging first of all one's basic spiritual indebtedness to God. The standard for such an attitude – the standard which most of the pilgrims (and most human beings) fail to live up to – is admirably stated by the Parson in his sermon.

'Deedly synne,' as seith Seint Augustyn, 'is when a man turneth his herte fro God, which that is verray sovereyn bountee that mey nat chaunge, and yeveth his herte to thyng that may chaunge and flitte.' And certes, that is everything save God of hevene. For sooth is that if a man yeve his love the which that he oweth al to God with al his herte unto a creature, certes, as muche as he yeveth of his love to thilke creature, so muche he bireveth fro God; and therfore doth he synne. For he that is dettour to God ne yeldeth nat to God al his dette, that is to seyn al the love of his herte.

(X, 368–70)

Because he was acutely interested in what motivates people, Chaucer saw clearly that both the best and the worst of human actions spring from people's willingness (or unwillingness) to acknowledge their various kinds of indebtedness, and he presented consistently in his characters the link between their dealings with human debtors and creditors and their sense of indebtedness to God. Certainly the four pilgrims whose tales we have examined (and the characters within their tales) may be evaluated by their degree of awareness that, as Shakespeare's Prince Hal put it to Falstaff, we all 'owe God a death', however much we manage to manipulate human debts to our advantage.

'QUHA WAIT GIF ALL THAT CHAUCEIR WRAIT WAS TREW?': HENRYSON'S *TESTAMENT OF CRESSEID*

DEREK PEARSALL

THIS ESSAY is in three parts. The first attempts to say something about Henryson's *Testament of Cresseid* as a poem, about its poeticness, and why it is that it is as a poem (and not, say, a didactic treatise, or a document in social history, or a psychoanalytic case-history) that it is important. The second and much the longest part offers a reading of the poem and an interpretation of what I take to be its meaning. The third part of the essay takes up some recent feminist readings of the poem in an attempt to find out how they bear upon the interpretation I offer.

I

Readings of medieval narrative poems do not often, these days, refer much to the fact that they are poems, or attribute the worthwhileness of talking about them to those features of form, style, language and imagery that constitute them as poems. Readings inspired by modern sociological and hermeneutic preoccupations – feminist, new historicist, psychoanalytic, deconstructionist – are interested in other things and could readily, it seems, manage with poems or prose texts on the right subjects that had not traditionally been admired as poems or formed part of the literary canon. Occasionally this happens, for particular reasons, as with Thomas Usk or William Thorpe, but generally it is the canonical poets who are endlessly recycled, even though the idea of a canon is supposedly one on the necessary casualties of the culture-wars. What is the reason for this?

It could be canonical inertia: these are the poets who are traditionally on the syllabus, and hard-pressed academics are bound to find it most economical to write about what they teach day by day. It could be a subtle long-term strategy: these are the commanding heights of the poetic economy, and to subdue them to a prevailing interpretative ideology is to win power over the cultural territory. It could be, as Marxist historians of culture have sometimes claimed, that the greatest poems emerge at the moments of greatest social and economic stress, as earthquakes accompany unseen tectonic shifts.[1] The ease with which virtually any period of history can be argued to be a time of specially stressful change makes this an attractive but uncompelling approach. A modification of this view sees the poems traditionally deemed to be worth reading as the ones in which the issues that interest the feminist or historicist or psychoanalytic reader are most fully and complexly explored. This is not true (witness the comparative neglect of Henryson's *Moral Fables* by comparison with the *Testament*), but it does bring us full circle back to the assumption that underlies all these possible ways of approaching the poems – that there is something about them that makes them worth reading even before we have decided what they mean and that inspires the desire to find out, or to decide.

How then to talk about what a very good poem the *Testament* is? There are a number of ways in which one knows this to be true, some of them physiological, as A. E. Housman once described,[2] but I think I can talk about two of them without recourse to spine-shudderings and toe-curlings.

One is intensity, the sense one has in reading the poem that everything that is happening is of enormous significance, or 'pendulation', as Auerbach (or rather his translator) called it.[3] Why the fate of this deceived and deluded young woman, who never even existed, should be more important than the fate of nations (remembering Hardy's poem 'In Time of "The Breaking of Nations"') is a mystery, but that's the way literature works and how Henryson makes it seem. Chaucer did the same, of course, and our sterner critics, historicist and new historicist, have not been entirely happy with such a state of affairs in relation to *Troilus and Criseyde*. They think that there is nothing more important than the fate of nations, and in trying to make something more of the poem they make something less – a warning to England of the political dangers of extra-marital sexual relationships, or a Theban omen of the repressive patterning of history, the iron law of recursion. One waits with leaden expectation for the *Testament* to have its history similarly dumped upon it (and there are signs of this happening, as we shall see).

But meanwhile there is Cresseid and her sadness, and the intensity with which we are made to care about it, and further, how every detail of the world around her has the same heightened significance. It is what I would call the 'gathering samphire/dreadful trade' effect.

Halfway down
Hangs one that gathers samphire, dreadful trade!

1 See Terry Eagleton, *Criticism and Ideology: A Study in Marxist Literary Theory*, London, 1978, p. 181.
2 A. E. Housman, *The Name and Nature of Poetry*, Cambridge, 1939, p. 47.
3 Erich Auerbach, *Mimesis: The Representation of Reality in Western Literature*, translated from the German (1946) by Willard Trask, 1953; New York, 1957, p. 36.

Such is the intensity of our engagement with the action of *King Lear* that our hearts momentarily miss a beat at the danger that the samphire-gatherer is in, even though his immediate dramatic function is just to be halfway down the cliff so as to impress us with its vertiginousness. (It would be a happy moment indeed if an unwary scholar, taking *dreadful* to mean 'deplorable' rather than 'fearful', proposed a short piece on Shakespeare and early agitation for an Industrial Injuries Act.)

So in the *Testament* everything that happens in the background, everyone who makes even the briefest appearance, stands out in our memories, affirmed in their life because of the extraordinary intensity of the life in the foreground. One thinks for instance of the tenderness and stoic resignation of Cresseid's father Calchas, in his unexpected role as a priest of Venus, or of the *chyld* or young servant-boy who comes to tell Cresseid, just after she has been stricken with leprosy, that supper is ready, and that her father grows impatient with her long and unnecessary communion with the gods:

> Madame, your father biddis yow cum in hy:
> He hes merwell sa lang on grouf ye ly,
> And sayis your beedes bene to lang sum-deill;
> The goddis wait all your intent full weill. (361–64)[4]

The unconscious irony of his words pierces to the heart, as does the cruelty of his innocence and ignorance, with its reminder of ordinary life going on at the back of the story, imperturbably. (Douglas Gray has written particularly well of the pathos and irony of this scene.[5]) One thinks also of the leper-woman who comes over to Cresseid on her first night in the leper-house and advises her to give up her noisy lamentation and make the best of a bad job:

> And said, 'Quhy spurnis thow aganis the wall
> To sla thy self and mend nathing at all?
> Sen thy weiping bot dowbillis thy wo,
> I counsall the mak vertew of ane neid:
> Go leir to clap thy clapper to and fro,
> And leif efter the law of lipper leid.' (475–80)

Henryson does not sentimentalise the leper-folk: they are pleased enough to find that their new recruit is of noble kin (and therefore more likely to bring money and food into the house) and they whisper enviously among themselves when they see how unfairly she has been favoured by Troilus. But the darkness of their world is momentarily illumined by that weary gesture of the *lipper-*

---

4   The *Testament* is cited, with some slight modification of spelling, from the edition by Denton Fox, Nelson's Medieval and Renaissance Library, London and Edinburgh, 1968.

5   Douglas Gray, *Robert Henryson*, Leiden, 1979, pp. 193–4.

lady in stirring herself in the night to comfort Cresseid.[6]

And it is not just people and events that have a heightened significance: the atmosphere of concentrated poetic intensity gives to every word the capacity to carry a great freight of meaning:

> Quhen Diomeid had all his appetyte,
> And mair, fulfillit of this fair ladie,
> Upon ane uther he set his haill delyte ...   (71–73)

What volumes are spoken of in *And mair* of the days and weeks of stale and forced lust. We already know everything, without Cresseid's own bleak explanation of events to her father:

> Fra Diomeid had gottin his desyre
> He wox werie and wald of me no moir.   (101–02)

Another thing that marks the *Testament* as a great poem is its connectivity, the way all its parts knit and work together to make of a linear narrative a *composition* full of echoes and anticipations. This compositional sense is not a non-medieval phenomenon or a sign that a Renaissance of perception is impending, as used to be argued in relation to paintings by art-historians like Wölfflin and Sypher. It is simply a quality of good writing, where the intensity of the engagement with the material makes the whole of the narrative simultaneously present in the mind of the reader. The story, literally, unfolds, and is revealed as a close-knit network of motifs, allusions, figures, phrases, words. One thinks, for comparison, of *Troilus and Criseyde*, or the Merchant's Tale, or *Sir Gawain and the Green Knight*, or *Piers Plowman*.

One of the patterns is that created by the repetition of the imagery of the flourishing and fading flower, of what is green contrasted with what is withered. It is there in the narrator's hope that his faded heart of love may be made green (line 24), in the description of the life of those ruled by Venus as *Now grene as leif, now widderit and ago* (238), and it is there in particular in the bitterly precise irony with which Cresseid's complaint against the gods is remembered in her punishment. She complains to Cupid that the seed of love that was sown in her face (that is, the beauty that made men desire her), and always flourished and grew green through Cupid's favour, is now slain by the frost of being forsaken (136–40). This killing frost is literally what is enacted in the punishment delivered by Saturn, who slays with cold and dry, and by Cynthia the moon, whose complexion is also cold and leaden and her garment spotted with black. It is she who delivers the sentence:

---

6   This is where one would wish to mention Douglas Duncan's final assessment of the poem, in one of the earliest and most influential accounts of it ('Henryson's *Testament of Cresseid*', *Essays in Criticism* 11 (1961), 128–35), as a meditation on 'the place of suffering outcasts in a Christian world' (p. 135).

> Thy cristall ene mingit with blude I mak,
> Thy voice sa cleir unplesand hoir and hace,
> Thy lustie lyre ouirspred with spottis blak,
> And lumpis haw appeirand in thy face.   (337–40)

The sowing of the seed of love in her face becomes the sprinkling of her face with the black spots and lumps of leprosy, as Cresseid takes on, grotesquely disfigured, the physical features of her two judges.

Intensity and connectivity are two of the ways in which Henryson's narrative poem makes its subject seem important to us. They are part of its poetic art, according to the terms in which the role of the artist was defined by Henry James. Replying to H. G. Wells's accusation that he had sacrificed his life to his art James replied, 'I live intensely, and am fed by life, and my value, whatever it be, is in my own kind of expression of that … It is art that makes life, makes interest, makes importance … and I know of no substitute whatever for the force and beauty of its process.'[7] What needs adding to James's formulation in this case is the essential part played by Chaucer in Henryson's poetic engagement with his material.

II

Henryson begins with Chaucer and what he perceives as Chaucer's failure to provide a satisfactory conclusion for the story of Criseyde. Chaucer refused to judge Criseyde, except by allowing her words and actions to speak for themselves. With a great deal of circumstantial detail and profound inwardness with an imagined consciousness, he made Criseyde's inconstancy pathetically understandable, but left her moral position unresolved. As far as we can see, she can be accorded only human compassion: there is no way of relating her unfaithfulness to any larger scheme of values – as there is for Troilus's constancy, through the ascent to the eighth sphere. It is an eddy in the flux of circumstance. Chaucer's refusal to judge, so carefully signalled and structured in the poem, is an act of great human and poetic significance, as Henryson recognised.

But, though he acknowledged the seriousness of Chaucer's purpose, Henryson was sure, as he began his thinking about his poem, that Chaucer's decision to allow Criseyde to go unpunished was insufficient, and determined that Chaucer's heroine should be brought to the bar of judgment. He plucks her out of the kindly oblivion in which Chaucer had left her, makes a spiteful insinuation about her subsequent career, loads her with infamy, punishes her, and then, as if under challenge to prove that humanity is never irredeemable, redeems her. The story that he invented is a machine to educate Cresseid

---

7   Letter of 10 July 1915, in Henry James, *Letters*, ed. L. Edel, Vol. IV, Cambridge, Mass., 1984, pp. 769–70.

through suffering toward self-knowledge: finding the story in 'another quire' that he picked up after reading *Troilus* is a form of textual authentication, designed to mimic Chaucer and to claim for his poem the same authority, the same truth, whatever it might be – 'Who knows if all that (even) Chaucer wrote was true?' (64) – as Chaucer's.

Henryson was aware, I think, of the sophistication of Chaucer's treatment of Criseyde, and of the vulgarity of the rush to judgment that arises from outrage at her behaviour, where the male reader is the cuckold or rejected lover whose wounded pride is disguised as moral outrage and sweetened with false compassion. The vanities of this reader can be detected even in the sympathetic and sensitive readings of C. S. Lewis and E. Talbot Donaldson,[8] and are embarrassingly present in the cruder ill-temper of some others. He was her man, and she done him wrong, is the burden of their complaint. All men know what she should have done – stayed in her tent, wrapped herself in an old blanket, and been faithful.

To accommodate this reader, Henryson incorporates him in the poem as a narrator and turns him into a figure of ridicule. He is an old man, who, like Criseyde, sees love only in terms of sexual desire, a heat of the blood, unfortunately in him enfeebled, despite the use of *physic*, so that when he goes to the window to make his avowal to Venus he has to retire hastily back to the fireside because of the draught. His lament for Cresseid is famously queasy:

> O fair Creisseid, the flour and A per se
> Of Troy and Grece, how was thow fortunait
> To change in filth all thy feminitie
> And be with fleschelie lust sa maculait
> And go amang the Greikis air and lait
> Sa giglotlike takand thy foull plesance!
> I have pietie thow suld fall sic mischance!   (78–84)

The narrator's professed sympathy is deeply suspect: the very syntax seems to pant with outrage, prurient relish, repressed ardour, and exhaustion at the imagining of rampant female sexuality, the horror of the woman seeking out pleasure, taking pleasure, the passionate desire to possess and to punish, in which the maculateness, the spottedness, of sinful lust so cruelly anticipates the ugly defilement of leprosy. The explanation of Cresseid's fall as being the result of bad luck is totally at odds with what has just been said of her wilful promiscuity, while the suggestion in the next stanza that it was malicious gossip (*wickit langage*, 91)[9] that brought her down is so shallow and trumpery

---

8   C. S. Lewis, *The Allegory of Love*, Oxford, 1936, pp. 182–90; E. Talbot Donaldson (ed.) *Chaucer's Poetry: An Anthology for the Modern Reader*, New York, 1958, pp. 967–71.

9   Henryson echoes Chaucer's Criseyde's specious self-exculpation, *For that I tarie is al for wikked speche* (*Troilus and Criseyde*, v.1610).

that it might seem to be ironical. But it's more like a belated and exhausted recognition of the need to be seen as fair-minded and sympathetic, which falls apart because it's so obviously spurious.

I do not want to take this narrator any further. I call him 'a narrator' rather than 'the narrator' because in describing what I think to be his function here I do not want to turn him into a hermeneutical principle, a key to the meaning of the poem. The narrative *persona* has perhaps now had its day; we used to hear a lot about them, but not any more. It grew to be recognised, I think, that *persona* was not a way of de-centring or complexifying authorial voice, but of asserting it more unequivocally. Fallible first-person narrators imply the existence somewhere else of someone manipulating their fallibility. Or, to put it another way, if Henryson is not Henryson when he's Henryson-the-narrator, then he's more than ever Henryson when he's Henryson, and the old conspiracy to pretend that the reader's opinion is the author's intention is fortified. Authors have lots of voices, and move in and out of them freely and not always distinguishably. We can manage with authors, I think, now that they are back from being prematurely buried by Foucault and others, and can see them to advantage as indeterminate signifiers rather than as empty functions. They and their intentions are of vital importance, even if we can never be entirely sure of what those intentions are.

Though he recognises, then, the suspect simplicities of condemnation, there is still no alternative for Henryson but an eschatological frame of reference. Cresseid must be punished before she can be saved. The punishment is carefully chosen – Cresseid's leprosy (this is Henryson's invention) is cruelly appropriate to her pride in her beauty – and the administration of it is carefully legitimated in relation to an apparatus of quasi-divine surveillance. Cresseid is not punished for being unfaithful to Troilus – how could that be a punishable offence? – but for blaspheming against the gods in blaming them for what has happened to her. This is like looking for the exact letter of the law under which someone who is known to be bad, or whom it is necessary to convict, but who cannot be proved to be guilty, can be convicted. All codes of law have some catch-all provision that can ensure this: in the RAF, in my day, it was called 'conduct prejudicial to good order and discipline'; the gods, naturally enough, call it 'blaspheming against the gods'.

The gods are not Christian gods, of course, nor do they stand for the Christian God, but as planetary influences they are *Participant of devyne sapience* (289), and they operate in a manner brutally similar to what goes under the name of divine justice.[10] Henryson seized eagerly upon the freedom that

10   The most careful explanation of the matter is in L. Patterson, 'Christian and Pagan in *The Testament of Cresseid*', *Philological Quarterly* 52 (1973), 696–714 (especially pp. 700–3), arguing against the view of E. M. W. Tillyard that the poem is 'the story of her salvation according to a Christian scheme' (*Poetry and Its Background*, London, 1955, p. 17), and of Duncan (see note 6 above) that the planets are 'an expression of the divine will' (p. 132).

Chaucer had given him in the pagan setting of the story (as well as in his more elaborate treatment of the planetary deities in the Knight's Tale) to meditate on questions of reward and punishment and human desert, and on the apparent ineluctability and impassivity of the circumstances that shape human destiny, without pre-empting the answers with the set formulae of the Christian faith – the freedom, as John Frankis so memorably put it, to explore 'the myth of mankind without God'.[11]

The freedom was needed because what Cresseid had done and what we recognise as 'wrong' and what she comes to recognise as wrong – her unfaithfulness to Troilus (her later promiscuity is an insulting aside) – is not normally thought of as susceptible of punishment according to any code of law. In Christian terms, how can infidelity to a kind of relationship which receives no Christian recognition anyway be said to be reprehensible? So she must be convicted on a technicality.[12] The logic of events, though, is deeper than any code of law, in the retribution that traces a moral in a physical corruption, a logic that was strengthened by the association commonly made between leprosy and venereal disease.

But the fearful machine that Henryson constructs to destroy Cresseid physically is not the instrument of her repentance and salvation: she learns nothing from it except to complain against her misfortune and warn others to learn by it. Her Complaint (407–69), in seven 9-line stanzas on two rhymes, is a formal poetic *tour de force*. It is a powerful warning of mortality in the tradition of the *memento mori*, given added pungency by being delivered – since we understand that lepers were regarded as legally and in effect dead – by a walking corpse. Her use of the formal complaint helps her, as Patterson points out in his excellent essay on the poem, already cited, to evade the full understanding of her experience; its extreme stylistic elaboration also creates a 'distance' between Cresseid and the reader, who is left free to see that her moralising upon her abject condition is the product of self-pity, not self-knowledge.

Here I have to disagree, I'm afraid, with Denton Fox, the editor of Henryson, and one of the greatest of medieval editors. 'Through suffering,' he says, 'comes knowledge, and the last part of the Testament is devoted, I think, to showing how Cresseid is brought, by *means of her leprosy*, into an understanding of herself and of the world.'[13] This is simply not true, or perhaps not

---

11 J. Frankis, 'Paganism and pagan love in Troilus and Criseyde', in *Essays on Troilus and Criseyde*, ed. M. Salu, Chaucer Studies III, Cambridge, 1979, pp. 57–72 (p. 72).

12 I hope it will not be thought improper to cite an odd parallel in the language used by S. Holmes in the *London Review of Books* (18 March 1999) to describe how Kenneth Starr, knowing that he could not topple Clinton or even damage him politically in a way that would be acceptable to the public, 'therefore set out to stage-manage a higher-level legal procedure, in order to alchemize Clinton's personal folly into an impeachable crime'.

13 *Testament*, ed. Fox (see note 4 above), p. 41 (my italics).

simply true. What may be true, and what may lie as another appalling hidden logic behind events is that leprosy does have an effect on Cresseid, not in teaching her self-knowledge, but in preparing her, against her will, for the administration of 'grace', with bitter allusion to the bruising of the body in inquisitional torture that 'softens' the victim into receptivity, as well as to the more comforting idea that lepers were chosen by God to be close to him through their suffering.

But Cresseid learns nothing from her punishment itself – not an uncommon situation. She complains that all her mirth is taken from her, that her fate is a warning to ladies of the fickleness of Fortune, but she cannot see herself as erring. Her progress through misery is untouched by self-knowledge until she meets Troilus, in a scene of overwhelming yet totally unsentimental poignancy such as few would have dared attempt. Only then does she recognise her offence against the truth of love, understanding having been bestowed not by punishment and suffering but by the recognition of what Troilus's love was and is. It is an extraordinary moment, and it shows how deeply Henryson had absorbed the ethos of Chaucer's poem whilst ostensibly correcting its morality: even with all its powerful Christian overtones and implications, the *Testament* is seen still to rest on the assertion of the 'holiness of the heart's affections', or rather on a system of organising and codifying those affections to the exclusive benefit of men. Troilus is the unflawed representative of an ideal code of love which Cresseid betrayed.

The scene in which the drama of self-recognition is played out, which one keeps wanting to call 'the recognition scene', is in fact a non-recognition scene, and it is vital that it should be so. Troilus does not recognise Cresseid, because of the deformity of her features, but he is reminded of her:

> Yit than hir luik into his mynd it brocht
> The sweit visage and amorous blenking
> Of fair Cresseid, sumtyme his awin darling.   (502–04)

Henryson has a little excursus on this act of partial recognition, and the manner in which fantasy, or imagination, plays the senses false, invoking the rather old-fashioned faculty psychology in which fantasy creates delusion:

> Na wonder was, suppois in mynd that he
> Tuik hir figure sa sone, and lo, now quhy:
> The idole of ane thing in cace may be
> So deip imprentit in the fantasy
> That it deludis the wittis outwardly,
> And sa appeiris in forme and lyke estait
> Within the mynd as it was figurait. (505–11)

This explanation does not work, of course, because in this case the fantasy is not a delusion but an intuition of a truth otherwise hidden – it *is* Cresseid, *sumtyme his awin darling.* Henryson, apparently speaking in so official and schoolmasterly a fashion about the illusory power of fantasy, could not offer a more powerful argument for its truth-telling power. It is a power that is given to Troilus because of his constancy as a lover and his constancy to the ideal of love. It is not a false illusion to be repudiated, but a true intuition that rekindles his passion and prompts him, as love should, to an act of selfless charity in pity of the lepers and in memory of his love. He rides on.

Cresseid has not recognised him either, nor had any glimmering of recognition, for physical reasons, and for symbolic reasons that hardly need explaining. Nor does she know or learn that he has remembered her through his partial recognition of her; as far as she understands, his charity is general to all the lepers:

> 'Quhat lord is yone,' quod scho, 'have ye na feill,
> Hes done to us so greit humanitie?'   (533–34)

When she finds out that it was Troilus, she has her own moment of epiphany when she has revealed to her for the first time the quality of truth in his love that she was blind to before, and enters upon her confessional lament, with its repeated refrain,

> 'O fals Cresseid and trew knicht Troylus!'

The last line of the confessional lament is the act of self-recognition that the poem has worked towards throughout:

> 'Nane but my self as now I will accuse.' (574)

This is the moment when Cresseid assumes responsibility for her own actions, albeit in a manner Chaucer would have thought excessively blunt and downright. It is represented to some extent as a form of redemptive self-knowledge, achieved through witnessing the truth of Troilus, through the mediation of Troilus's truth. If he is one of love's martyrs, then she is one of love's apostates, who is brought back to the faith by being witness of living faith.

The poem, however, even with the eschatological pressures that bear upon it, and encourage the kind of language I have just used, holds to its paradox: it is neither sin nor salvation that is the subject but the responsibility of human beings, men and women, for their own actions, which I take to be a principal subject of Chaucer's *Troilus*.

I speak persistently, through habit, of Henryson as the author of the poem and the intentionality that shapes it. It would be better perhaps to speak, in the old-fashioned way, of his 'unconscious meanings', or, in the modern way, of 'the meaning of the text', for Henryson has not contrived his machine consistently to the concluding purpose I have described. There is a sense perhaps that a more traditional eschatology of sin and punishment has been swayed out of orbit by the enormous gravitational pull of Chaucer's poem, so that the cause of offence is located in a sin against what he, and he only nervously and waveringly, had identified and elevated as a moral virtue. But Chaucer had repudiated his own poem, and the tentative sanction it had offered to faithful human love, and ended by blowing the trumpets for Jesus Christ. This is where Chaucer made the compromise – 'Who knows if all that Chaucer wrote was true?' – that Henryson does not make.

III

Two recent feminist readings of the poem[14] provide the opportunity to put the reading that has just been offered, which is a version of the 'redemptive' account of the poem which has long been broadly accepted, to the test. Susan Aronstein agrees that the poem is redemptive in its purpose, but argues that what it seeks is 'the redemption of the patriarchal order' (p. 20). 'The real concern of the text', she says, is 'the need to reassert the pre-Chaucerian Criseyde of earlier misogynist tradition and thus to recover a social order based on that tradition' (p. 5). What Cresseid learns is not self-knowledge, nor redemptive understanding, but 'to read herself "correctly", that is, in terms of the era's prevalent misogynist writings' (p. 8). Aronstein concludes: 'Henryson's "reading" of Cresseid and her story not only closes down what were seen as the dangerous ambiguities of Chaucer's text but also directly participates in the reinvigorated misogynist discourse of the late fifteenth century' (pp. 10–11).

This is a powerful polemic, easy to understand, and easy to summarise. It is of course true that Henryson's poem is immersed in the world of patriarchal discourse (as I acknowledge in a probably insufficiently emphatic aside in my account of it) and it is healthy to be reminded of this from time to time. Henryson's original intention, dictated to him by his position as an agent in the patriarchal discourse, may not have been very different from what Aronstein describes. But his poem is nothing like what she describes, and the energies of her account seem to be derived from other experiences than that of reading the poem. One of them is the experience of reading a book on medieval prostitution, to which she devotes several pages, probably irrelevantly, since Cresseid is insinuated to have become promiscuous (*commoun*, line 77) but not to have become a prostitute: there is a difference, in terms of both class and agency.[15]

---

14   S. Aronstein, 'Cresseid Reading Cresseid: Redemption and Translation in Henryson's *Testament*', *Scottish Literary Journal* 21 (1994), 5–22; F. Riddy, '"Abject odious": Feminine and Masculine in Henryson's *Testament of Cresseid*', in *The Long Fifteenth Century: Essays for Douglas Gray*, eds H. Cooper and S. Mapstone, Oxford, 1997, pp. 228–48. (I want to thank Isobel Armstrong for helping me to see how I might read these pieces.)

15   See Patterson (note 10 above), p. 699.

The attempt, likewise, to associate the poem with a specifically 'late fifteenth-century misogynist backlash' (p. 19) is flimsily supported, and no evidence at all is advanced for Scotland. Aronstein does, however, recognise in passing that the most important relation of Henryson's poem is with Chaucer's poem, when she speaks of the 'pre-Chaucerian Criseyde' and the attempt to close down the 'dangerous ambiguities' of his poem. This, one should understand, is the highest praise that a modern feminist criticism can offer of Chaucer's poem: it recognises something in it which, as I claim, arises from its power as a poem and not from any historically more liberal or less misogynist attitudes attributable to Chaucer or his age. Henryson's poem has a similar power, which Aronstein has forced herself to neglect.

The account of Henryson's poem by Felicity Riddy is more responsive to its particularities as a poem, but is similarly insistent upon its role in confirming the patriarchal order. Kristeva's idea of abjection – 'the process whereby the infant begins to found an identity separate from the mother' (Riddy, p. 235) – is used as a means to arguing that Cresseid too must be abjected in order to establish Troilus's identity and with that the traditional patriarchal order. His truth and consistency is constituted through the expulsion and defilement of the feminine (p. 236). Riddy concludes: 'What the *Testament of Cresseid* shows is the struggle to constitute a stable masculine identity; its constant risk of dissolution; its relation to repression, law, and punishment; and above all, its need to exclude the feminine ... What is obscurely at stake in the story of the much-loved woman who is cast out is the very making of masculinity' (p. 244).

Like Aronstein, Riddy tries to find a specific historical place for the poem in late fifteenth-century Scotland, alluding to presumed evidence in Scotland of roundels used in domestic glazing in which cautionary tales of female promiscuity might have been represented (pp. 241–2) and to 'The Spectacle of Lufe' in the Asloan MS (p. 242). Again, too, the energy of interpretation seems to derive from sources outside the poem, in this case from the intoxicating combination of an exceptionally horrible late fifteenth-century painting of *Les amants trépassés* and the apparently lucky use in the poem of the Kristevan 'abject' (line 133).[16]

---

16   It may not be so lucky as it looks. There is Denton Fox's authority for the meaning 'outcast' for the substantive *abject*, but the earliest supporting evidence is 1534, and the word, when it begins to be then used substantively, retains relically the character of a former participial adjective. The usage here would be highly unidiomatic as well as exceptionally early. Meanwhile, *Middle English Dictionary* records spellings of *abject* for 'object' and *object* for 'abject', which suggest that the two forms sometimes fell together: 'object odious' would be a perfectly idiomatic example of *Oxford English Dictionary*, s.v. *object*, sb. sign.3b, 'something which on being seen excites a particular emotion, as admiration, horror, disdain, commiseration, amusement' (this in its turn is not recorded until 1588, but is directly related to the more neutral use in sign.3a, attested in Trevisa).

It is at first difficult to know what to do with the poem when analyses of this kind have been completed. There is no point in trying to refute an argument which is so obviously true – that Henryson's poem is immersed in patriarchal discourse – and 'abjection' is certainly a convenient term. Riddy's essay opens the poem up to some extent to further investigation of the nature of identity, but Aronstein's closes it down: there is nothing to do now but erect warning signs around the poem – 'Hateful Discourse'.

In seeking the common ground that one presumes to exist between readers of the same poem (if it is indeed the same poem that they have been reading), even if they have approached it from different points of view, one might offer a number of pointers. They would *not* lead, via a fallible narrator, in the direction of a systemic irony in which all the assumptions that the poem seems to make are implicitly subverted and a subtext is opened up which confirms the modern interpreter's opinion of the poem. One would look rather for the differences *within* the discourse of the poem and within what it represents. There are on the one hand the elements of contradiction within the patriarchal discourse itself and the elements of self-reflexivity within the poem that enable us to be aware of them. There are on the other hand those aspects of the poem as a formal structure – the role of the narrator, the role of the gods, the portrayal of the persons – which are not fully contained within the strictly 'redemptive' plan of the poem.

The poem, in this view, is not an acquiescence in the uncompromising violence and power of the patriarchal order, nor a self-consciously subversive questioning of it, but a poetic representation of it which reveals, through the powers invested in such poetic representation, what is customarily concealed. There are fractures and fissures within this ostensibly monolithic patriarchal order which betray its meanness, its contradictions, its weakness, its denial of the humanity of the humans over whom it presumes to preside. In particular, all the figures in the poem who might be supposed to represent the patriarchal order, and therefore to be complicit in its violence, are portrayed as inconsistent, weak, or vulnerable; the authority that dispenses torment and punishment is constantly compromised, criticised, redefined.

The narrator himself, in certain respects the most powerful male figure present, is vulnerable to many contrary impulses, weak, wanton (in his daydreams), prone to surges of pity, irrational, preoccupied with his physical body, in ways that would, in the world of conventional patriarchal discourse, be thought 'feminine'. Calchas is Cresseid's father and eponym of the patriarch, but he is tender and loving towards his daughter, tries to comfort rather than condemn her, in a way that seems more conventionally characteristic of the kindly woman in the leper-house. The planetary gods, Saturn, Cynthia and Venus, done as lavishly detailed pictorial grotesque personifications, are ghastly parodies of male/female stereotypes, projections on a large screen of the kind of thinking that keeps Cresseid and the narrator imprisoned. Troilus, finally, is the man whose 'impressionable' nature (to use a word often applied to Chaucer's Criseyde as the epitome of femininity) and constancy in loving enable him to perceive, through the power of the explicitly non-authoritative and 'dangerous' faculty of 'fantasy', what is really there but not apparent.

All these complexities within the poem, which are an essential part of its beauty and its power over us, are made possible by the fact that it is a poem, working under a pressure of engagement with its material that stimulates unexpected feats and activities of imagining. This is the manner of poetic representation: not a cloak or disguise for a hidden meaning but, simply, a different way of seeing. Further than that there is the vital importance to the poem of its literary ancestry, of the inherited literary culture through which the world is irresistibly refracted. Chaucer is much more important here than late fifteenth-century Scottish history. 'What Chaucer wrote' was truer than Henryson knew, as he came to realise in the process of 'realising' further the experience of Chaucer's poem.

INDEX

TABULA GRATULATORIA

The editors are grateful for financial support from King's College, London, Glasgow University and the University of Salford.

Rosamund Allen
Dr John Anderson
Professor Malcolm Andrew
Dr W.R.J. Barron
Janet Bately
Larry D. Benson
Professor Norman Blake
Julia Boffey
Dr Elizabeth M. Brennan
John Burrow
Dr Wendy Collier
Dr Margaret Connolly
Helen Cooper
Janet Cowen
Roger Dahood
Professor W.A. Davenport
Dr Eirian Davies
Terence Patrick Dolan
Brian Donaghey
A.I. Doyle
Martha W. Driver
Valerie Edden
A.S.G. Edwards
Roger Ellis
P.J.C. Field
Rosalind Field
Professor David C. Fowler
Dr Vincent Gillespie
Manfred Görlach

Professor Douglas Gray
John Gray
Richard Hamer
Ralph Hanna
Phillipa and Christopher Hardman
Elton D. Higgs
Terry Hoad
Karen Hodder
Stanley Hussey
Professor Tadahiro Ikegami
Nicolas Jacobs
George Kane
Professor C.J. Kay
Geoff Lester
Peter and Angela Lucas
Dr Sally Mapstone
William Marx
Professor David Mills
Maldwyn Mills
Dr Gerald Morgan
Veronica O'Mara
Professor Leonee Ormond
Derek Pearsall
Helen Phillips
Oliver Pickering
Susan Powell
Kari Anne Rand Schmidt
Christine Rees
Professor Paul G. Remley

Felicity Riddy
Jane Roberts
Victoria Rothschild
James Simpson
Jeremy Smith
Dr Louise Sylvester
Professor Toshiyuki Takamiya

John J. Thompson
Thorlac Turville-Petre
Professor Meg Twycross
Míceál F. Vaughan
Professor Yoko Wada
S. Carole Weinberg
Elizabeth Williams

Department of English Language and Literature, King's College, London
Leeds University Library
McGowin Library, Pembroke College, Oxford